Mixed Enterprise

Mixed Enterprise

A Developmental Perspective

Lloyd D. Musolf
University of California, Davis

Lexington Books
D.C. Heath and Company
Lexington, Massachusetts
Toronto   London

For Stephanie

Contents

List of Tables

Preface

One of the features of traditional societies is a lack of differentiation between "government" and "economy." Societies engaged in modernization soon make such a distinction. Yet the more complex a society becomes, the more its interdependence grows. Links are forged between government and economy, no matter what the form of government.

This volume furnishes a glimpse of one such link, the mixed enterprise. It has drawn scant attention even though its more glamorous sister—the international joint venture—has attracted much. Mixed enterprise refers to direct government participation in an undertaking with the domestic private sector. Here the context in which this institution is studied is development planning, a common preoccupation of nations, especially those wishing to modernize. The approach is that of an introductory survey.

The first glimmer of an idea for this volume sprang from two requests received in 1966. In September of that year, the Public Administration Division of the United Nations held an interregional conference of twenty-odd developing nations in Geneva. As one of the consultants, I was asked to prepare a paper on "Public Enterprise and Economic Development (Mixed Economy)," which was eventually published in *Organization and Administration of Public Enterprises: Selected Papers* (United Nations, New York, 1968). Though public enterprise had long been an interest, the UN request prompted a special look at mixed enterprise. As development plans generally assumed the necessity of cooperation between the public and private sectors, a natural focus was an institution that, on the surface at least, institutionalized this cooperation. Conversations with representatives of the developing nations at Geneva reinforced the notion that mixed enterprise was worth studying. A second request that prompted thinking about the topic was made by the *George Washington Law Review*, which suggested an article for an issue celebrating the twentieth anniversary of the Employment Act of 1946. ("Public Enterprise and Economic Planning: A Comparative Perspective," appeared in the December, 1966 issue.) The second and fourth chapters of the present volume benefit from some of this early speculation.

These initial efforts revealed a paucity of writings on the subject of mixed enterprise, whether considered alone or in conjunction with development planning. Stimulated in part by a reading of Daniel L. Spencer's *India, Mixed Enterprise and Western Business*, I conceived the idea of a survey that would cover both developed and less-developed countries. An opportunity to explore its feasibility came in 1968-1969 with the aid of sabbatical funds and a Senior Scholar award from the East-West Center in Honolulu. The Center's research assistance and scholarly atmosphere facilitated progress. After the inevitable resumption of teaching and administrative duties, several publishing opportunities helped to regain momentum for the project. The *Journal of Comparative Administration* published a piece on "Mixed Enterprise in a Developmental Perspective: France, Italy, and Japan" in August, 1971, an earlier version of the third chapter of the present volume. In December of last year the *Western Political Quarterly* published a portion of what was to become Chapter IV under the title of "Mixed Enterprise and Government Responsibility." Permission to publish revised versions of those pieces as portions of the book was graciously granted by both journals.

In a project involving an enormous canvassing of published sources, there is no hope of expressing adequate appreciation to all the individuals and organizations who provided assistance of one kind or another, but a few of those who were of particular help should be singled out for mention. Research assistants Diane Henley at the East-West Center and George Goerl at the University of California, Davis, searched out numerous pertinent references in sources both prominent and obscure. Two members of the Institute of Governmental Affairs staff at UC Davis who patiently dealt with the onerous task of editing and footnoting and with outlandish requests for materials, respectively, were Mrs. Elizabeth Owen, editor, and Mr. Ned Suljak, librarian. In its various manifestations, the manuscript passed through the efficient typewriters of Mrs. Florence Nelson, Miss Lauri Flynn, and Mrs. Judith Stone. The refinement and testing of information and ideas also involved many persons who can only be listed in part. The Senior Scholars who shared a pleasant year at the East-West Center kindly listened to a presentation of Chapter I and evaluated it. The chapter on the United States owes much to the wisdom of Mr. Harold Seidman, former assistant director of the U.S. Bureau of the Budget. Mr. Toshiyuki Masujima of the Administrative Management Agency, Office of the Prime Minister, furnished vital information and advice about mixed enterprise in Japan. A preliminary draft of Chapter III benefited from the criticisms of Professors Nobutaka Ike of Stanford University and Joseph LaPalombara of Yale University. For material on Pakistan, Mr. M.A.K. Beg, then director of the National Institute of Public Administration at Lahore, is owed a debt of thanks, especially as he circulated a draft among Pakistani civil servants. Professor Henry H. Schloss of the Graduate School of Business, University of Southern California, provided useful criticism of the section on India. For Chapter VI, Mr. S. Shapiro, then deputy director of the Government Companies Authority, Israel, and Assistant Professor William Tuohy, University of California, Davis, were helpful in providing materials and criticizing sections, respectively. The final chapter benefited from the scrutiny of Professor Richard W. Gable, another UCD colleague. Encouragement from Mr. Geoffrey Gunn, director of Lexington Books, D.C. Health and Company, helped the project to fruition. So did the patience of my wife, Berdyne, here gratefully acknowledged. Kind as all these individuals and organizations have been, the responsibility for the shortcomings of this book is mine alone.

Davis, California
February, 1972

Mixed Enterprise

1 Mixed Enterprise: Contour and Context

The world contains an amazing variety of commercial ventures, some of which cross national borders and often involve cooperation between the public and private spheres. To give only a small random sample of items noted in the press and periodicals: the Canadian government has formed an oil exploration company to which it contributes 45 percent of the equity and Canadian private capital the rest; in the United Kingdom, the enactment of the Industrial Expansion Act of 1968 enables the government to aid industry by means which include taking up shareholdings or purchasing all or part of enterprises; International Harvester has seven joint ventures among its huge overseas operations; the state of Israel uses government-to-government joint commercial enterprises as a vehicle for extending technical aid; in India, there is "a heavy reliance on what are called private limited companies" in which the government holds 51 percent or more of the shares; after land reform in Taiwan, the former large landlords have found themselves to be investors in four former government industrial corporations through the process of receiving 30 percent of the sale price of their land in the form of shares; in Chile, the copper industry is moving from private foreign ownership through various phases of steadily growing government ownership and control; in the People's Republic of China, a system of joint government-private enterprise has been used as a way station to state socialism; Fiat, a private Italian automobile manufacturer, supplies the technology and much of the equipment for a big Soviet automobile plant; Renault, a French government-owned automobile firm, has made an arrangement with the Rumanian government to produce cars; and by 1970, Hungary had forty-two joint industrial ventures with Western European firms, and Yugoslavia, twenty-eight.[1]

Such phenomena, increasingly prevalent these days, test the bounds of traditional analyses of economic forms. Thus, in his brilliant presentation of ten ownership models in *The Political Economy of Communism*,[2] Peter Wiles quite naturally did not include combinations such as those above. His models do, however, suggest the immense range of politico-economic institutional models of the economy, and these are summarized here to throw the present study into relief:

1. Primitive capitalism: the private individual.
2. Managerial capitalism: the anonymous shareholders in a large limited liability company.

1

3. Managerial socialism: the public board of a nationalized industry or firm, operating in a free market independently of the state.
4. State socialism: the state machine, operating the economy through regular organs of state. (The Soviet Union is the paradigm.)
5. Consumers' cooperative: the owners are the consumers of the enterprise's product.
6. Producers' cooperative: the owners are the workers in an enterprise.
7. Syndicalism: the owners are the workers in a nationalized establishment.
8. Municipal socialism: the owners are the people organized in a local authority.
9. Community socialism: the people are both consumers and producers at once (Israeli kibbutz).
10. Full communism: the whole nation is a single commune in which planning embraces all activities from consumption to the choice of a job.

There are a theoretically infinite number of institutional models for industrialization, as Wiles noted in choosing those above for discussion. As the present study deals with an institution (mixed enterprise), an additional example of an attempt to describe an "institutional framework for the organizations which might successfully promote industrialization" is warranted. Richard L. Meier has set out five different policy alternatives for industrial development:

1. The government might initiate and itself operate in the public interest a series of key manufacturing activities, adding one after another in order of priority [U.S.S.R. and Communist China].
2. The government might encourage (through subsidies, credit, guaranteed markets, and other aids) the local entrepreneurs who wish to enter the manufacturing field or modernize the traditional and obsolete plants they already operate [Western Europe and North and South America, during the nineteenth and early twentieth centuries].
3. The government might attract competent industrialists from the outside; with extra incentives, it may also attract some outside capital to accompany the imported skills [developing countries since World War II].
4. A politically neutral "development council," either completely independent of government or established as a semiofficial body, might take on the detailed task of information gathering and expediting associated with the establishment of industry within a given territory [depressed areas of a nation].
5. A mixed strategy, including several of the above, might be followed, with the creation of widely different instrumentalities by the government and by firms in the private sector [more widely applicable than any pure strategy].[3]

When nations mix their development strategies, they often open the way for public-private collaboration in commercial enterprises. Thus, Eugene Staley, after detailing a range of possibilities similar to Meier's, has commented: "An additional possibility, often a part of the combination, is production and distribution by various kinds of co-operatives or by special corporate bodies in which the public sector and the private sector participate jointly."[4]

This volume deals with a variant of joint operation known as mixed enterprise. Loosely speaking, the term could conceivably be applied to any body in which there is an informal mixture of public and private influence; regulatory boards, such as this country's Interstate Commerce Commission, come to mind. In a somewhat more restricted sense, agencies in which there is formal representation from different sources, such as the United States wartime wage and price stabilization boards composed of business, labor, and public representatives, might qualify for the name. In a still more restricted sense—and taking the word "enterprise" seriously—the term would be restricted to commercial or quasicommercial units. This is the sense in which the term is used here, but even more narrowing is necessary. The name "international joint venture," for example, has been applied by one writer to undertakings in which there is the sharing of technical information, and skills, management talent, and patents and trademarks, but not necessarily the sharing of ownership.[5]

Even after joint operations that do not require ownership are eliminated, further narrowing is necessary in order to reach a manageable definition of mixed enterprise. Terminological distinctions employed by Daniel L. Spencer are useful in achieving this purpose.[6] Their use here will also avoid adding still other appellations to the confusing area of joint commercial operations. By stressing participation in internal structure, attention falls on the aforementioned ownership of shares and also on membership on the board of directors. For each of these, it can be asked whether parties of different origin, i.e., foreign or domestic, public or private, participate in some degree.[7] Where participation is entirely from either the public or private sector, the term *joint* enterprise is employed. A *composite* enterprise is one in which there is intersectoral linkage across national boundary lines. *Mixed* enterprise is reserved for a venture which is both domestic and intersectoral. Theoretically, the following combinations are then possible:

Joint enterprise	Foreign private - Domestic private
	Foreign public - Domestic public
Composite enterprise	Foreign public - Domestic private
	Foreign private - Domestic public
	Foreign public - Foreign private - Domestic public
	Foreign private - Domestic public - Domestic private
Mixed enterprise	Domestic public - Domestic private

Mixed enterprise, then, has the participation—in the form of capital, or appointments to the board of directors, or both—of a nation's government and its private enterprise. The country surveys that follow the next chapter will focus on such mixtures, though they will also take account of such peripheral arrangements as the fourth type of composite enterprise listed above, or the rare case when a mixed enterprise itself undertakes foreign operations in which it participates jointly with a foreign government.

To concentrate on intersectoral combinations within a country is not intended to imply any lack of importance for joint or composite enterprises; these have already received elaborate attention.[8] A much-publicized question related to these other types of enterprises concerns the aggressive stance taken by American business abroad. Of the five hundred largest United States companies in 1967, nearly half had extensive overseas investments totaling about 50 billion dollars.[9] So substantial is this investment that Jean Jacques Servan-Schreiber's view of it as "The American Challenge" has received worldwide attention.[10]

Though the term "mixed enterprise" describes an economic concept rather than a legal or organizational form, its relation to the latter should be briefly noted. Public enterprise is usually administered under one of three forms: the ordinary government department, the government corporation, and the joint-stock company. The first is widely used in Communist countries but is now regarded as somewhat anomalous in Western nations except for revenue-producing purposes, such as lotteries, salt, tobacco, or match monopolies. The government corporation has achieved great popularity both in developed and underdeveloped countries because it presumably recognizes the need for special status for business-type activities of government. Conventionally, a government corporation has a separate legal existence, the right to sue and be sued, and a measure of financial and personnel autonomy. In recent years, some Western governments have reacted against the notion of autonomy and have tried to increase the corporations' responsiveness and accountability by passing general statutes setting forth controls to which they are subject.

The joint-stock company is of most interest here because it is a handy device for public-private entrepreneurial action. This is accomplished through the sharing of capital and assigning seats on the board of directors. The company is essentially a creature of private law, with its origins going back at least as far as the mercantilist era.[11] The company form has been widely used on the European continent, and in the Commonwealth (aside from Great Britain, which has preferred the government corporation).[12] Though the company device makes for flexibility, it has also drawn criticism for giving too much freedom to the executive branch or the company executives.

Despite the vast literature about these legal or organizational forms, a functional approach is appropriate to a study which seeks to discover what public-private undertakings do and to relate these activities to national development efforts. Legal forms are tools, and their employment is dependent on purpose. For example, concerning the three forms of public enterprise mentioned above, the United Nations *Handbook of Public Administration* opines that each achieves "a different balance between the objectives of operating autonomy and government control of their major policies."[13]

The research needs for the topic of mixed enterprise in a developmental perspective—and the extent to which the present study meets these needs—should now be explained. By way of introduction, two general comments are in order. First, the topic manifestly requires that far more attention be given to certain areas of the economy than others. Industry is the principal area dealt with, simply because it frequently harbors mixed enterprises, whereas they are relatively rare in most other areas, such as agriculture. Finance is an exception, for many financial institutions that have been created to aid development have the participation of both the public and private sectors. Secondly, the study makes no pretense at economic analysis. Whether industrialization was the wise course for a country to follow, or even whether industrialization was a success, are not proper questions for this study by a noneconomist. But development goals—largely economic and social, but with political overtones—do provide an appropriate focus.

Economic development—especially industrialization—involves a choice as to the degree of reliance on the public and private sectors. The prominence of either of these sectors in a country's mixed enterprises presumably bears some relation to their prominence in the economy at large. Thus, a survey of mixed enterprise may itself constitute a rough measure of economic development philosophy. The element of deliberativeness in national development should not, of course, be overstated. For example, though a country may have a preference for using private enterprise, its inadequacies in various developing countries are such that government may be compelled to begin undertakings itself. To give another example, in using national economic plans as evidence of developmental goals, as this study does, one must bear in mind that the implementation of plans has conventionally been much weaker than their formulation.

Whatever the significance of mixed enterprise as a measure of the public-private "mix" in national economies, the study recommends itself on other grounds. Mixed enterprise has received little popular, or even scholarly, discussion. The literature on development, with a few outstanding exceptions that will be noted in the final chapter, largely passes it by. Writings on public administration in English have tended to treat mixed enterprise as a type of public or government corporation.[14] Secondly, there is a dearth of empirical information as to whether nations fit mixed enterprise into their developmental goals and, if so, how?[15] Finally, there should be value in attempting generalizations about mixed enterprise in a developmental perspective. Several areas of investigation and their relation to the present study may be noted.

The first concerns a typology of mixed enterprise. One variable would be the degree of permanence intended for mixed enterprise. One can hypothesize that this dimension is affected by the national vision of a desirable economy: the less intended permanence, the less intended reliance on the public sector. One must also ask whether there is likely to be anything that interferes with this vision in practice. A second variable is the source of leadership in establishing mixed enterprise. In the context of development, the public sector is ordinarily the originator, one suspects. Even if this be granted, the character of the present and future role of the private sector should be revealing as to a developmental perspective. It can be seen that the implications of typology extend far beyond the mere cataloguing of varieties of mixed enterprise.

A second area to explore is the purported connection between mixed enterprise and planned economic development. One might ask whether mixed enterprise is likely to be sufficiently significant to affect economic development substantially. If government actively manipulates the economy in order to obtain compliance with a national plan, then it can probably be assumed that mixed enterprise will be regarded as one of the instruments to manipulate. The working out of this hypothesis might depend in part upon whether mixed enterprise is overbalanced toward government or toward the private sector. One might postulate that the greater the degree of governmental dominance of mixed enterprise, the greater the degree of coordination with plans.

A related area for investigation is the connection of mixed enterprise with economic development philosophy, particularly its political overtones. We might hypothesize, first, that there will be a conscious transfer of mixed enterprise ideas from one country to another, especially from relatively developed nations to the less developed. Secondly, within nations, one can postulate that a balance of power between the public and private sectors in mixed enterprise will be difficult to establish and perhaps harder to maintain once established. This hypothesis is based upon the general instability of power relationships and, more particularly, upon the assumption that there will not be an identity of interests between the sectors if both are vigorous. A third hypothesis is that, in the less-developed countries, the government will tend to dominate mixed enterprise because of the usual weakness of the private sector. This weakness is the very reason that governments in these countries begin mixed enterprises. At the extreme, such a disparity of power would mean the enterprise is not "mixed" in a meaningful sense, that it is relatively formalistic.[16] Still, one would anticipate that even a minimum of private participation would make *some* behavioral difference.

Especially in underdeveloped countries, the government dominance of mixed enterprise is likely to occur through executive or bureaucratic hegemony. This, in turn, would tend to remove mixed enterprise from effective public, or at least, legislative, scrutiny. Actions concerning mixed enterprise might also be affected. The sale of mixed enterprises to the private sector, for example, might be frustrated by the reluctance of the bureaucracy to lose part of its empire or by the temptation of government leaders to sell only to favorites at give-away prices. The net effect of formalistic mixed enterprise could be to help delay political development along the lines of a participatory society. This is on the assumption that building viable economic interest groups is an essential part of building participation.

At least theoretically, overwhelming government domination is not the only type of mixed enterprise formalism. From what has been said about the probable weakness of the private sector in underdeveloped countries, one would hypothesize that immense private sector dominance of mixed enterprise is far more likely to occur in developed countries. In practice, examples of this kind of formalism are likely to be much rarer than the first type. The reason is the likelihood that the governments of developed nations, even when exceptionally compliant, would not be as weak as private enterprise in underdeveloped countries.

In testing such hypotheses, it would be interesting to see the effects of changing conditions. For example, as private enterprise becomes stronger in an underdeveloped country, what happens to mixed enterprise? Does it, too, become stronger because of an infusion of vitality from private enterprise? Does it, instead, become weaker because private enterprise pours its energies into projects closer to its corporate heart? On the basis of limited experience, one is inclined to lean toward the latter, but the degree of permanence envisaged for mixed enterprise would probably affect the answer.

It is appropriate to state the degree to which the present study, which is essentially a survey, responds to the needs for research outlined above. In all probability, answering them fully would require the cooperation of officials and scholars in a number of countries and the services of a well-coordinated research team. What can be done in a survey is to suggest the dimensions of the concept of mixed enterprise in a developmental context; to undertake a preliminary sketch of practices in a small number of developed and less-developed countries; and to relate these practices to the highly tentative hypotheses listed above. To do more, a great deal of refining based on field studies and research on the development process will be needed. In-depth country studies, for example, should get beyond the national economic plans and the secondary sources on which the present volume must rely and uncover the extent of, and reasons for, departures from planned roles for mixed enterprise. Such research should also provide reports on the internal operations of mixed enterprises. The present study does not attempt to deal with such vital organizational aspects as management, finance, accountability, pricing and profitability, labor relations, and consumer representation. Their bearing on the developmental theme would need to be assayed carefully.

The approach to the subject is roughly as follows. In the absence of an adequate literature on mixed enterprise and development, the next chapter sketches the general relationship between public enterprise and economic development. Why is government involved in commercial ventures? What are the dimensions of the growing interest in economic planning? From what vantage points may the relationship between public enterprise and national development be viewed? What differences in approach are found in developed and under-developed nations? What problems arise in relating public enterprise to national development?

Turning next to mixed enterprise, the little-known, but surprising, variety of country experiences with this instrument is surveyed in a series of chapters. The selection of nations, though having an inevitable element of arbitrariness, is partially channeled by circumstances. Mixed enterprise is found chiefly in mixed economies. Countries are grouped roughly according to their state of economic development.

Two chapters report the experiences of the developed nations. The initial chapter summarizes the diverse experiences of three countries that pioneered mixed enterprise in markedly different ways. French mixed enterprise encountered a strong *dirigiste* tradition which most recently resulted in vigorous, though democratic, planning. In Italy, mixed enterprise passed through the period of Mussolini's drive for autarchy, but chiefly it came up against the substantially cartelized character of the Italian economy. Japan's unprecedented modernization after 1868 is world famous, but the place of mixed enterprise then and now is little known. The subsequent chapter is devoted to the unusual form and role of American mixed enterprise. Its difficult identification, problems associated with government participation in its governance, financial ambiguities, and planning questions are successively treated.

Two chapters briefly review the record of mixed enterprise in certain less-developed countries. One compares and contrasts the experiences of the neighboring rivals on the Indian subcontinent. Their similarities in approaches to planning, their differences in attitudes toward private enterprise, and Pakistan's apparent use of the Japanese model, make their employment of mixed enterprise particularly intriguing. The other chapter recounts the experiences of three geographically-dispersed nations that have been especially imaginative in relating mixed enterprise to development goals. Mixed enterprise is widely used in the intricate and carefully concerted economy of Israel. Mexico has made use of mixed enterprise in basic industries so as to shape them in desired patterns. Taiwan has attempted to link the industrial and agricultural sectors through transactions involving mixed enterprise.

In the final chapter, an effort is made to place the reported country experiences in perspective. The relatively sparse literature on mixed enterprise in a developmental context is noted and related to the country reports. Both literature and reports are then discussed against the backdrop of the hypotheses described above.

2

Public Enterprise and Development Planning

The purpose of this chapter is to establish a framework for discussing mixed enterprise in a context of national planning. To do so, it becomes necessary to focus on *public* enterprise in relation to planning because of the paucity of writings about mixed enterprise. Even so, it must be noted that the literature that links public enterprise and development is minor compared to the extensive writings that consider them separately. Though mixed enterprise often is something more than a division of public enterprise, it will be helpful to consider it so in the present chapter.

Much of the ensuing discussion centers on national economic planning as a formal sign of intended development. Obviously, this approach does not penetrate to the heart of such questions as the meaning of "development," the extent to which stated development goals are appropriate, and the extent to which the goals have been achieved. These are appropriately the subjects of other studies, a few of which are cited below. Even the loosest form of planning requires a government to consider ways of manipulating economic actions to achieve stated purposes. There are factors, as we shall see, that complicate any attempt to have public enterprises automatically follow government orders relating to the direction of the economy. Still, guiding the activities of the public sphere is easier than guiding those of private enterprise. The situation facing an enterprise with mixed public-private ownership is thus intriguing. Particularly is this so because governments with ambitions to plan tend to regard enterprises in which they have a total or partial interest as instruments with which to influence the private sector.

Some Dimensions of Planning

Although national economic planning has been a common phenomenon through-out the world since the second World War, its origins stem from the era after the first worldwide holocaust. The Soviet Union (and considerably later, its East European satellites) used national planning to create a heavy industry. The term "economic plan" was first employed when the Soviets introduced the "First Five-Year Plan" in 1928, and it was not until the 1940s that economic plans were actually introduced in other countries.[1] There were also non-Communist roots for planning. Great Britain and Scandinavia, under the stimulus of the unprecedented unemployment of the 1930s, flirted with ideas for a gradualistic and less totalitarian planning oriented toward social justice.[2] Even in the United States, the vague outlines of a school of planning can be traced from Frederick W. Taylor through the New Deal era, including the abortive experiment with the National Resources Planning Board from 1939 to 1943, when a jealous Congress abolished it. The actual institution of plans proceeded much more slowly. In Western Europe, France, the Netherlands, Norway, and perhaps Sweden began planning in the 1950s.[3] The Organization of European Economic Cooperation, created to administer the Marshall Plan, acted as a catalyst for various countries.[4] By 1966, an observer counted fourteen countries in Western Europe with "forward plans."[5] Planning as "the intellectual matrix of the entire modernization ideology" in South Asia has been emphasized by Gunnar Myrdal in his massive three-volume study of the area.[6]

In the postwar era, planning has often been regarded by the less-developed countries as a panacea for their ills. These countries have had to deal with inadequate infrastructures, shortages of investment capital and managerial and technological skills, and a lack of means for stimulating productive investment and increased productivity. These formidable challenges have produced various responses. Three of the most common are economic planning, assisting and guiding the private sector, and initiating those investments and managing those activities which comprise the public sector of the economy.[7]

The precise combination of these functions selected by a developing nation varies widely, of course. The choice will be a function of the character, range, and variety of developmental goals, as well as the level to be attained; the time horizon in economic development; the means available for attaining the ends sought; the structure and character of social, economic and political institutions; and the current level of development of the economy.[8]

Despite its popularity, developmental planning remains a controversial tool. Some economists hold, with Friedrich A. Hayek, that planning requires a complete listing of economic priorities in a society, and is therefore unsuitable to a democracy and an economy in which private enterprise is prominent.[9] A similar criticism of planning in a mixed economy has sometimes come from the Communists, who believe that only total planning brings economic growth and that mixed economies cannot plan totally (but recent experiments with decentralized planning in the Soviet Union and Eastern Europe tend to mitigate the harshness of this view). Without entering into these controversies, one may find persuasive A.H. Hanson's moderate view that "Economic planning, as such, offers no infallible recipe for achieving a high rate of growth. Nor, on the other hand, does lack of economic planning."[10] Some of the initial flush of enthusiasm for development planning appears to be receding in the face of discouraging experiences.[11]

Even if still controversial, economic planning is considerably less so than a generation ago. In Neil W. Chamberlain's phrase, it is "less ideological and more technical."[12] American corporate giants have been involved in this shift of focus. They have instituted extensive planning themselves, and their European subsidiaries have encountered government planning and found it tolerable. Chamberlain even suggests that planning may now be viewed from a technical aspect because of the widespread interest in, and use of, systems analysis in business, a development which has revived interest in Adam Smith's concept of the economy as a system.[13]

An irksome problem is the confusion surrounding the term planning, which has many meanings, all, within their respective contexts, valid.[14] Richard L. Meier has noted that, *inter alia*, it can refer: "(1) to a set of theoretical procedures that conform to socialist ideologies, (2) to the practice of resource allocation and programming of production as typified by the Soviet Union, (3) to the use of long-range forecasting devices and administrative controls in large organizations, in order to avoid pitfalls and prevent substantial losses over the long run and (4) to the orderly exploration of alternative paths of action by government, such as those undertaken specifically by military staffs who test proposed alternatives by laying out the logistics and making assessments of feasibility."[15] Helpful at this point is Joan Mitchell's distinction: "Economic planning by Governments then, while it has to include forecasting, must also include some intention to change the use of economic (scarce) resources."[16]

Some economists seize upon the governmental methods employed as the key to whether planning exists. Jacob Viner, for example, defines national economic planning as "the extensive use by government of direct controls over specific categories of individuals, firms, and transactions as a means of regulating a national economy."[17] By emphasizing "direct controls" and distinguishing them from "indirect" or "compensatory" controls, Viner finds Soviet Russia, the United Kingdom, and Norway operating under planned economies, while nonplanning countries include the United States, Canada, Belgium, and Switzerland.[18] Political economist Hanson, in distinguishing countries that attempt coherent economic planning from others that merely pursue interventionist policies of one kind or another, suggests that: "The planning, as distinct from the mere stimulation, of growth involves the formulation of economic goals and the manipulation of the factors of production to secure their attainment."[19]

From these and other works, several tentative conclusions emerge. First, there is little agreement on a precise definition, and it may not be useful to attempt a highly refined one. National economic planning is more than mere governmental interventionism and more than mere forecasting without attempted manipulation, but, in both cases, it is not clear how much more is required to deserve the name of planning. For example, stabilization planning, or the management of aggregate demand, is included by some economists but excluded by others.[20] Second, though economic growth is the leading goal of planning, there are enough additional objectives to require some ordering of rank among them.[21] Finally, the political, or bargaining, element in planning is crucial. This impression is reinforced by Andrew Shonfield's summary of the approaches to planning employed by Western European nations.[22] The first, the intellectual approach, he considers "indicative" planning in its purest form because "the quality of the analysis done by the planners convinces the men wielding economic power, in the private and public sectors alike, that the conclusions offered to them provide good advice." As put by another scholar, the " 'indication' of what is possible in each industry may itself serve to induce a higher level of private investment than would otherwise occur."[23] A second approach relies on reinforced governmental powers and permits planners to use the extensive governmental control of the economy to guide the remainder of the economy toward any objective chosen by the government. Thirdly, government may eschew direct intervention whenever possible and instead rely on bargaining with interest groups as a device to move the economy along the intended path. Shonfield found that most of the Western European planning efforts at the time he wrote (1965) contained elements of all three approaches.

From formulation to implementation of a plan is a critical step. The higher incidence of what Douglas Ashford and Bertram Gross call "symbolic" or "ritualistic" planning greatly affects the generalization that planning is almost universal among the less-developed nations.[24] Obvious as it may seem, little attention was paid to the implementation of plans until fairly recently.[25] Perhaps because of the prominence of economists in national planning efforts and in technical assistance in its support, major emphasis was placed upon the formulation of an economically consistent plan. This oversight seems now to have been corrected, although actually achieving high-quality administration in the implementation of plans is an exceedingly complex matter.[26] The lesson of flexibility needs frequent emphasis; if the actual economic behavior departs from the assumptions in the plan—a virtually inevitable occurrence—then the corrected intentions must be fed back into the plan.[27]

Roles of Public Enterprise in National Planning

Economic planning would seem to lessen the distinction between public and private enterprise. In addition, the extent to which public enterprise is employed undoubtedly affects the nature and degree of this blurring process. Thus, public enterprise may be limited to the provision of social and economic overhead, i.e., educational, health, and social welfare facilities, banking, transportation, and communications facilities, or it may extend beyond the overhead sectors and manage entire industries, ignoring others. It may cover a few firms in different industries or it may virtually blanket productive enterprise.[28]

There appears to be a worldwide trend away from positions at either theoretical extreme in the relationship between public enterprise and national planning. Centrally-planned economies have recently enlarged the sphere of autonomy for public enterprises, permitting more initiative on their part in both

the formation and the execution of the national plan. By contrast, predominant-
ly private-enterprise economies have steadily tended to relate their public
enterprises more consistently to a concept of national planning. Although the
"move toward the middle" is of great interest, obviously it will not result in an
obliteration of differences. Ideology alone will see to that. In addition,
"Differences in institutional structure and in stage of development," as
Edward S. Mason has pointed out, "will always dictate differences in optimal
arrangement."[29] Though these differences complicate any description of the
relationship between public enterprise and national planning, the problem is
somewhat minimized when the focus is upon the mixed-economy countries.
Tentatively, at least, this includes many of the new nations.

Often the less-developed countries harbor a spirit of complementarity
between public and private actions. A United Nations study of planning found a
considerable contrast between the eagerness with which the public sector is
viewed in developed countries with mixed economies and in less-developed
countries: "While these developed countries . . . look upon private enterprise as
the main source of economic growth and many of these regard the principal
tasks of the government as ensuring economic stability and providing a
favourable economic climate for the private sector, the under-developed countries have generally viewed the public sector as the key instrument for securing
economic development."[30] An illustration of the differing circumstances is
provided by a commentator on the Commonwealth countries: "In Canada and
Australia the private sector of the economy was already developed before active
public economic action came into vogue. In the newer federation where the
private sector has been less developed, the governmental policies could be more
directive and the instrumentalities chosen had less need to adapt to the habits
and mores of an already well developed private sector."[31]

Within the category of the less-developed countries, there are naturally many
differences. Though the share of public to total investment has grown in all
regions of the world, public investment has been especially high in a number of
African and Asian countries and generally rather low in Latin America, where
the infrastructure was better developed.[32] Nor is substantial public investment a
unique characteristic of nations where private investment is limited. It has been
estimated that the nationalized industries in France account for perhaps
one-third of total investment.[33] And where, as in the United States, public
enterprise occupies only a small portion of the economy, the government still
controls and disposes of about 20 percent of the gross national product.[34]

To the extent that nations are preoccupied with economic and social
development, they are likely to discourage the isolation of public enterprise.
Ideally, a concentration on planning leads to an analysis of weakness in the
sectors of the economy, and finally to a multiinstrument attack upon factors
contributing to lack of success in a sector. When public enterprise is available as
a contact point for a sector, a development-oriented government is not likely to

overlook the fact. This situation creates various subtleties, as we shall see later.

Although public enterprise is often associated with a drive for development these days, it would be unwise to assume that this association is always present. Public enterprises were a common phenomenon long before economic growth became a popular aim, some governments are still not growth-oriented, and various public enterprises have been created for such purposes as bringing in revenue to the state, providing a favorable display, or as locales for partronage appointments.[35]

Criteria in Relating Public Enterprise to Development

Before some of the problems that arise in relating public enterprise to economic and social development are considered, it will be helpful to review some criteria that might be employed to assess the relationship. What relevance is there in the number of public enterprises, the intent in establishing them, and in their degree of permanence? Should one insist upon the importance of national planning as a criterion for relating public enterprise to national development? Is public ownership itself crucial to the national development process?

The presence of large *numbers* of public enterprises in a developing country probably testifies to an eagerness to establish social and economic overheads and to achieve an economic "takeoff." If the enterprises are being run for profit and become a source of financing for the establishment of additional enterprise, this judgment may be even more apt. On the other hand, we have already noted that public enterprises may be created for many purposes other than development. Furthermore, though India has numerous public enterprises, "in many respects the Indian government plays a smaller role in her economy than do the Governments of the so-called 'mixed' economies of the Western world."[36]

The *intent* announced in creating enterprises exhibits difficulties in providing a sure criterion. Ideology has played a prominent role in certain cases, practical circumstances in others. Important as ideology is, one suspects that practical circumstances are even more critical in the choice of public enterprise. Pragmatic considerations often overtake stated intent and circumscribe it sharply. The state of Israel, for example, established various public enterprises because, even though it gave every encouragement to private enterprise, including remitting taxes and loaning money, the response from the private sector was, in the opinion of the country's leaders, inadequate.[37]

Shall one place lower on the scale a country whose public enterprises are in process of flux as opposed to one with a stable, permanent public enterprise sector? Certainly, it can be argued that *permanence* in public enterprises affords the opportunity for gearing operations to a national plan. But what is to be said of a country such as Japan, which developed rapidly in the late nineteenth century while investing its resources only temporarily in enterprises that were later placed in private hands? The process has the advantage of permitting the constant reuse of government capital in areas of the economy that are presumably in the greatest need of bolstering. Granted that the coordination of enterprises turned over to private ownership is more difficult, can one go so far as to say that a disservice has been done to national development? A more accurate judgment is one given in a United Nations bulletin. After noting the Pakistan government's unsuccessful attempt to induce private enterprise to take over more than a quarter or so of the fifty enterprises established by the Industrial Development Corporation, the report commented: "Thus, the scope of the public sector may be temporarily expanded as a matter of expedience and in spite of ideological considerations in order to initiate and accelerate economic development."[38] As already indicated, ideology is heavily tempered with necessity, and this makes the question of intention—whether enterprises shall be permanent or temporary—somewhat moot, at least as to those enterprises requiring heavy investments.[39]

The amount of *planning* is undoubtedly influential in relating public enterprise to national development. In the centrally-planned economies of the Soviet bloc, the correlation between planning and public enterprise has traditionally been almost perfect. Yet, the experiences of Yugoslavia and, more recently, the Soviet Union would seem to suggest that there are practical limits to the amount of central planning for public enterprises. In the former country, according to a United Nations report dating from the first half of the 1960s, "Broad autonomy was granted . . . to enterprises," and "plans no longer specify detailed targets for individual enterprises."[40] As to changes in the Soviet economy, the same report observed: "Generally wider use has been made of incentives to encourage better performance on the part of both individuals and enterprises and to achieve a more rational use of resources."[41]

Commentators on mixed economies sometimes overstate the authority of the government in directing public enterprise to follow a national plan. Enterprises may not follow meekly along with a statement that "Since the government has full jurisdiction over the activities of the public sector, it lends itself to direct planning in the form of investment programmes and construction and production schedules."[42] Hopes may be falsely raised by the assertion that "If the commodity is to be produced by a public enterprise, or by a public-private partnership, the targets tell officials what they are supposed to do. . . ."[43] As Mason has emphasized, "Even in countries which have extensive nationalized industries, these are usually under the control of managements that enjoy most of the freedom of action of private enterprises."[44]

In another sense, it is conceivable that public enterprise can even have a negative effect on the use of planning, if we are to believe the report of a competent observer of the Philippine economy. After reviewing the stormy history of public enterprise and national development efforts in the Philippines,

Frank Golay concluded that "economic planning was discredited by Philippine experiences with public commercial and manufacturing enterprises as well as agricultural marketing corporations with price functions. In the commercial enterprises, management left much to be desired; nepotism and overstaffing were rampant. Productivity proved to be so low that optimistic estimates of competitive costs of production were not realized."[45] John K. Galbraith has spoken of the need of the corporate personality, whether public or private, for sufficient autonomy to work out its own destiny."[46] His comment touches on an issue that will be examined in the next section. Aside from the autonomy question, there is the fact, already noted above, that public enterprises may have been established for reasons other than development. To the extent that this situation exists in any given country, to that degree will a concordance of planning and public enterprise be difficult to achieve.

Public ownership itself would seem to be an unchallengeable criterion for relating business-type enterprises to national development, but even its adequacy can be challenged. Undeniably, it facilitates direct governmental action favoring development, and it may be indispensable where the private sector is moribund. The limits of this criterion, however, are of several kinds. First, it is difficult to contrast public and private ownership when there are so many variations of each. Raymond Aron, in fact, denies that "Forms of ownership can be reduced to the simple alternative of public or private," and names five patterns in Western countries alone.[a] Secondly, various governments, especially those of the democratic socialist type, have come to realize that wherever ownership resides, the management of an enterprise is more critical, and ownership often does not decide its caliber.

Thirdly, there is less stress on public ownership when, as today, governments have a great range of weapons geared to development. Thus, almost a decade ago, a well-known spokesman for the British Labor Party argued in print that further nationalization was unnecessary in England because governmental influence over the economy no longer rested on ownership to the extent it once had. An active government could use "numerous selective methods of controlling particular private firms or industries—discriminating taxes or subsidies, legislative action . . . selective physical or financial controls . . . the exploitation of its power as a final buyer, and generally the uninhibited use (often most effective) of bullying, cajolery, and political pressure."[48] Thus, the privately-owned American agricultural industry has operated under a measure of governmental direction for a generation (though with farmer referenda as an assumed democratic safeguard). A fourth factor that limits the influence of ownership is

---

[a]The types named are: "individual ownership, with an owner-manager; ownership by shareholders of limited companies, the manager or director not always being a major shareholder; state ownership of large firms (for instance Renault) or public service; ownership by consumers' cooperatives or producers' cooperatives; ownership by municipalities which are custodians and managers of the public services."[47]

related to the foregoing one. Under today's active governments, a giant private corporation may be more responsive to the government's wishes than a public enterprise. The steel industries of Great Britain and the United States demonstrate the point. One economist has noted that in Britian "During its brief life, government-owned steel was virtually indistinguishable from privately-owned steel," whereas the privately-owned American steel companies have justified price increases by arguments often used by nationalized industries and have in turn been subjected to successful government pressure to roll back prices.[49] A corollary of such behavior is that a public enterprise may, under some circumstances, be more vigilant in guarding its independence from governmental direction than is a private enterprise.

It is reasonable to conclude that placing complete reliance on any single criterion that relates public enterprise to national development is unwise. All of the headings discussed above have some relevance and must be considered a part of the picture. A broad perspective is undoubtedly useful in this instance. Though public enterprise is a strong, or at least a popular, instrument for countries bent on development, it is only one among many where government is hyperactive.

Problems in Relating Public Enterprise to Development

A much-discussed dilemma in the public enterprise literature of the last generation was that of autonomy versus control.[50] For public enterprise, achieving accountability is complicated by the need to permit sufficient freedom for a commercial enterprise to operate, its very *raison d'etre*.

The trend toward governmental planning further complicates the picture. Against the traditional right of an enterprise to manage its own finances, there is posed the right of the government, under planning, to use all of its resources in the best way possible. The contrasts in the situation before and after planning can be overemphasized. Many writers on public enterprise would maintain that governments have always had the duty to prevent enterprises from becoming isolated islands unresponsive to governmental wishes. This issue has been prominent in discussing the future of public authorities at the state and local government levels in the United States, for example.

Recent trends relating to public enterprise may be summarized. First, there are signs that complete autonomy is increasingly regarded as inconsistent with the idea that public agencies of whatever sort shall be responsible to the elected representatives of the people. In Canada and the United States, for example, the postwar period witnessed the passage of legislation regularizing the creation of public enterprises, imposing certain operating rules, and improving the surveillance of enterprises. The last-named includes a variety of ministerial and financial controls. Secondly, the establishment of a public enterprise is today less frequently an isolated event and more frequently one correlated with the birth of other enterprises and related to a national plan. In proportion to the amount of national planning undertaken, decisions will be reached on such questions as the following: what kind of balance shall be sought among segments of the economy (i.e., balanced versus unbalanced growth)? Which industries shall be developed in the public sector? What shall be the scale of effort for individual enterprises in the public sector? The effect of such questioning is to create an atmosphere more conducive than before to fitting the operation of public enterprises into a national framework.

Although these trends have stifled an earlier movement toward rather complete autonomy for enterprises, they have only intensified the search for a proper relationship of government and public enterprise, particularly under a developmental perspective. There are really two separate questions at issue, as suggested by the trends just discussed. The first, and older, concerns the degree of governmental control over the actions of enterprises. The second, associated with planning, asks how far-reaching and how specific national guidelines for public enterprise should be. In the following discussion, these questions are considered together.

One way of dealing with them is to insist, with Galbraith, that the fragile corporate personality is the critical element, and that accountability must be "not for method, procedure, or individual action, but for result."[51] Outside authority must be "unremittingly firm in what it asks of the corporation," but it must not intrude upon its decisions. The measure of performance for an enterprise would be its success in developing earnings "that allow it the greatest growth." Although Galbraith suggests that this enterprise expansion would take place within the "framework of plan," he does not seem to have allowed for the possibility that a plan might have other goals for an enterprise than to make the most money possible.

Proplanning writers on public enterprise provide a somewhat different perspective. They tend to view profitmaking somewhat differently and to emphasize national goals more. Hanson would permit profitmaking "only if the enterprise is able to make its profits as a result of efficiency and not through exploiting a monopoly position and also if it can do so without putting up prices to the consumer to such an extent that demand becomes unreasonably depressed."[52] He can visualize a situation where the national economic interest might require an enterprise to be run at a loss, as, for instance, to enable impoverished rural dwellers to purchase fertilizer or electricity. If profits are made by public enterprises, he would not permit them to dispose of them freely but would leave this for government decision. Ben W. Lewis, like Hanson, stresses the planning strategy implicit in price-setting for public enterprise: "The 'profit' return of nationalized industries is not a residual representing the favor or disfavor in which the product of the industry is held by the market; it is to all intents and purposes an explicit cost calculated to provide the industry with as much investment capital as the government believes should be forthcoming from this source."[53] Both Lewis and Hanson urge governmental restraint in requiring approval of decisions and delegation of authority to a public enterprise with the notion of stimulating imaginative experimentation, but both insist that government must be free to interfere when it chooses.

The differences in emphasis reviewed above illustrate an unresolved dilemma in the relationship of public enterprise to national development planning. In the words of a National Planning Association pamphlet: "Where important public enterprises have such a degree of independence that governments cannot fit their activities into plans for the public sector, the effectiveness of planning suffers. At the same time, of course, there exists the opposite danger, that of bureaucratic or political interference with effective management."[54] "The most common compromise," a United Nations study points out, "has been a semiautonomous profit-conscious entity subject to a varying degree of control over broad policy matters ... but free to take day-to-day decisions."[55] Relating such public enterprises to the private sector has also raised problems about national development, as the same report makes clear. Their hiring and purchasing policies are in many cases "a spur to private producers of the inputs and sometimes a source of improvement in respect of the quality of labour, providing training and experience not obtainable elsewhere."[56] The public enterprises may, on the other hand, serve as a deterrent to private investment if it is regarded as an unfair competitor for scarce labor and raw materials.

What has been said needs to be supplemented with political realities to give a more-rounded picture. Government planning can be a euphemism for plain political dealing. As the United Nations study mentioned above observes, "Unsuitable, politically determined plant location and undue intervention in operations—particularly in price policy—have been among the principal causes of low efficiency, though there are also many instances of poor management, stemming sometimes from the political nature of top-echelon appointments."[57] There is, of course, an opposite danger: a tendency of economic planners to regard political factors as automatically inferior to economic factors.

Within the central issue of public enterprise autonomy under planning, there are several subsidiary questions whose ramifications can perhaps be suggested in a brief discussion. One important issue revolves around the incorporation of social service aims into the operation of public enterprises. Shall a publicly-owned railroad or airline, for instance, be required to develop "uneconomic" routes in the interest of national defense or regional economic development? If so, shall the public enterprise be paid an operational subsidy? If such a subsidy is paid, shall it be shown as such on the balance sheet?

There is no doubt that the addition of social service aims complicates the operations of public enterprises immensely. "By economic criteria," says the United Nations study mentioned above, "they have been most successful when freed from the need to serve political or social ends: when saddled with employment policies or price policies that are out of line with market requirements their efficiency has usually tended to suffer."[58] Yet, public enterprises, because they are public, often are required to go beyond purely economic factors, especially in underdeveloped countries. A lack of alternatives may make this unavoidable in some cases, desirable in others, especially when broad social benefits result. It would seem to be advantageous to keep the record straight, if at all possible. Though the difficulty of placing cash values on social services is great, an attempt to do so and clearly to identify governmental subsidy payments on a public enterprise's balance sheet is desirable; the financial record of an enterprise becomes clearer, probably to the benefit of those responsible for scrutinizing that record, as well as to the morale of the management and staff. Another important benefit may be that the planners will be forced, by the process of calculating subsidies, to consider the merits of each claim for social service and to assess its legitimacy. Presumably, this process can improve planning for national development. If a public enterprise is an outstanding money-maker, a reverse subsidy issue is presented. Does good planning dictate that some of the revenues should be diverted to less profitable public enterprises, or should the enterprise be entitled to keep its revenues for expansion?

As public enterprises often sell goods or services, relatively slight differences in a single price can have a significant effect on consumption and, hence, on a national plan. Certain enterprises offer articles or services much in demand; others do not. Sometimes, as in England, pricing is further complicated by the fact that the nationalized coal, gas, and electricity industries are in competition with each other. Hard-pressed government planners cannot be blamed for taking such factors into account. And yet, whose goals and what considerations shall prevail in the hundreds of individual prices that may be involved? Where the public enterprise is a monopoly or nearly so, "price is to some extent a policy variable."[b] A planning emphasis would suggest that public enterprise prices be related to the government's price and wage policies and that "price policies for public enterprise can be designed which will improve the performance and prospects of private enterprises."[60]

Another financial question of interest to planners and public enterprises alike involves the rate at which public enterprises may borrow. If they borrow from the private money market, it may provide the answer, but in an underdeveloped

---

[b]The fuller explanation is as follows: "In such cases, recent experience tends to show that Governments are apt to hold prices down when they enter directly and significantly into costs—particularly the costs of consumers and of the Government itself—and to hold prices up when they can more readily be absorbed. Thus rail and urban road passenger fares have often been held low in the interest of short-run social objectives, even at the cost of subsidies to the transport enterprises. In some cases, steel and cement prices have also been kept low—in the interest of holding down the cost of public works. Electricity and telephone tariffs, on the other hand, have often been held high: their impact on costs tends to be small and their production can bring into the treasury a useful profit."[59]

country, this alternative may not exist. If the enterprise borrows from the government, an interest rate less than the rate at which the government borrows constitutes a subsidy to the enterprise. An interest rate identical to the cost of money to the government allows "the government to act as guarantor. Such a policy must leave out of account any differences in the riskiness of lending to the government and lending to enterprises of the kind being considered, and must fail to distinguish between the different riskiness of public enterprises of different kinds."[61] Though, again, policies will differ, the terms of government loans to public enterprises will vitally affect the borrowers and the calculations of planners.

Conclusion

By way of background, this review has tried to suggest the subtlety and complexity of the relationship between public enterprise and economic planning for national development. Because of its structural characteristics, mixed enterprise can be expected to have an even more perplexing planning context. When the public and private sectors have roughly equal influence over a mixed enterprise, ambivalence in its treatment under planning (which often has different procedures for the two sectors) might be expected. When one sector dominates, one would expect the mixed enterprise to be submerged in the organizations and procedures associated with that sector under planning.

Subsequent chapters will attempt to depict the relationship of mixed enterprise and national economic planning with the background described here in mind. Although relatively brief country surveys are limited in what they can convey, sufficient information to sketch country profiles with a broad brush is available.

3 Pioneers in Mixed Enterprise and Development: France, Italy, and Japan

In a sense, "pioneers in mixed enterprise and development" could probably be found without difficulty in the history of earlier ages. There were, for example, the age of discovery, when kings and some of their bolder subjects formed partnerships to explore the New World, and the age of mercantilism, when the exploitation of the New World's resources also produced liaisons between "public" and "private" individuals and groups. Somewhat arbitrarily, but in accord with the definitions employed in the introductory chapter, a decision has been made to concentrate on modern times and especially on industrialization.

Even within this broad context, the selection of countries and their experiences cannot escape elements of arbitrariness. The earliest European experiments with mixed enterprise in the twentieth century apparently took place in Germany.[1] Other European nations having some experience with mixed enterprise include Austria, Hungary, Czechoslovakia, Sweden, England, and Holland.[2] The choice of France and Italy over the other European countries stemmed from such factors as the following: the relatively greater prominence they have given to mixed enterprise; their continuity of experience (Germany is now divided); their emphasis on development; and their importance as models for developing nations. The last factor influenced the choice of Japan. In addition, the fame of both its modernizing drive after 1868 and its reconstruction after 1945 make it a fascinating case study, especially when mixed enterprise has had more of a role than is perhaps generally realized.

Taken together, the experiences here all too briefly summarized hint at the variety that is possible in the use of mixed enterprise in a developmental context. For each country, this survey will attempt to clarify the circumstances under which mixed enterprise originated and developed; the extent of a movement toward national economic planning; and the manner in which mixed enterprise relates to efforts at planning.

France

Mixed enterprise loomed on the French scene in the interwar period, though not markedly with the aid of ideology. *Ad hoc* measures by the government in meeting various situations resulted in the creation of public enterprises, some of which were public-private mixtures.[3] Thus, the return of Alsace to France was the occasion for the formation of two Alsatian shipping and shipyard firms in which the government owned a minority of shares and participated in management. The financial difficulties of a major shipping company which had been subsidized for a long time led the government, in 1933, to take majority ownership in order to protect the savings of many small investors. As the owner of 87 percent of the capital stock of the *Compagnie Générale Transatlantique*, the government took over ten of the nineteen seats on the board of directors. Financial difficulties also led to the significant governmental acquisition of a controlling interest in the railroads in 1937. The private companies making up the French rail network ceded to the *Société Nationale des Chemins de Fer Français* (SNCF) the franchises previously granted by the state, receiving in return 49 percent of the shares of the new company. Because private enterprise was unable by itself to finance hydroelectric development of the Rhone river, the *Compagnie Nationale du Rhône* was formed. Although local governments subscribed capital to the venture, along with private enterprise, the national government did not, receiving, nevertheless, two-fifths of the positions on the board of directors in return for granting a concession and guaranteeing the public loan floated by the company.

The circumstances recounted above suggest that the French government used mixed enterprise as a tool to assure economic progress, especially when the private sector faltered. Governmental activity for economic development extended back several centuries, of course. What was different in the interwar period was the use of shared ventures with private enterprise, rather than the grant of exclusive concessions.

During this period it also became clear that the mixture might be in terms of ownership or control, and that in either case, the state tended to be aggressive in its use of the companies. To do battle with foreign oil companies, the government joined private enterprise in setting up the *Compagnie Français des Pétroles*. Although the government held only a minority of the shares, it insisted on management rights; by contrast, the British government abdicated such rights, even though it held most of the shares.[4] The *Crédit National*, a privately-owned bank formed to finance industrial development, permitted governmental appointment of the managing director and his two deputies in return for certain privileges and the assurance of much government business.

For the decade after 1936, nationalization became much more an ideological issue than it had been, with adverse effects upon attitudes toward mixed enterprise. Several reasons may be identified. In the first place, when the Popular Front coalition of left-wing parties came to power, mixed enterprise suggested too many echoes of a business-dominated past. Greater financial flexibility, a touted advantage of mixed enterprise, was not working well because of the reluctance of business to advance additional funds to firms dominated by the government. Even though the railroads were set up as a mixed enterprise during the Popular Front period, the signs of transition to a more clear-cut form of public ownership were evident. The government's agreement to purchase the railroad companies' stock over a period of time drew little criticism from the traditional opponents of nationalization, but nationalization advocates were vocal in stating their belief that the arrangement favored the companies. Another link to nationalization in the railroad case involved its board of directors. After 1944, the SNCF board employed interest representation on its board, a trademark of the postwar nationalized industries in France. In a loose sense, the railroad re-organization of 1937 is sometimes considered the most important nationalization act of 1936-1939.

Reaction to the dramatic political issues of the day constituted a second reason for the widespread preference for more dramatic public ownership action than that suggested by mixed enterprise. The pacifism of the thirties and the popular indignation at the "merchants of death" led to the nationalization of part of the armaments industry in prewar France. Punitive measures toward firms which had collaborated with the Germans affected the Renault Works, the Gnome and Rhone Aircraft Engine Company, the Berliet Automobile Company, the film industry, a chemical factory and many newspapers which had continued to appear during the Occupation. The complexity of managing these enterprises led to the adoption of a variety of devices; mixed enterprise was employed for two, the film companies and the successor to the Gnome and Rhone Company. The determination of Resistance elements and Leftist parties to build a new France free of decadent capitalism, stimulated the complete takeover, in 1946, of key industries (coal, electricity, gas) in the energy sector as well as banks and insurance companies. Tripartite management was installed. Its backers had mixed reasons, including, for some, a desire to avoid excessive government control and to give broad representation in the new nationalized industries. In practice, the system of representing government, workers, and consumers equally on the boards broke down under the strain of politics and interest group conflicts.

An eagerness to create corporations wholly owned by the government did not survive beyond 1946. Because of the fame achieved by the nationalization drive, it is easy to overlook the firm position mixed enterprise had achieved by that year. A study published by Minister of Finance Robert Schuman listed forty-two *sociétés d'économie mixte* in the fields of transportation, communications, energy, chemicals, manufacturing, mining, film-making, as well as several miscellaneous enterprises. The government equity ranged from under 3 percent to 99 percent and amounted to 50 percent or more in nineteen enterprises. After 1946, mixed companies were substituted for several proposed nationalized companies. In 1948, two maritime shipping companies were retained as mixed enterprises instead of becoming fully nationalized companies, as the Communists and Socialists had proposed. Air France was transformed from a company in which the state had been the sole shareholder to one in which it shared ownership.

Planning

Economic planning, like nationalization, was a major—and more consistent—goal of the immediate postwar era.[5] Postwar France was remarkably receptive to the idea of planning. There were acute shortages everywhere, industry was in chaos, and a spirit of reform prevailed. The organized effort demanded by the Marshall Plan furnished the final stimulus. If the postwar strain made planning almost inevitable, other forces sustained it in later years. The cooperative methods inaugurated by Jean Monnet, the first head of the *Commissariat Général du Plan*, are often credited. "Monnet understood," a later head of the agency has written, "that despite the political situation (a majority leaning toward socialism) and despite the economic situation (the *'dirigiste'* state having all the powers), the French plan would only work if it was a collective enterprise, and if all those who were going to implement it took part in drawing it up."[6] Through the modernization (or planning) commissions set up for each of the main sectors of the economy, this aim was largely realized. For the Fifth Plan (1966-1970), there were twenty-five "vertical" commissions organized on an industry basis and six "horizontal" commissions with the tasks of dealing with common problems and synthesizing the data supplied by the vertical commissions. The commissions have included representatives of private and public business enterprises, industrial and trade associations, agriculture, and labor unions, as well as civil servants and other experts. Little importance has been attached to representation strictly in proportion to numbers. Through this extensive participation, the central planning agency was kept small; its membership was under 200, while about 3,000 individuals actually took part in framing the plan in 1960-61.

In seeing that the plan is carried out by the private sector, the state has powerful instruments for compliance. These include: subsidies, tax reductions, credit arrangements, special agreements, and other devices to persuade the private sector to follow the plan. In addition, government investment directly or indirectly controls, or is the principal influence over, one-half of total investment. One nationalized industry, *Electricité de France*, is France's biggest industrial investor. A pioneering mixed enterprise, the *Crédit National*, is used by the Ministry of Finance and the *Commissariat Général du Plan* to guide discreetly the issuance of medium-term credit according to purposes of the plan. Yet, the adequacy of the means of enforcement has been challenged. "If the threat of setting up public companies were added to these measures," a prominent French authority has written, "investment could undoubtedly be guided along the desired lines."[7] Survey data indicate, as expected, that planning is more influential when government investment is involved. In a survey of 371 French firms, 51 percent of those under public ownership assessed the Plan's influence as "very important," 31 percent as "important," 12 percent as "of little importance," and only 4 percent as "of no importance."[8] By comparison, the respective percentages given by respondents from French-owned private industry were 22, 28, 26, and 24. Some commentators, nevertheless, warn against assuming supineness on the part of the nationalized industries or simplicity in coordinating the public sector.[9]

Although the French form of planning—variously labeled "indicative," "concerted," "active," or "the modified market model"—has gained widespread attention and generally favorable notices in Western circles, there is considerable disagreement on precisely how well it has met its objectives. For any plan, implementation is not a matter of simple arithmetic, for forecasts may need to be adjusted and targets may have to be reached by different means than originally considered. With reference to performance, Jean Ripert has concluded that although the French economy substantially achieved its intended annual growth rate of about 5 percent for the years 1947-1966, prices rose about the same amount in defiance of the aim of price stability; that apart from the figures, "French economic growth in the last twenty years has been accompanied by a certain number of transformations in structure and mentality on which the plans had laid stress"; and that, nevertheless, "these transformations were neither as rapid nor as profound as would have been desirable in the light of the serious lag of the French economy at the end of the Second World War."[10] In a recent study, Stephen Cohen concluded that the actual pattern of sectoral development has differed significantly from the planned pattern, that implementation of the plan has been only a marginal consideration to the government for day-to-day economic decisions, and that the most important role of French planning is in providing conscious choice of the direction of development.[11] Another American commentator has argued that French planning declined in quality after 1952, the decline accelerating after the return of de Gaulle in 1958, because "the economic, social, and political unity of the plan has been disintegrating."[12] Events in France after this comment appeared in early 1968 lent some credence to this judgment. Unrest and riots shook the de Gaulle regime; in response, the General proposed a radical decentralization and regional autonomy, a proposal which produced sufficient opposition to lead to his resignation. In various ways, the successor government of President Georges Pompidou and Premier Jacques Chaban-Delmas worked toward a loosening of state control over the economy. At the same time, the government actively promoted industrial growth. In 1970, it proposed the establishment of an Industrial Development Institute to modernize and expand medium-sized industry. It was to spend state-supplied funds under the direction of private businessmen with a minimum of government interference. The implications of all this for planning await the passage of time.

Planning and Mixed Enterprise

If the complexities of French planning are difficult to capsulize, it is even more difficult to explain the position of mixed enterprise with reference to planning. In general, mixed companies appear to be lumped with the nationalized industries as part of the public sector, where both formulation and execution of the plan employ more direct methods than for the private sector. The degree to which mixed enterprises tend to be considered in the same breath as wholly-owned government corporations can be illustrated. Under the Economic and Social Development Fund (FEDS), which was created in 1955 to channel public investments, a dozen specialized committees were established to aid in the process. In listing the membership of the committees, no apparent distinction between the nationalized industries and mixed enterprises (at least some of the more prominent ones) was made by the Fund. For example, the Fund's Specialized Committee No. 4 included, under the heading of representatives from "nationalized industries," such mixed enterprises as the *Compagnie Nationale du Rhône* and *Société Nationale des Pétroles d'Aquitaine.* This lack of distinction for planning purposes may not occasion much surprise in the light of the previously mentioned fact that the mixed enterprise French railroads are frequently thought of in French circles as one of the first "nationalized industries." An example from the shipping industry further reinforces the notion that mixed enterprise is treated like an enterprise wholly-owned by the government. The *Compagnie générale transalantique* and the *Messageries maritimes*, in which the public sector has majority holdings, are compelled by the government "to operate some not very profitable lines or to maintain uneconomic service frequencies. . . ."[13]

It is reasonable to ask whether, in terms of planning, a distinction should be drawn between those mixed enterprises in which the state has a majority of the shares and those in which it does not. There are numerous enterprises in the latter category. French law requires that Parliament receive information on any company in which the state or nationalized enterprises singly or together hold at least 30 percent of the capital. A source published in 1963 states that 496 companies were placed on this list but adds that "there are many others where the share is below that figure."[14]

There are indications that the lack of majority control does not deter the French government, but it is less certain that the government has always moved aggressively. As noted above, even before formal planning was instituted, the government was not reluctant to direct the actions of the *Crédit National*, despite a lack of equity in it. When the government has an equity, even when it has only a minority of shares, Warren C. Baum found that it "may nevertheless exercise a significant, if not dominant voice in management decisions."[15] Another observer has theorized that where the government share is less than 30 percent, the French executive has an especially free hand because the management put in by the state is not accountable to Parliament.[16] Yet, even though mixed enterprise has been brought heavily into the extensive planning cycle, the process may not have been carried out to its full potential. "Many minority shareholdings," say John and Anne-Marie Hackett, "have been created by the participation of the nationalized industries in private firms. Up to now, the State has not used this situation in order to facilitate the achievement of the four-year Plans although it has often been suggested that it should do so."[17]

Aside from its somewhat ambiguous role in planning at the national level, mixed enterprise plays an important part in the rather feeble French regional planning. Instituted in the 1950s but given prominence only in the Fifth Plan, regional planning has as its principal object overcoming "le Désert Français," the rather descriptive name for the phenomenon of economic underdevelopment in the provinces. There are twenty-one regions, each including from two to eight departments. Regional commissions for economic development, which include representatives from employers' organizations, chambers of commerce, and trade unions, in addition to central and local government representatives, are to assist a regional prefect in planning. Regional improvement projects are carried out through a form of mixed enterprise, the *société d'économie mixte.* In the early 1960s, at least 50 percent of the capital came from local authorities (departments or communes), specialized governmental financial institutions, or private banks supplied from 30 to 40 percent, and the remainder flowed from various departmental organizations (chambers of commerce or chambers of agriculture). The scope of the seventy or so *sociétés* varies greatly, and the model for this form of organization goes back to the *Compagnie National du Rhône*, a mixed enterprise of the 1920s. The *Crédit National*, another pioneering mixed enterprise, also has a hand in regional development through its coordination of, and financial participation in, regional development societies, which are regional investment trusts having the purpose of attracting local savings and making them available to industry and trade by investing in private firms and making loans to them.

This cursory review would suggest that mixed enterprise in France fits well into the prevalent context of *dirigisme.* Although state influence over mixed enterprise did not await the arrival of formal planning, planning probably has firmed up governmental control and made it more systematic. It has not been possible to depict private influence over mixed enterprise. Yet, in the French context, it is apparent that the government works hand in glove with powerful elements in the private sphere. One would not expect to find public and private representatives at loggerheads in mixed enterprises when influential private business is drawn so fully into the planning picture and responds so well to the granting of governmental favors.

The variety of means of governmental influence over the economy may, however, raise the question of why the government should bother with mixed enterprise at all. Answers can only be speculative, but Andrew Shonfield's reasoning is suggestive on two levels.[18] On the practical level, he believes that planning which relies on cooperation requires a core of enterprises more responsive than those that are purely private, although they should show initiative and make profits (three of the four most profitable French firms in 1961 were mixed companies in the oil business). On a more mystical level, Shonfield suggests the French effort to unify investment under a single national plan may relate to the perennial French longing for the emergence of a Rousseauean general will. It is only fair to mention, however, that French planning, as Shonfield points out, has tended in the direction of using other instruments (the incentives noted above) than public ownership, whether mixed or not. In conclusion, then, mixed enterprise in France may be characterized as being thoroughly enmeshed in governmental direction of the economy, but in this it is far from unique in France.

Italy

Italian mixed enterprise is highly idiosyncratic and full of contradictions. It is ubiquitous, but it is not readily identified in the public mind as mixed enterprise. On paper, it is subject to governmentwide controls, but in practice they seem to be little used. Although the extent and variety of mixed enterprise create broad opportunities for governmental direction of the economy through planning, it is only at an embryonic stage. The accidental origin of mixed enterprise—in a haphazard rescue of failing businesses during the worldwide depression of the thirties—contrasts sharply with the deliberate use of mixed enterprise today to further the development of selected industries, services and areas.

In Italy, unified only in 1870, classical economic liberalism did not long remain the prevailing government philosophy.[19] The first notable departure was a mixed enterprise *manqué*. Although private capital was to share the cost, government money and initiative created the first modern steel works in 1884. In the first decades of the present century, the state moved into the public utility area. The railroads, begun with mixed public and private financing, were nationalized in 1905, and corporations were created in the 1920s to administer state forests, long-distance telephones, the postal and telegraph service, state monopolies, and roads. The private economy that struggled to grow in Italy's formative years leaned heavily on banks which not only extended credit but invested short-term deposits in industrial enterprises; and the banks, unequal to the task, joined industry in looking for public support.

The calamitous depression of the 1930s aggravated the drift toward deep government involvement in industry and laid the basis for today's curiously mixed economy. Initially, Mussolini tried to meet the crisis by setting up an agency to provide medium-term credit to industry and to substitute for the banks as an instrument for financing industry. When this step quickly proved inadequate, the *Istituto per la Ricostruzione Industriale* (IRI), which bore some resemblance to the Reconstruction Finance Corporation of New Deal days, was established in 1933. The Italians were less successful in extricating themselves from bankrupt enterprises than the Americans, however, and thus there occurred, as Shonfield has called it, "perhaps the most absentminded act of nationalization in history."[20] The IRI's relative lack of success in disposing of its assets, plus its usefulness for an autarchic policy and in preparing for a war economy, led to its transformation into a permanent industrial holding body in 1937. From 1933 onward, IRI had tried to make its holdings more homogeneous by creating financial holding companies to coordinate and finance investments in such sectors as iron and steel, shipping, and telephones. Even after it was made a permanent agency, however, IRI's attempt to streamline its holdings and put its house in order were gravely handicapped by two factors. It could easily sell enterprises where (as in electricity) the risk of losses was not great, but not where (as in shipyards and iron and steel) private enterprise was unwilling to risk losses. The second rigidity stemmed from the government's order to keep certain enterprises—and even to acquire some—because of their essentiality for autarchy and war.

Mixed enterprise was not confined to IRI during this era. Other, smaller corporations were created, chiefly for reasons just mentioned. *Azienda Generale Italiana Petroli* (AGIP)—founded in 1926 to encourage oil prospecting, and *Azienda Nazionale Idrogenazione Combustibili* (ANIC)—created a decade later for the refining, processing, and marketing of crude oil—were established as joint-stock companies, permitting private interests to buy shares. Unlike France, Italy did not turn to the public corporation after the second World War, and the joint-stock company, which operates under private law, increasingly became the accepted form for the public sector in industry. The state has holdings in various engineering industries, health resorts, film companies, and other firms.[21]

At this point, it is useful to briefly examine mixed enterprise as it relates to IRI and the other giant conglomerate in the public enterprise field, *Ente Nationale Idrocarburi* (ENI). Although the flamboyance of ENI, especially under its spectacular first leader (and, in a real sense, founder) Enrico Mattei, contrasts sharply with the gray anonymity of IRI, the two can be treated together here.

Created in 1953 as a wholly-owned state holding company with the task of developing the oil and natural gas industries, ENI combined AGIP and ANIC, two holding companies already mentioned, with *Società Nazionale Metandotti* (SNAM), which is both an operating and holding company. ENI owns all of SNAM, 80 percent of AGIP, and 60 percent of ANIC. Although the rest of AGIP's shares are owned by the state insurance companies, private shareholders—including notably, Montecatini, the giant chemical firm—own the other 40 percent of ANIC's shares. (In the complex Italian economy, Montecatini has itself recently fallen into the ENI-IRI orbit, as the discussion below will document.) As for the operating companies under the three intermediate companies, most are both owned and entirely controlled by ENI directly or through its subsidiary companies. There are, however, considerable outside holdings in many of the operating companies.

The IRI, which is about twice the size of ENI, pioneered the three-tiered structure in the 1930s. At the apex of IRI is the wholly-owned state holding company; in the middle are subsidiary financial holding companies whose share capital is fully or principally subscribed to by the state holding company at the apex; and at the base are the operating enterprises in which the state has either a majority- or minority-share interest. A majority shareholding apparently is not essential for control because many of the shares are frequently widely dispersed. The financial holding companies issue equity shares, of which IRI owns a majority interest, and in turn, the companies control the enterprises through ownership of shares.

In actuality, the IRI structure is even more complicated than this. An analysis of IRI's 1966 annual report reveals, for example, (1) that the state holdings in the financial companies—Finmare (shipping), Fincantieri (shipyards), Finnemeccanica (engineering), Finsider (steel), and STET (communications)—vary from 54.1 to 100 percent, with an average of 75.2 percent; (2) that the number of enterprises under a financial company ranges from six to twenty-four; (3) that the companies at the base of the pyramid sometimes have subsidiaries of their own; (4) that an operating company more often than not has multiple ownership drawn from two or more of the levels in IRI and, frequently, from the private sector; (5) that numerous enterprises, including the powerful banks and such important enterprises as airlines, toll motorways, and radio and television, are not under financial holding companies but under IRI directly; and (6) that it is the rare IRI operating enterprise in which private shareholders have a majority of the shares. Subsequent annual reports suggest no marked shifts in this picture, except for an extension of the organizational principle of making a financial holding company responsible for defined groups of subsidiary companies. An IRI subsidiary was converted into a financial holding company with supervision over thirteen small firms formerly under direct IRI control.

After World War II, when IRI was virtually leaderless and floundering to find a new direction after the years under Fascism, the structure was hardly equal to the task. Ernesto Rossi has observed that there were various shortsighted or questionable practices, such as "agreements with private industry for the joint exploitation of consumers, the adoption of legal subterfuges to escape price regulations imposed by the government, cutthroat competition among IRI industries in foreign markets, or the secrecy with which each IRI manager surrounded his own plants and manufacturing programs, with resulting duplication and excess capacity."[22] Even in more recent years, it is questionable whether IRI's view that its firms "must operate on an equal footing with private-owned firms in the same branch of production" is entirely accurate.[23] A less official, but perhaps truer view is that IRI acts as a "centralized risk-taker: shaky and unprofitable concerns are shielded by the Institute's benevolent umbrella from the stormy and unsympathetic market."[24] Yet, it may be asked whether this practice is essentially different from the practice of many large businesses in the United States in reporting only companywide (as opposed to divisional) financial results in their annual reports.

Planning

Before considering Italian mixed enterprise in a developmental context, it is desirable to note briefly the nature of governmental planning in Italy.[25] Unlike France, Italy chose to rely mainly on market forces to bring about a postwar economic recovery. Yet, the Italian government has repeatedly flirted with planning. In 1947, a Ministry of the Budget was created to coordinate all economic planning, but its subordination to the Treasury caused it to fail. The so-called Vanoni Plan laid out a ten-year development program in 1954, but national planning was not the outcome. Again in the early 1960s, the Fanfani government moved in the direction of planning. A National Committee for Economic Programming was created and a five-year plan was announced, but parliamentary inaction proved to be an obstacle. A national economic program was developed for 1966-70—the Pieraccini Plan—but, in Nigel Dispicht's apt phrase it "tagged along after the events it was designed to direct."[26] Given conditions of political drift and administrative inertia, there is little basis for optimism that the second national economic plan for the years 1971-75 will actually direct development.

Why has planning been so persistently (if ineffectually) considered when there has been unprecedented prosperity in postwar Italy? Joseph LaPalombara has suggested a multipronged answer: "rapid economic expansion has done nothing to alleviate the economic disequilibrium between North and South"; public intervention was necessary to guarantee that a high rate of economic growth, which is essential to the solution of the disequilibrium problem, be maintained; such essential features as schools, health and recreational facilities, and low-cost housing were not assured by rapid economic growth alone; and the swift development of the North aggravated the twin problems of absorbing hordes of industrial workers there and finding useful activity for individuals remaining in the backward South.[27] The government, it should be noted, did not neglect the long-festering problem of the South after World War II. In 1950, it had created the *Cassa per il Mezzogiorno*, a regional planning and development agency whose purpose was to raise the South's economic level.[28]

Planning and Mixed Enterprise

To the limited extent that governmental planning has been a reality, public enterprise, especially IRI and ENI, has occupied a prominent position in it. Thus, one might view the creation of ENI in 1953 as an effort to bring oil and natural gas exploration and development within a planning orbit. A more clear-cut measure was the passage of a law in 1957 which obliged public enterprises to invest at least 40 percent of their total investment and 60 percent of their industrial investment in the Mezzogiorno, the depressed South. There is controversy over the degree of compliance with these statutory investment proportions, but some Italians would argue that good planning required even higher proportions of Southern investments.

Another law that at least laid the basis for relating public enterprise to planning established the Ministry for State Holdings in 1956. The statute brought even the giant IRI and ENI complexes under the nominal control of a single agency. By the Ministry's interpretation, the law covered all firms in which the state held a majority of the stock or where its financial position enabled it to name a governing portion of the board of directors. The 1956 legislation also broke the tradition, left over from Fascist days, that IRI industries would be under the *de facto* control of private industry. Until then, IRI firms were dues paying members of the General Confederation of Italian Industries and were represented by it in collective bargaining negotiations.

The significance of the creation of the Ministry of State Holdings for planning can easily be overstated. It had a long way to go to overcome the confusion in the public enterprise field before 1956. The La Malfa report of 1951 noted the existence of over a thousand different undertakings and confusion over legal status and degrees of accountability. "The shares of one economic enterprise," Rossi observed in 1955, "may be owned by IRI, by the Public Domain, and by other government agencies, so that on their boards of directors the government is represented by different persons speaking with clashing voices and perhaps representing conflicting centers of political and administrative power."[29] The coming of the Ministry did not change the situation radically. Direction by a cabinet-level committee has been minimal, as is noted below. In addition, by the terms of the 1956 statute, the Ministry of State Holdings does not manage the state holding companies and their subsidiaries. Instead, the law provided for management institutions. IRI and ENI received such a designation; others are the Engineering Industries Finance Board, the Autonomous Board for the Management of Spas, and the Autonomous Board for the Film Industry.

The rationale of planning was employed by the Fanfani government in justifying the highly controversial nationalization of electricity in 1962. From a realistic planning standpoint, however, there were serious limitations. *Ente Nationale di Energia Elettricita* (ENEL) was not given jurisdiction over municipal electric companies and gained control of only 70 percent of national production, most of the rest remaining under IRI. Nor was ENEL placed under the Ministry of State Holdings but under the Ministry of Industry and Commerce.

It appears fair to say that a consistent connection between mixed enterprise and government-directed development efforts does not exist. The Mezzogiorno law did mark such a connection—and a most important one—but it has stood virtually alone. According to informed observers, the governmental organs set up to plan, coordinate, or control have had a limited impact. The Ministry of State Holdings lacks economic and technical expertise. A permanent ministerial committee, composed of the Minister of State Holdings and three other ministers, was set up in 1956 to lay out general directives for state holding companies and, indirectly, their subsidiaries to follow. The committee, one observer has noted, "has confined itself for all practical purposes to the *permissive* role of approving actions initiated by the Minister of State Participations or the managements of IRI and ENI."[30] That IRI—and especially ENI under the aggressive Mattei—have been the actual source of many important directives is often suggested.[31] George C. Maniatis, though disputing this judgment, appears to concede its force by suggesting that what IRI and ENI do has the approval of the majority of Italians, as reflected in the composition of Parliament and the ruling governments.[32] In any event, the directive power of both Parliament and ministers is inevitably restricted because IRI and ENI have relied overwhelmingly on the market rather than the government for funds.

The limited amount of governmental direction of IRI and ENI helped turn the government toward the public corporation form in bringing electricity production into the public sector in 1962. In effect, this amounted to a turning away from mixed enterprise, and it is therefore interesting to review some of the circumstances in ENEL's creation. The left-of-center parties favored nationalization in order to eliminate the private companies' political power, but they did not want to spawn another ENI, that is, a power center in the public sphere. Proponents of nationalization also criticized IRI—for failing to lead the electricity sector though it produced, through its subsidiaries, one-fourth of the nation's electricity. Previously, in 1954, IRI had been the subject of a tug-of-war about its position in the Italian economy and its relationship to government superiors. The majority of a commission appointed by the Minister of Industry and Commerce to study ways to tighten the connections between IRI and the superior authorities, referred, according to Vera Lutz, "to the necessity for ever-increasing government intervention in economic affairs, and spoke of state shareholding as a transitional stage in the process of evolution toward forms of public management."[33] By contrast, the minority enunciated the older view that IRI, rather than extending its activities, "should gradually liquidate its holdings in sectors where there was no special reason of public interest for retaining them, and where private buyers at a reasonable price could be found."

From all this, it is apparent that the decentralized form of mixed enterprise in Italy is giving way only slowly to the notion of governmental direction of the economy, to say nothing of institutionalized global planning. There is probably considerable truth in the idea that ENI, which defends Italian honor in the international oil market and has had a clever and aggressive leader, still can gain considerable popular support and freedom to follow its own expansionist course. After Mattei's death in 1962, however, ENI's financial difficulties have made it far more dependent upon the government and thus more amenable to its direction. To a degree, IRI may retain something of its earlier image of a benevolent boss employing more people than needed in order to prevent their conscription or their deportation to Germany during the war, or their unemployment after the war, but, given IRI's constructive work in the south in recent years, that image, too, may be changing.

IRI's perception of its relationship to national planning might be more accurately conveyed, however, through a summary of some items in recent annual reports. After detailing its heavy investment program for the Mezzogiorno ("of a scale and scope without precedent"), the 1968 report commented: "For this very reason, IRI has a vital interest in the current review both of the government's incentive policy for the South, which must be judged inadequate for today's requirements, and of the whole system of the so-called 'negotiated planning' which is still at its beginnings."[34] The disproportionate investment in the south in the interest of national policy and the inclusion of marginal firms in IRI ranks were cited as two important factors adversely affecting profit margins. Plainly in return for these departures from economic rationality, IRI asked in the report for an increase of 15 percent in the government endowment so that "the ratio between government funds appropriated to the [IRI] Group and capital raised on the market would be raised to about 1:6 by the end of 1972."[35] In a later report, IRI characterized its role in the formulation of the 1971-75 national economic plan as one of defining major investment projects and of working out a strategy of sectoral development in which these would find their place.[36]

Has the economic power of IRI and ENI been used to open up Italy's tightly held business establishment? Until recently, at least, there was little evidence to suggest such a course of action. Of nineteen Italian manufacturing industries surveyed by Joe S. Bain in 1959-1960, fourteen were significantly more concentrated than counterpart industries in the United States, and only one was significantly less concentrated.[37] Whether the presence of government firms altered competition and market performance, or whether government influenced or controlled prices, output, and investment policies through its firms were questions to which he could find no clear-cut answers. "The general character of [the government's] policy," he concluded, "is such that it would not be expected to employ public enterprise in manufacturing industries as a means of limiting private monopoly power."[38] The situation may be changing. In 1969, IRI and ENI used their holdings in Montecatini-Edison, Italy's largest private industrial corporation and Europe's second largest chemical company, to wrest control of the corporation away from two private financial holding companies, which are among about twenty that have interwoven ownership and dominate the Italian stock market. IRI had had holdings in the company since 1933, but, upon specific authorization from the Ministry of State Holdings, it increased its share.

The reputed lack of planning inclinations or capability among the Italian bureaucracy may be an element in slowing any move toward more integrated planning. Even if formal planning became a reality, some doubt whether the administrators would be able and willing to direct and coordinate economic planning on a national scale.[39] Senior officials already have personally rewarding connections with the industrial public sector, and without the onerous task of planning. Years ago, it was already apparent that "in certain ministries, such as the Treasury, Finance and the Interior, senior officials regard appointment as directors as almost a vested right, and the additional salaries, bonuses, expense accounts, and so on, form an important part of the emoluments of high administrative office."[40]

Despite the absence of integrated planning, a case can be made for the view that the government greatly aids development by dealing with IRI and ENI in a benevolent manner. In contributing to the investment programs of both, Shonfield argues that investment was accelerated "and so presumably the rate of growth of the whole Italian economy would have been less."[41] The forbearance of the government in not pressing for dividend payments, at least from IRI, facilitates attracting private investors and, by so doing, to expand investment programs greatly. The government's tolerance also enables IRI in particular to nurse along weak enterprises "until they have become sufficiently profitable to be able to go directly to the capital market for finance on favourable terms."[42] Whatever the merit of Shonfield's argument, IRI and ENI brought a far more systematized approach to economic development than when the government was constantly required to aid a banking system deeply involved in industrial commitments. The existence and actions of the two giants (especially ENI, under Mattei) constitute far less evident contributions to political development.

Probably in Italy alone does mixed enterprise have so central a position in the economy that it can be a critical instrument for governmental direction of the economy. As reviewed above, a complex combination of facts has inhibited the realization of this potential. So gigantic and influential are the leading mixed-enterprise aggregations, however, that Italy still emerges as a remarkable example of the use of public-private enterprise. The size and multifarious activities of IRI and ENI makes them developmental forces to be reckoned with. Against the backdrop of concentrated economic power in the private sector, they have a logic of their own. Whether Italian mixed enterprise primarily cooperates with the private giants or primarily resists their influence is a question on which the evidence appears to be mixed. A mild trend in the latter direction may be emerging, along with somewhat closer cooperation with governmental purposes and plans than in the past.

Japan

The brilliant success of Japan's concerted drive to become a modern nation can be largely attributed to a high degree of cooperation between the public and private spheres.[43] For example, in reviewing the financing of Japanese economic development, Gustav Ranis states: "The fact that [the landlord industrial group] abstained from diverting resources to nondevelopmental purposes is evidence of a degree of cooperation—or discipline—which makes it difficult to ascertain where the public sector ended and the private began."[44] The inbred nature of Japanese economic development provides the backdrop for a discussion of her mixed enterprise, but the same feature inevitably complicates the identification of such enterprise. In Japan's early industrializing history, most industry employed the closed corporate system, controlled by either the Zaibatsu, the government, or some form of coalition of the two. Japanese mixed enterprise is thus both subtle and interesting.

Although the government's activist policies after the Meiji Restoration (1867-68) are often taken as the signal for Japan's economic take-off attempt, conditioning factors apparently were at work earlier. Among these were 250 years of peace and an economizing middle class of urban merchants and money lenders—together with a good system of harbors, roads, and rudimentary schools, a large reservoir of skilled labor, both urban and rural, a highly developed tradition of cultural receptivity, and the existence of a world silk market. In the latter Tokugawa Period, the shogunate followed mercantilist policies, using proceeds from taxes for investment and exercising some measure of control over almost every aspect of economic life. The government also owned and operated or controlled all major mines and forests and attempted, without success, to participate directly in production and marketing on a national scale. Though the shogunate was thus highly active in the economy, a concerted attempt to modernize the economy awaited the appearance of a less feudalistic government able and willing to launch the heavy industries and build the infrastructure required of a modern state.

The extent of government activity along these lines after 1868 is suggested by G.C. Allen's statement that "there was scarcely any important Japanese industry of the Western type during the latter decades of the nineteenth century which did not owe its establishment to State initiative."[45] In 1880, the government owned three shipyards, fifty-one merchant ships, five munition works, fifty-two other factories, ten mines, seventy-five miles of railroads, and a telegraph system.

Public enterprise, it should be realized, was only a part of the program of a regime with the slogan of "a rich country, a strong army." Government subsidization and encouragement of private operations, the importation of equipment and technicians from abroad, and experimentation with the manufacture of various Western-type goods were all part of the picture. What fueled the economy most of all was the high proportion of military investment to the central government's total investment. Between 1875 and 1900, this amounted to a mean figure of 57 percent, with a range from 30 to 83 percent, according to Henry Rosovsky.[46]

Military considerations were also a strong factor in deciding what industries should be kept when the government, as early as 1880, began disposing of industries it had begun. Although a number of model factories, textile mills, mines, and certain shipbuilding installations were transferred to private industry, the government retained the railroads, a shipyard, the telegraph, and enterprises supplying military materials. Through the official and semiofficial banks and the bureaucracy's close relationship to big business, the government continued to chart industrial development.

Direct action by government in the industrial field resulted less from dogma than from the inadequacy of private enterprise. There were various explanations for this inadequacy.[47] The considerable wealth of merchants of the Tokugawa Period was insufficient for the demands of long-term investment in capital-intensive industries. High interest rates and private investors' expectations of quick dividends discouraged the formation of such light industries as cotton spinning. The slowness, uncertainty, and high cost of transport added a serious obstacle to the building of private factories. Another barrier, at least initially, was unfamiliarity with foreign machinery. Finally, the conservatism of merchants and their ignorance of international financial practices, as well as of technology and production, also played a part. The prospect for getting effective action in the private sphere appeared so discouraging by 1880 that some voices urged the abolition of governmental subsidies on the ground that they had failed.

From 1868 onward, the government, in stepping into the breach, had sought to involve private capital in the industries that were beginning. For example, in 1871, a government-inspired company was formed to build the Osaka-Kyota railroad with private funds. Although the government guaranteed the owners 7 percent a year on their investment, the company could raise only half the capital required for the 27-mile line. The company was dissolved in 1873, and government capital built the railroad. To get the first private railroad built, almost a decade later, the government had to promise to have its own engineers do it, to free the land of taxes, and to guarantee an annual net return of 8 percent for a number of years.[48]

In view of this dismal record of private capital in joining in a mixed enterprise system, why did the government begin to sell off its nonstrategic enterprises at such an early date and at a fraction of their initial cost? Explanations vary. A Marxist interpretation is that the firms were begun by the government in order to repay powerful merchants for their support in the 1868 Revolution and that "The state coped with all the risks involved in the construction of the first modern plants and the Zaibatsu took them over as soon as they proved to be profit-making."[49] At the time of sale, the government justified its actions on the ground that its entrepreneurial activities were no longer needed. Thomas Smith's thorough examination of the evidence led him to conclude that the enterprises were sold because the government badly needed capital to promote exports, this being one of the few ways to get it, and that, though the sales admittedly were made to privileged insiders at bargain prices and on easy terms, the government nevertheless had difficulty disposing of the firms because they were losing money.[50] On the value of the government's effort in beginning the factories, there is broader agreement. The industrial age had been launched, a nucleus of managers, engineers, and workers trained, embryo markets developed, and a base laid for further industrial growth.

Although the government's short-lived attempt to found plants in conjunction with private entrepreneurs can qualify as a failure of mixed enterprise, there were also instances of successful collaboration. A few dated from the early era just reviewed, but most were the product of Japan's imperialist surge in the 1930s. In 1885, the government joined with private interests to form a shipping firm and assured it a government-guaranteed dividend of 8 percent—preferential treatment whose effect was lost when the government began subsidizing all ocean shipping in 1896. More crucial to development were the special banks, which were subject to official control and to appointment of their chief officers by the government. These included the Yokohama Specie Bank, which conducted most of the foreign exchange business of the country; the Industrial Bank of Japan, which made long-term loans to industry; several banks to make agricultural loans; the Hokkaido Development Bank; and various colonial banks for operating in Korea and Formosa. "These Special Banks," an observer has noted, "became important instruments of national policy both in Japan Proper and overseas."[51] As to the Bank of Japan, created as a central bank in 1882, the government owned the majority of its shares and appointed its chief executives.

The close—but nonideological—link between the government and the Zaibatsu in basic industries can be illustrated by the example of a mixed enterprise in iron and steel. In 1896, the government formed the Imperial Iron Works at Yawata, soon the leading producer of iron and steel. Merged with six Zaibatsu firms in 1934, it became a mixed enterprise with three-fourths government capitalization. Yet, after 1896, the government also subsidized a number of private iron and steel firms, and, after 1934, the official manufacturing statistics apparently classified the mixed enterprise in the category of private industry.

Colonial development and the Sino-Japanese hostilities of 1937 sparked the establishment of other mixed enterprises. The largest investor in the South Manchuria Railway, acquired from Russia as a war prize, was the government. It also obtained part-ownership or special legal rights in other colonial development companies. After the flare-up in China in 1937, scores of "national policy companies" were organized to expand Japan's productive capacity, especially in war goods, and the government soon held shares in a dozen trading and industrial companies. Despite the scope of this effort, William W. Lockwood has stated his belief that "the stimulation and control of Japan's war economy in its first phase were achieved less by direct public financing than by legislation giving the government sweeping control powers over private industry and trade."[52] It should also be noted that the conversion to a war economy came, not under the old government-Zaibatsu alliance, but through the military cliques, now in the ascendant, who strengthened new capital groups and tried to free small manufacturers and traders from the domination of the Zaibatsu.

In the postwar economy, mixed enterprise initially declined as a part of the diminution of the public sector sought by Japan's conquerors.[53] The Occupation authorities closed the special colonial banks and the Yokohama Specie Bank. Three debenture-raising banks, including the Industrial Bank of Japan and the Hokkaido Development Bank, lost their privileges and their close connections with the government. The national policy companies were dissolved, along with the Zaibatsu companies. The giant mixed enterprise in steel was broken up and its properties divided between two private companies. "The shares owned by the government were sold on the market, and many of them passed into the hands of banks and financial institutions formerly part of the Zaibatsu."[a]

A marked revival of mixed enterprise occurred after Japan regained her full sovereignty. It took place as a part of the establishment of numerous government corporations, which in turn stemmed from the government's use of a whole battery of devices—including tax benefits, subsidies, and restrictive legislation—to promote economic development. Particularly after 1958, when the government decided to invest heavily in infrastructure, various government corporations dealing with transportation, communications, and natural resources were created. The corporate form had begun to be favored at least a decade earlier when the largest public concern in Japan, the National Railways, was changed from a government department into a government corporation. The pace of growth is indicated by decennial statistics: the nineteen government corporations in 1948 rose to fifty-three ten years later, and reached one hundred and nine in 1968. For various reasons, including growing doubts about relying on the corporations so heavily, growth slowed dramatically by 1966; in 1970, there were 112 corporations. They ranged in size from the Japanese National Railways, with 460,000 employees, and three other major public corporations—the Nippon Telegraph & Telephone Public Corporation, the Japan Monopoly [tobacco and salt] Corporation, and the Japan Development Bank—down to some corporations with only twenty or thirty employees. Their purposes were also diverse, including supplying funds for industrial development, aiding low-productivity sectors (the largest group) such as agriculture, small business, and welfare enterprises, promoting infrastructural development, and aiding regional development.

It is perhaps one sign of the close, informal bond between government and the private sector that the existence of numerous mixed enterprises among the government corporations is so little known and so little stressed. Of the 65 government corporations (out of a total of 110 in 1969) considered by the Administrative Management Agency of the Prime Minister's Office to be directly associated with economic development, 25 are enterprises in which both the

[a]In passing, it may be noted that the two companies recombined in 1970 under the government's urging that business grow stronger by merging.[54]

government and the private sector have invested (see Table 3-1). Sixteen of these were created after 1958, a period when the government pushed hard for economic development through providing infrastructure. As of 1969, the government held a majority interest in seventeen of the mixed enterprises, shared a 50-50 interest with the private sector in four others, and held a minority interest in four. In ten of the mixed enterprises, the government investment was over 90 percent. For the mixed enterprises with "company" in their titles, capital is owned in the form of shares and directors are chosen by a general meeting of shareholders unless there are special provisions concerning appointment.[55] For the other mixed enterprises in Table 3-1, the government directly or indirectly appoints all directors.

Table 3-1
Japanese Mixed Enterprises Associated with Economic Development

Name and Year Established	Employees (1968)	Government Investment/ Total Investment (million yen)	Government Investment as Percent of Total Investment
Japan Housing Corp. (1955)	4,086	75,472/77,473	97.4
Tokyo Express Way Public Corp. (1959)	1,447	12,799/25,598	50
Hanshin Express Way Public Corp. (1959)	841	6,850/13,700	50
Japan Railway Construction Corp. (1964)	2,121	16,800/62,929	26.6
Keihin (Tokyo Bay) Port Development Authority (1962)	173	647/1,294	50
Hanshin (Osaka Bay) Port Development Authority (1962)	178	790/1,580	50
Employment Promotion Projects Corp. (1961)	2,360	73,742/74,660	98.7
Livestock Industry Promotion Corp. (1961)	93	2,700/3,075	88
Japan Nuclear Ship Development Agency (1963)	79	2,253/2,636	85
Japan Raw Silk Corp. (1966)	25	2,030/2,933	69
Power Reactor and Nuclear Fuel Development Corp. (1967)	888	18,884/18,925	99
Bank for Commerce and Industrial Cooperatives (1936)	5,484	18,402/29,700	61.9
Tohoku District Development Co. (1936)	968	10,408/10,510	99
Electric Power Development Co. (1952)	2,790	66,500/66,600	99.8
Japan Air Lines Co. (1953)	10,963	15,600/26,905	58
Nihon Aeroplane Manufacturing Co. (1959)	444	4,200/7,800	53.8

Table 3-1 (cont.)

Name and Year Established	Employees (1968)	Government Investment/ Total Investment (million yen)	Government Investment as Percent of Total Investment
Small Business Investment Co. (1963)	124	600/5,500	10
Japan Motor Terminal Co. (1965)	76	750/2,150	34.8
Anami Gunto Promotion Fund (1953)	28	1,111/1,172	94.8
Forestry Credit Fund (1963)	46	800/2,277	35.1
Japan Atomic Energy Research Institute (1956)	2,124	64,113/65,900	97.2
The Institute of Physical and Chemical Research (1958)	567	12,241/12,735	96.1
The Institute of Asian Economic Affairs (1960)	226	300/376	79.8
Institute of Agricultural Machinery (1962)	85	2,333/2,517	92.6
The Japan Information Center of Science and Technology (1957)	319	1,733/2,068	98

Source: Adapted from Toshiyuki Masujima, "Government Corporations in Japan," Office of the Prime Minister, Tokyo, 1969 (mimeo).

Planning

As in France, the emphasis in Japanese indicative national planning is on long-term growth rather than on the analysis of short-term policy decisions.[56] Postwar emergency controls gave way to indirect methods as the private economy boomed and as social overhead capital needed to be provided. Indirect methods, Shuntaro Shishido has argued, increased rather than diminished government influence "because of the strong interdependence of the public and private sectors."[57]

Long-term economic plans are drafted by the Economic Deliberation Council, an advisory organ to the Prime Minister consisting of about thirty leading industrial, banking, and scholarly experts who can draw on a wider circle. Technically, the Council advises the Economic Planning Agency, but the latter acts as a secretariat for the prestigious Council. In the immediate postwar period, the Ministry of International Trade and Industry was influential in drafting plans for the industrial sector, and its influence in the execution stage of the plan was even larger than in the preparation stage.

Economic planning has played tag with Japan's unprecedented economic expansion. A long-range plan was drafted in December 1957, but Japan's economic growth was so rapid that the goals set for 1962 were actually reached by 1960. By the latter date, however, a new plan had already been drafted (by thirty formal, and eighteen temporary Council members as well as 191 members of specialized committees) and was approved by the Cabinet in December 1960. It provided for doubling the national income in the 1961-1970 period. It was expected that industries would be guided by the projections in making their own plans and that government would stimulate, encourage, and guide private economic activities. Economic growth during the 1960s consistently exceeded the estimates in the plan.

The inaccurate projections of the "Doubling National Income Plan" of 1961-1970 and changing perspectives led to the creation of medium-term plans at various chronological points. The first of these was published in 1965 to cover the period from 1964 to 1968. It lasted only a year, principally because of a change in governments. The title of the plan that replaced it, the "Economic and Social Development Plan, 1967-1971," suggested a move away from unqualified economic growth. This plan's emphasis on price stability, economic efficiency, and social development was, however, not considered completely adequate, and in 1969 a "New Economic and Social Development Plan" covering the 1970-1975 period was authorized. Japan's burgeoning international trade and an accompanying expansion in the scale of the economy, and popular concern about pollution and about slowness in providing amenities all contributed to the government's decision to issue still another medium-term plan.

The surface looseness of Japanese economic planning and the frequency with which its projections have been exceeded leads to inevitable skepticism about its effectiveness or even its utility. For example, after reviewing more than a dozen postwar plans, Shigeto Tsuru concluded, "The lesson is that optimism of the government *can* be highly contagious, but real planning requires more than slogan-making, in fact, more than paper work, no matter how realistic it may be."[58] Another commentator believes, nevertheless, that rapid economic growth may indeed have been facilitated by the planning process: "... a kind of coordination between mutually conflicting interests has been implemented by the overall national plan and, for that purpose, the quantitative projections have been very necessary, even though the coordination realized might not be the most desirable one."[59]

Planning and Mixed Enterprise

Little of a precise nature can be said of the relationship between national economic planning and mixed enterprise. The most specific references are in the 1961-70 plan, but it gave only slight direction to public enterprise and did not mention mixed enterprise separately. Government investments were divided into "government enterprise" and "public investments." Though the latter was scheduled to rise from 27.3 to 34.0 percent of total capital formation, "government enterprise" was scheduled to rise only slightly, from 8.6 percent in the "basic year" (an average of 1956-1958) to 9.1 percent in 1970.[60] Few public corporations and only one mixed enterprise, the Japanese Housing Corporation, were mentioned by name in the document. The annual national budget is only slightly more informative. The Diet must approve the annual budget for wholly-owned bodies, though not for units using the company form, most of which are mixed enterprises.

Although official references to planning in relation to mixed enterprise are skimpy, the skein of public-private interdependence must affect this area as it does others. Various signs noted by observers point in this direction: organized business, party government, and the government bureaucracy are the "legs of the tripod" on which the Japanese political system now rests; University of Tokyo graduates, who have frequently studied under the same professors, dominate leadership of all three, as well as of the government corporations (with which, as we have seen, mixed enterprise is indiscriminately mingled); and the frequent second careers of government bureaucrats, who tend to retire between ages 48 and 55, are in politics, big business, or public corporations (in the last-named case, to the point where employee morale is said to be adversely affected).[61]

One can conclude that mixed enterprise has been a humble handmaiden of Japanese modernization. Over a frenetic century, it has served a variety of immediate governmental aims, but these aims have been mere variations of the abiding, aggressive drive toward catching up with the West and surpassing it.

Conclusion

The context of mixed enterprise in these three countries, different as their approaches are, suggests a strong developmental perspective of a nonideological nature. In all three, mixed enterprise has largely emerged from such situations as the following: financial difficulties of private firms, which are then bailed out by the government; inability of private firms to finance projects requiring large amounts of private capital and where returns are low; a need to meet foreign competition, as in the oil industry; and assertions of national prestige, as in the case of airlines. For Japan, there was, in addition, the element of military expansion.

Both in its origins and in the manner in which it is fitted into national economic planning, mixed enterprise in these countries bears a considerable resemblance to wholly-owned government enterprise, at least when the latter is not associated with a nationalization movement. This implies an orientation of mixed enterprise toward government goals.

Whether it also implies clear-cut government domination of mixed enterprise or merely a strong community of interest between government and the private sector is less clear. In favor of the latter interpretation is the fact that cartelized industries appear to be common to all three countries and that none has a meaningful antitrust or procompetitive policy.[62] On the side of the government domination of mixed enterprise in these countries is the slighting of private interests, especially in France and Japan. The Italian government—perhaps out of its own irresolution and the size and power of IRI and ENI—has made a decided effort to balance the government's developmental purposes and private investor concerns. Thus, the government's exhortations to IRI for development of the south have been offset by its forbearance in collecting on its investment in IRI. Further encouragement to the private sector comes from its option of investing only in the most profitable IRI undertakings and in IRI's established policy of subsidizing its losers so as to retain the allegiance of private shareholders.[63] Yet, the dispersion of private shares means IRI holding companies can usually retain policy control, even when they own only a minority of the shares of the operating companies. It is perhaps unsurprising that, of the three, the country with the weakest planning and least authoritative directions to its public enterprises and mixed enterprises should also have extended the strongest incentives to the private sector to invest.

4 The United States: Private Power and Partial Planning

Inclusion of the United States in this survey may occasion surprise. Even if France, Italy, and Japan have found mixed enterprise useful in their national development, what should one expect from a nation so antithetical to "government in business"? A moment's reflection, of course, dissipates wonder. America prides itself on its pragmatism, TVA is hardly a household word for private enterprise, and, before the War between the States, state and local governments invested heavily in such basic enterprises as canals, railroads, and banks.[a] In our own day, there is wide disagreement on the significance—but not the fact—of the growing interdependence of the public and private sectors.[b]

A more realistic question, then, is, what kind of mixed enterprise and what kind of integration with development aims can be expected in the United States? Given its reputation as a country with an aggressive private sector and a well-articulated interest group structure, unusual features might be expected. They exist, in fact, and to attempt to explain them, an unorthodox approach will be employed. It responds to the difficulty, in a business civilization, of fixing a clear-cut role for the government partner in mixed enterprise. Specifically, before looking at the developmental context of mixed enterprise directly, it will be desirable to approach this topic obliquely by considering three apparent hurdles in defining government responsibility: (1) the murky identification of American mixed enterprise; (2) problems associated with government participation in the governance of mixed enterprise; and (3) complications centering on financial arrangements for mixed enterprise.

Identification of Mixed Enterprise

Three items may be singled out as contributing to the difficulty of clearly identifying mixed enterprise and, hence, to the question of clarifying govern-

---

[a]Little ideological significance was attached to these actions, for it was widely felt that if the private sphere could not furnish capital, it was proper that the public sphere do so, just so long as economic progress was made.[1]

[b]For example, economists differ on the ultimate significance of close connections between the government and its contractors. Thus, Andrew Shonfield, Walter Adams, Murray Weidenbaum, and John K. Galbraith have regarded these relationships, respectively, as an important step toward rational economic planning, a bestowing of "royal" franchises upon privileged recipients, a fruitful partnership for important and otherwise unattainable purposes, or a stage in the merger of large corporations into the governmental administrative complex.[2]

ment responsibility: the complexity of the economy, a recent tendency toward novel forms of sectoral mixing, and the whimsicality of the government's own classification system for units with some mixed enterprise characteristics.

Complexity of the Economy. The existence of a mixed economy is now generally recognized, even in the midst of routine obeisance to free enterprise. Well publicized are the pervasiveness of government subsidies for economic interests; the Keynesianism characteristic of the Nixon administration (deficit spending in the guise of a "full-employment budget"); and the countless links between big government, big business, big labor, and big agriculture.

The intertwining of public and private efforts spreads across the spectrum of government activities: promoting (farmer-elected county committees locally administer certain farm programs); regulating (trade practice conferences evolve rules which the Federal Trade Commission may accept); buying (nonprofit corporations chartered by the government conduct research and development for the government); and managing (the Atomic Energy Commission administers nearly all of its programs through private contractors). Mixed enterprise is thus part of a larger phenomenon.

To mention only the public and private sectors, however, is a grave oversimplification of the intricate American economy. As Ginzberg and his associates have pointed out, "In the decade 1950-1960, nine out of every ten net new jobs added to the economy reflected, directly and indirectly, the activities of the not-for-profit sector."[3] The authors include in this sector mutual insurance companies, savings and loan associations, trade associations, chambers of commerce, professional societies, farmers' cooperatives, consumers' cooperatives, trade unions, private colleges or universities, foundations, voluntary hospitals, research organizations, churches, social clubs, Blue Cross and Blue Shield insurance programs, and museums and libraries.

A further complexity is that the country may be undergoing shifts in notions as to the proper role of the public and private sectors. "The federal government," says an observer who sees the shift as a possible source of strength, "is taking on functions that have often been performed elsewhere, at least in the past, and private organizations increasingly are being oriented to serving governmental, rather than private, customers or clients."[4]

Novel Forms of Sectoral Mixing. Given the variety in the economy, the possibility of novel combinations is probably enhanced. To illustrate, a relatively recent annual report by the head of the Carnegie Foundation referred to "quasinongovernmental organizations" as a new social form that is legally incorporated in the private sector, has private employees, and a tax-exempt status.[5] Yet, these organizations have been created through federal initiative to meet urgent public needs, and they are financed by the national government. The main categories suggested by the report include: the "not-for-profit corporation" which provides advice to the military services; agencies which provide educational, informational, cultural, and technical assistance overseas on behalf of the Department of State and the Agency for International Development; regional educational laboratories set up by the Office of Education; and most of the community-action centers supported by the Office of Economic Opportunity. The first and the last of these have been the center of some controversy. The status of the Rand Corporation and its imitators as tax-exempt institutions earning handsome fees has led to criticisms from business as to the unfairness of such competition and from Congress as to the seeming delegation of policy functions to nongovernment bodies.[6] Community-action centers have been the object of a notable tug-of-war between minority groups and local politicians.[7]

Judging by recent events, novel forms of linkage between the public and private sectors are proliferating. Among the events of 1970, for example, were various governmental actions to meet the problems of the railroad industry:

—The Emergency Rail Services Act of 1970 authorized up to $125 million in federal loan guarantees for the bankrupt Penn Central Railroad;
—This action followed congressional passage of a statute mandating a rail-wage increase to avoid a national railroad strike;
—The National Railroad Passenger Corporation was created to take over and run intercity passenger trains.

The same year also witnessed the following actions:

—The venerable U.S. Post Office was transformed by statute into the Postal Service, a government-owned corporation;
—A Securities Investor Protection Corporation was established by statute as a private nonprofit corporation to provide financial protection for investors against loss due to brokerage insolvencies;
—The Department of Defense began negotiations with Lockheed Aircraft Corporation over payments in connection with cost overruns on 81 C-5A jumbo jet transports that threatened the solvency of the corporation.

Slightly earlier, a single statute, the Housing and Urban Development Act of 1968, had spawned the following unusual mechanisms:

—The Federal National Mortgage Association, previously a "mixed-ownership government corporation," was made into a "Government-sponsored private corporation"; but one-third of the directors were to be appointed by the President and governmental regulation was to continue;
—The National Home Ownership Foundation, with the mission of encouraging public and private organizations to supply more housing, was set up

with a governmentally-appointed board of directors selected from the private area and directions to use donated funds as well as appropriations;
–The National Corporation for Housing Partnerships was created as a federally-chartered, privately-funded corporation with the task of mobilizing private investment and business skills for the creation of low- and moderate-income housing.

It is the fact that these actions have taken place in times of economic affluence that catches the eye. Economic depressions (as well as wartime mobilization) have traditionally acted as a catalyst in the sector-mixing process. Thus, the Reconstruction Finance Corporation undertook a massive infusion of government capital into the nation's banks beginning at the time of the depression, an interesting example of temporary mixed enterprise.[8]

There are various units, both old and new, which almost, but not quite, meet one mixed-enterprise criterion, that of boards appointed by both the government and private interests. Perhaps the closest miss is the Securities Investor Protection Corporation (SIPC), created in December 1970 to provide protection against the bankruptcy of stockbroker firms. The House bill provided for an intricate and fascinating mixed-enterprise formula. Two board members were to be appointed by segments of the securities industry and five by the President, with Senate confirmation. This was straightforward enough, but a condition of obtaining loans from the Securities and Exchange Commission (via the Treasury) would have been the addition of four more presidential appointees to the SIPC board.[9] The bill that finally became law, however, provided that five board members were to be appointed by the President—three representing the securities industry and two representing the general public—and one each by the Secretary of the Treasury from the Treasury Department and by the Federal Reserve Board from its officials and employees. The notion of interest group representation was thus preserved but not appointment by the interests themselves. (Whether this makes a behavioral difference is obviously interesting, but not the subject of the present study.)

Complexities of Government Classification. A final obstacle in identifying American mixed enterprise and clarifying government responsibility is the seeming inadequacy of the classification system established by the Government Corporation Control Act of 1945. It lists government corporations in one of two categories, "wholly-owned" or "mixed-ownership." Corporations in the latter category are described in the legislative history as those "in which part of the capital stock is owned by the United States and part by borrowers or other private holders."[10] Because the statute is primarily concerned with fiscal accountability through budget and audit controls, there is no reason for it to deal with units having mixed boards—the other part of the mixed enterprise definition employed in this study.

Even the financial criterion appears not to have been applied consistently, however, though this failure may sometimes have been a matter of congressional carelessness in keeping the act up to date. The Federal Intermediate Credit Banks were shifted to the mixed-ownership category by Congress in 1956 when the banks were instructed to begin the retirement of government capital. Also, mixed-ownership corporations that have passed into private ownership have not always been promptly removed from the category. A later section will describe how Congress failed to change the categorization of the Federal Deposit Insurance Corporation, even though the error was pointed out to a congressional committee.

If the Government Corporation Control Act classifications are compared with others used by the national government, further confusion results. Thus, the "Special Analyses" section of the 1971 Budget states that "Six major types of *Government-sponsored privately owned institution* administer credit programs."[11] These six are the Federal National Mortgage Association, the Banks for Cooperatives, the Federal Intermediate Credit Banks, the Federal Land Banks, the Federal Home Loan Banks, and the Federal Reserve Banks. All but the first and last of these are listed in the Government Corporation Control Act as mixed-ownership government corporations. The Budget description is accurate in the sense that there is no government capital in any of the institutions. The overall impression of classification undertaken by the federal government, however, is of great confusion, an impression lent special credence when stated by the government's former expert on government corporations in a recent perceptive book.[12]

Current Mixed Enterprises

There is now no unit in the national government that meets the first mixed-enterprise criterion, public-private ownership. Paradoxically, none of the "mixed-ownership" government corporations listed in the Government Corporation Control Act are that. The three farm credit corporations and the Federal Home Loan Banks, whose capital was once owned in part by the government, now are entirely owned by member institutions. The Federal Deposit Insurance Corporation is self-supporting from user charges, though it is empowered to borrow from the Treasury in case of need. Although the National Railroad Passenger Corporation was granted $40 million in government funds, its common and preferred stock issues will be entirely in private hands.[13] Of units not listed in the Government Corporation Control Act, none has partial government ownership.

As to the second criterion, mixed boards, the story is quite different (see Table 4-1). Admittedly, the degree of government representation on some of the boards is so slight as to raise questions about classifying the units as mixed enterprises. It is not, however, the proportion but the existence of government

Table 4-1
U.S. Mixed Enterprises Based upon the Mixed Board Concept

Unit	Statutory Description	Selection of Board Members
A. Pre-1960		
Farm Credit Corporations Federal Land Banks Federal Intermediate Credit Banks (12) Banks for Cooperatives (12 regional, 1 Central)	(None. Organized and chartered by Governor of the Farm Credit Administration)	A part-time policy-making board in each of 12 farm credit districts is composed of six representatives elected by the associations and cooperatives which own the stock of the 3 types of banks; the seventh member is appointed by the Governor of the Farm Credit Administration with the advice and consent of the Federal Farm Credit Board.
Federal Home Loan Banks (12)	(None. Established by Federal Home Loan Bank Board)	The Federal Home Loan Bank Board appoints 4 of each bank's board members. The others—varying in members from 8 to 11—are elected by the member institutions.
Federal Reserve Banks	(None)	The Board of Governors appoints 3 members of each bank's board of directors. The other six members, though divided into 2 categories, are elected by the stockholding member banks.
B. Post-1960		
Communications Satellite Corporation	"a . . . corporation for profit." Not a U.S. agency	Three directors are appointed by the President, with senatorial confirmation. The other twelve directors are elected by communications common carriers stockholders and other stockholders.
Federal National Mortgage Association	"a government-sponsored private corporation"	Five of the 15 directors are appointed annually by the President, the rest being elected annually by the common stockholders. The President's appointees must include one from each of the following industries: homebuilding, mortgage-lending, and real estate.
National Corporation for Housing Partnerships	"a private corporation for profit." Not a U.S. agency	Three directors are appointed by the President, with senatorial confirmation; the other twelve are elected by the stockholders.
National Railroad Passenger Corporation	"a for profit corporation." Not a U.S. agency	Eight directors are appointed for 4-year terms by the President with senatorial confirmation; 3 are elected annually by the common stockholders and 4 by the preferred stockholders. The presidential appointees must include the Secretary of Transportation and a consumer representative and cannot include anyone connected with a railroad.

representation that is the criterion. Table 4-1 also suggests the wide range of subject matter to which the mixture of public and private membership has been applied. Finally, it may be noted that the more recent mixed enterprises are most often carefully labeled as not being agencies or establishments of the United States.

Government Participation in Mixed Enterprise

In our business civilization, it is particularly appropriate to ask how active government is when it joins private interests in an enterprise as an investor, or as participant on a board of directors, or both. So as to gain a time perspective on the question, relevant material on shareholding and director appointment will be reviewed for two early American institutions (the first and second Banks of the United States), one established a century ago (the Union Pacific Railroad), and one contemporary mixed enterprise (the Communications Satellite Corporation).

The First and Second Banks of the United States. The first Bank of the United States reflected Secretary of the Treasury Alexander Hamilton's belief that such an instrument would not be "a mere matter of private property, but a political machine of the greatest importance to the State."[14] Though Hamilton emphasized the public purpose inherent in the proposed Bank of the United States, he told Congress in his response to its request to develop a program for establishing the public credit that the Bank should "be under a *private* not a *public* direction—under the guidance of *individual interest*, not of *public policy*; which would be supposed to be, and, in certain emergencies, under a feeble or too sanguine administration, would really be, liable to being too much influenced by *public necessity*."[15] Directors chosen by the stockholders could be relied on to seek the prosperity of the institution.

What, then, was to be the role of government? "It will not follow, from what has been said," Hamilton argued, "that the State may not be the holder of a part of the stock of a bank, and consequently a sharer in the profits of it. It will only follow that it ought not to desire any participation in the direction of it, and therefore ought not to own the whole or a principal part of the stock. . . ."[16] If it did and management were in private hands, "this would be to commit the interests of the State to persons not interested, or not enough interested in their personal management." Only the right of inspection should be retained by government.

When Congress authorized a twenty-year charter for the bank in 1791, $2 million constituted the government's share of the bank's scheduled $10 million in capital. By authorizing the government to contribute its share out of money borrowed from the bank, Hamilton hoped to give the bank a firm specie base and enable it to get underway quickly. "Though," he conceded, "it is proposed to borrow with one hand what is lent with the other, yet the disbursement of what is borrowed will be progressive, and bank notes may be thrown into circulation instead of the gold and silver."[1][7]

Though the bank's charter was for twenty years, the government's stock holdings lasted a much shorter time. In addition to the $2 million the Treasury had borrowed to pay for its subscription to the stock of the bank, it borrowed an additional $4 million by the end of 1795.[18] As the bank's large loan to the government restricted its freedom to make private loans, the bank asked that the debt be reduced. The Treasury was unsuccessful in raising money through a bond issue and therefore had to resort to selling part of its stock in 1796 and 1797. In 1802, aided by the doubts of the Jeffersonians about the bank, the rest of the stock was sold and the proceeds used to pay off the debt to the bank. The government's profit on all the sales was $672,000, or 30 percent, and it had received dividends of over $1 million.

Secretary of the Treasury Albert Gallatin's handling of the bank's application for a renewal of the charter in 1809 showed both his Jeffersonian principles and a variation on the mixed-enterprise theme. To reduce the bank's private and centralized control, he proposed that the national government appoint some of the directors and that the states be allowed to furnish as much as half the capital as well as appoint some of the directors of the branches of the bank. All this went for naught when Congress refused to renew the charter.

In addition to participating in the capital subscription ($7 million out of 35 million) of the second Bank of the United States, established in 1816, the government was represented on the board of directors (five seats out of twenty-five). These two features were approved despite the fears of some congressmen about extending governmental power or alliance with a privileged aristocracy. Arguments in favor of the new arrangement for government membership on the board included reference to similar experience in the states. The reporter for the House debate noted that "some State banks were cited, in which the State possessed an entire control, from which no disadvantage had been realized."[19] The fate of several amendments showed the pattern of congressional sentiment about government directors. It was decided to permit selection of the president of the bank from the entire roster of directors, rather than from those chosen by the President and Senate, as the bill had originally stated. A proposal to pay the government directors ($3,000 per year was suggested) and to forbid their borrowing from the bank was voted down. In the Senate, a motion to eliminate or reduce the number of the government directors if the government shares were eliminated or reduced also lost, as did a move to require a minimum of stockholding by government directors. An amendment specifying that government directors should have no voice in choosing other directors was victorious.

Both forms of government participation, shareholding and directorships, figured in the stormy twenty-year history and demise of the second Bank of the United States. Though space does not permit a review, several incidents may be mentioned. One involved Bank President Nicholas Biddle's attempt to collect a bill from the government by withholding part of the dividends due on the government's bank stock. In September 1833, President Andrew Jackson, who had feuded with Biddle earlier, announced that he would withdraw government deposits from the bank. The ensuing years saw no diminution of the conflict. In a message to Congress on December 1, 1834, Jackson complained of "exclusion of the public directors from a knowledge of its most important proceedings."[20] After reviewing the ways in which he had striven to sever the connection between the government and "this faithless corporation," he made the recommendation "that a law be passed authorizing the sale of the public stock." A historian strongly sympathetic to Biddle and the bank has put forth another version of this controversy: "The government directors, chosen by the President, used their powers to obtain information to be handed to the Bank's enemies, with the natural result that the Bank's management instead of confiding in the board of directors, concealed all it could from them."[21] In his farewell address to Congress in December 1836, Jackson noted that, though the bank's charter had expired on March 1, the bank "has made no payment on account of the stock held by the government in that institution, although urged to pay any portion which might suit its convenience, and . . . it has given no information when payment may be expected."[22]

The Union Pacific Railroad. This bit of American history especially suggests the fuzziness of the public-private boundary. Between 1852 and 1860, a great variety of schemes were put forward in Congress for the construction of an urgently needed transcontinental railroad. The proposals ranged from government construction to subsidized private construction, but "Often these two elements were woven into patterns that were far too intricate to permit a categorical classification into 'government work,' 'private work,' or even 'private work aided by government.' They were proposals for mixed enterprise in every sense of the term."[23] The advocates of mixed enterprise were not socialistically inclined but were calling for extraordinary governmental intervention "in the name of private enterprise and of American commercial supremacy. . . ."[24]

The final statutory arrangements for the Union Pacific venture did not involve government stock ownership, despite huge land grants and loans. but the statutes of 1862 and 1864 did authorize government directors on the board. The inclusion of two directors on the 1862 board of fifteen members has been characterized by one historian as "a small enough concession to make to those who favored a government road or some provision for eventual surrender to government."[25] The 1864 statute, which bolstered financial support for railroad construction, then halted, also enlarged the proportion of government directors (now five out of twenty) and gave them specific tasks: to inspect books and records; to have a representative on each standing committee; and to file annual reports with the Secretary of the Interior.

The government directors' experience with the Union Pacific was, if anything, more turbulent and controversial than under the arrangements for the second Bank of the United States. As "directors on the part of the government," their statutory designation, they were forbidden to own Union Pacific stock. Their annual reports stated they often were not invited to meetings, rarely were heeded or consulted as to policy decisions, and were treated as spies or antagonists by the rest of the board.[26] Their frequent lack of experience, interest, and zeal as well as their high turnover rate and often poor relations with the government further detracted from their influence. Yet, it must be said their reports at least kept government officials who read them abreast of such matters as the rapid development of the West, the progressive increase in the amount of goods destined for the Orient handled by the railroad, and even the directors' opinion, in 1878, that the Union Pacific's rates were fixed on the principle of charging what the traffic would bear. In their 1894 report, the government directors also proposed a plan of reorganization for the railroad; it was one among many proposed at the time and apparently made no special impression. The total experience was sufficiently discouraging to lead some of the government directors themselves, in the 1887 report, to call for their own abolition. In 1897, when the railroad went into receivership, this wish was granted.

The Communications Satellite Corporation. The most widely-publicized and hotly-contested battle involving mixed enterprise in the twentieth century occurred over the creation of the Communications Satellite Corporation (Comsat) in 1962.[27] As with the transcontinental railroad, controversy centered on the precise mixture of public and private interests in the proposed corporation.

This question is only a part of the complications about the significance of this mixed-enterprise arrangement. A second complication arose out of statements made about the presidentially-appointed directors when the 1962 statute was being debated and during the subsequent senatorial confirmation proceedings for the incorporators and directors. Originally, the Kennedy administration had contemplated having only one government director. This was rejected, according to Robert F. Kennedy, then Attorney General, "for fear that he would be considered as the representative of the President and spokesman for the Government."[28] Apparently, the administration was sensitive to some congressional criticism that a single representative would be a "czar."

As to the precise role of the three presidentially-appointed directors provided for in the administration bill and adopted in the final statute, there was considerable confusion. Some of the advocates of a government corporation felt that these directors owed a fiduciary obligation only to the corporation and that even Senate confirmation of their appointment was inappropriate. The floor manager for the legislation in the Senate, on the other hand, saw the directors as potential conduits for the President's views. In advising Congress, Attorney General Robert F. Kennedy had to tread gingerly. As the Constitution provides for Senate confirmation of "Officers of the United States," he had to justify confirmation for incorporators and directors of what the statute called a "corporation for profit which will not be an agency or establishment of the United States Government." He also felt compelled, however, to show enough public purpose inherent in the corporation to justify legislative action. His letter to the President, printed in the *Congressional Record*, took account of testimony before Congress that the directors were to represent the public interest and not the government. From this, and the rejection of a single director, he concluded, "there appears to have been no intention on the part of the originators of the legislation to create directors who would be officers of the Government but rather an intention to dissociate the Government from the directors."[29] To offset the contention that the corporation was purely private, he pointed to the "key functions" it was to perform in major areas of public policy.

The provision for a few presidentially-appointed directors on the board probably represented a sop to those who had urged a government corporation or felt that the huge government investment in the space program needed tangible acknowledgement. Unlike the Union Pacific arrangement, however, the presence of three government directors on a board of fifteen was only one evidence of government involvement with the corporation. Other features included: (1) the furnishing of booster and tracking facilities for communications satellites by the National Aeronautics and Space Administration; (2) advice from the State Department in foreign negotiations or interconnection and frequency allocation, and on assistance to developing nations in building their communications facilities; (3) regulation by the Federal Communications Commission of rates and competitive procurement; and (4) an annual report by the President to Congress on the activities of the corporation. The still unanswered question raised by this pattern of extensive government involvement with Comsat is whether more or less significance than usual should be attached to government appointment of one-fifth of its directors.

A final complication concerns the duties of the three directors on the Comsat board. As Herman Schwartz has noted, they do not even have the supporting measures that their counterparts on the Union Pacific had: mandatory membership on committees; the requirement of an annual report; and such a specific task as seeing that debt repayment is accomplished.[30] The Comsat bylaws provide that at least one government director is to sit on the executive committee and on a contract committee, but the corporate charter declares that *all* directors have the same fiduciary duty to the corporation.[31] Yet, it would be shortsighted to pretend the interests of the corporation and the government are identical or even similar. Contracts between the two for communications services or for launching satellites, the corporation's search for profitability vs. the government's concern for service to less profitable areas, rate regulation, and competition in procurement—these are but a few examples of potential conflict of interest. In practice, the three presidentially-appointed directors seem to have been undifferentiated from their colleagues on the board.[c] Neither Comsat's annual reports nor the President's annual reports to Congress are revealing as to the views or role of the three directors. On the record, at least, there is little to dispute the statutory description of Comsat as "a private corporation, subject to appropriate governmental regulations."

Summary

These four examples of American mixed enterprise, spread over the history of the republic, portray a relatively unassertive role for government in participating with the private sector in ventures. Quite naturally, government's financial contribution in the form of capital has been more welcome than its participation in the direction of the enterprise. Hamilton apparently thought this quite proper, even to the point of doubting the propriety of having government representatives on the board. The involvement of the Second Bank's government directors in controversy related to the Jacksonians and their political rivals did nothing to legitimate the notion of government participation in the direction of the enterprise. For the Union Pacific, and even more for Comsat, government directors were little more than a bow in the direction of vast governmental financing (but not in the form of share capital) of costly undertakings.

Financial Arrangements for Mixed Enterprise

Though financial arrangements were touched on in the discussion about identifying mixed enterprise, four matters—some more controversial than others—that contribute to the vagueness of government responsibility were left unmentioned. In dealing with them, it will be necessary at times to discuss entities beyond mixed enterprise to supply the context.

One important source of confusion appears to be the practice mentioned above of establishing mixed enterprises that have *no evidence of government ownership* in the form of share capital, as is commonplace in mixed enterprise in foreign lands. Shares appear to be a more precise measure of ownership than board membership, judging by the historical review in the preceding section, but there are at least two formidable obstacles blocking their use. Private, profit-seeking corporations with presidentially-appointed directors but no government equity (see Table 4-1) can be said to recognize a government interest without the more disturbing thought that government is part-owner. To the business-civilization bias against government stock ownership in mixed enterprises, there must be added the long-standing policy of the Bureau of the Budget (now incorporated in the Office of Management and Budget) in favor of "no-stock" government corporations. This policy was developed soon after passage of the

[c]The appointees have usually been prominent men, such as George Meany and Frederic G. Donner, both of whom have served three three-year terms. William W. Hagerty served as a presidentially-appointed director from 1965 until his election as a Series 1 (i.e., noncarrier) director in 1970; this is presumably another sign of lack of differentiation.

Government Corporation Control Act of 1945 despite the act's assumption of continued stock ownership in its categories of "wholly-owned" and "mixed-ownership" corporations.

A situation involving the Federal Deposit Insurance Corporation (FDIC) may well have stimulated the adoption of the practices of retiring stock and of not beginning new corporations with ownership shares. From the viewpoint of the Bureau of the Budget in 1960, Congress had incorrectly placed the FDIC in the mixed-ownership category. The action had occurred because at the time the corporation began (in 1933), the Federal Reserve Banks were required to subscribe to stock in the FDIC in an amount equal to one-half of their surplus. As private banks must by law subscribe to the capital of the Federal Reserve Banks, the action of the latter in investing in the FDIC created "an appearance of mixed ownership," as a Bureau spokesman noted.[32] It lacked genuineness, however, because, again by law, the Federal Reserve Banks' surpluses belong to the national government, a fact recognized by Congress in the procedure it established for retirement of FDIC stock between 1946 and 1948.[d] Retirement of all of the stock had opposite effects upon the government financial agencies and the FDIC. Both the Budget Bureau and the General Accounting Office (GAO) intensified their pleas that the FDIC be moved to the "wholly-owned" category and thereby become subject to annual budget review.[34] Repayment of the entire investment, whether from the Treasury directly or from the Federal Reserve Banks, only reinforced the FDIC's conviction of the inappropriateness of classification as a "wholly-owned government corporation."[35] The FDIC has continued as a mixed-ownership government corporation. All in all, the experience with the FDIC was not calculated to make the Office of Management and Budget regard reinstitution of stock ownership a contribution toward ending confusion.

A second matter that has drawn controversy centers on the *ownership of financial surplus and reserves* in instances where the mixed enterprises initially had been heavily capitalized by the government. This question has especially arisen in connection with the peculiarly American institution of "disappearing" mixed enterprise. The process of permitting borrowers from a mixed enterprise to acquire complete ownership over a period of time has been applied to the pre-1968 Federal National Mortgage Association and the farm credit corporations. Taking the latter as an example, the Federal Land Banks retired their government capital by 1947, and the Federal Intermediate Credit Banks and the Banks for Cooperatives, spurred on by statutes in the 1950s that urged mutualization, finally retired theirs by the end of 1968.[e]

---

[d]Congress "directed the corporation to retire its capital stock by paying the amount received therefor, whether received from the Secretary of the Treasury or the Federal Reserve Banks, to the Secretary of the Treasury for deposit in the Treasury as miscellaneous receipts."[33]

[e]Farmers who borrowed from an association or cooperative were required to purchase stock in it in an amount equal to a fixed percentage—5 percent for the production credit associations—of their loans. The association or cooperative in turn purchased a like amount of stock in the bank. When the loan was repaid, the stock in the bank and the association or cooperative was retired.

As early as 1945, the GAO challenged the Federal Land Bank's approach to the question of surpluses: "The land banks have been enabled to reduce the amounts designated as Government capital by the use of accumulated income, a large portion of which was devised from such Government capital. This raises the question whether the accumulated income derived from Government capital should not be regarded as capital provided by the Government, rather than as a fund accumulated exclusively for the benefit of borrowers."[36] A subsequent GAO report noted that, in addition, all of the farm credit corporations enjoyed such government services as "interest-free and dividend-free Government capital and . . . the proper share of the Government's contribution to the civil service retirement and disability fund and to the Federal employees' compensation fund and other costs of Government."[37]

Though the farm credit statutes of the 1950s that started the Federal Intermediate Credit Banks and the Banks for Cooperatives on the path to private ownership stimulated discussion of the disposition of surplus and reserves, Congress basically upheld the position of the powerful farm groups that the banks were the owners. The 1953 act did make the net earnings of the Federal Intermediate Credit Banks and Banks for Cooperatives subject to a 25 percent franchise tax, as long as they had government capital in them. Criticism of the Banks for Cooperatives came from the second Hoover Commission. It noted that the banks were adding to their surplus by collecting interest on government bonds which they had purchased through an interest-free $150 million investment by the government, "a hidden subsidy from the taxpayers at large to a small group of beneficiaries."[38] In the Farm Credit Acts of 1955 and 1956, nevertheless, Congress voted to give up any government interest in the surplus and reserves of the corporations, once the government capital had been retired. Then and subsequently, the lawmakers were unmoved by criticism from one of their number along the following lines

Can it be argued that surpluses accumulated by private banking institutions belong to the depositors and borrowers because the banks did business with them? . . . Under the same reasoning, would not the gentleman say that the Home Owners Loan Corporation, which was liquidated with a profit of over $14 million to the Government, should return this money to the homeowners? Would the gentleman say, under the same line of reasoning, that the small firms which pay interest to the Small Business Administration upon loans made to them should also share in accumulations derived from interest paid . . . ?[39]

Though the first two items have centered on ownership, the third—the question of *financial commitments* made by the government—deemphasizes it. Borrowing authorizations and revolving funds are involved rather than government stock investment. In a sense, there is no issue here because it is highly unlikely the government would permit a government-sponsored banking or credit system to collapse whether or not commitments were made explicit. This is thoroughly understood by the financial community in dealing with the commercial paper of the credit agencies.[40]

In any event, the existence of governmental commitments promoted one notable but unsuccessful attempt by the Eisenhower administration to increase financial supervision over the units involved. The President's budget message of 1958 recommended "budget and audit control over Government corporations which are authorized, directly or indirectly, to obtain or utilize Federal funds."[41] In support of a bill to accomplish this purpose, the Bureau of the Budget urged upon Congress a criterion of control "based not on private ownership of capital stock, but on the use of Federal funds and the financial responsibilities assumed by the United States Government."[42] The Bureau emphasized the irrelevance of ownership in this context by pointing out, "The Government's financial stake in most of the mixed-ownership corporations is far greater than that in many of the wholly-owned corporations."

The government's direct financial commitments derive from mandatory borrowing authorizations possessed by corporate units. If the boards of government corporations that insure deposits (FDIC and Federal Savings and Loan Insurance Corporation) decide to borrow against their authorized funds, the Treasury has no choice but to make the loan.[43] Even though neither agency has made use of its respective funds of $3 billion and $750 million, the bureau argued before Congress that such powerful authorizations warranted budget and audit controls even without partial government ownership.[44]

Mixed enterprises have been involved in more indirect commitments. The Federal National Mortgage Association and the Federal Home Loan Banks are required to obtain Treasury approval of the terms and timing of specific offerings, and the Treasury is authorized but not required to purchase limited amounts of their obligations.[45] Indirect commitments of a different kind produced the Budget Bureau's request to Congress in 1958. The Bureau expressed concern that the money from retirement of the government stock in the Federal Intermediate Credit Banks and the Banks for Cooperatives was not being paid into the Treasury directly but into revolving funds that were available for reinvestment if needed.[46] Not only did Congress retain this arrangement, but, a decade later, when it passed a law (Public Law 90-582) accelerating the retirement of the remaining government stock, it again stipulated that stock retirement money should be credited to the revolving funds. The statute also provided that if the government makes short-term investments in any of the banks in an emergency, their private ownership status will not be changed, though they will once again be subject to the Government Corporation Control Act.

The last—and currently the major—question of financial responsibility is the growing use of *extrabudgetary credit programs*. Of all the questions, this has the most direct bearing on development planning. Federal and federally-assisted credit outstanding has grown from about $100 billion in fiscal 1961 to a projected $250 billion in fiscal 1974.[47] Loans by mixed enterprises in the credit field make up over one-fifth of this huge total and have more than doubled since 1969. Along with the category known as guaranteed and insured loans (mainly mortgage insurance commitments, guarantee commitments for community development, insured student loans, and Export-Import Bank guarantees, loans by government-sponsored enterprises have not been listed in the budget since fiscal 1969. This was in line with a recommendation in 1967 of the President's Commission on Budget Concepts that the activities of government-sponsored enterprises be excluded if the agencies are privately-owned.[48] Though the Federal Land Banks and the Federal Home Loan Banks had completed the transition to private ownership decades earlier, statutes in 1968 facilitated the quick passage of three other entities, the Federal Intermediate Credit Banks, the Banks for Cooperatives, and the Secondary Market Operations Trust of the Federal National Mortgage Association.

Although extrabudgetary credit has been attractive because it does not affect budgetary expenditures or contribute to the budgetary deficit, already swollen from the Vietnam war, the rapid expansion of the programs has recently produced plans to bring them under better control. President Nixon's budget message for fiscal 1972 declared his intention to "propose legislation to enable these credit programs to be reviewed and coordinated along with other Federal programs."[49] Concern about their impact was at the heart of the President's stand, though he may also have been influenced by growing criticism in the business community about the rapid expansion of the five credit enterprises.[50] Speaking of all of the extrabudgetary credit programs, he said: "Their effects on fiscal policy have not been rigorously included in the overall budget process. And their effects on overall debt management are not coordinated well with the overall public debt policy."[51]

The means proposed by the Treasury to carry out the President's intent of achieving greater coordination were much milder than the means that might have been suggested, i.e., bringing the credit mixed enterprises back into the budget. Instead, the Treasury prepared draft legislation to create a federal financing bank.[52] It would serve as a vehicle to consolidate the mass of federally-assisted credit. Securities issued by federal or federally-sponsored agencies would be sold to the bank; it would finance these purchases by issuing its own securities in the market. The bank would not make decisions as to the level of credit programs. Its function would be to facilitate management and control of the credit programs by reducing their costs and market impact and by aiding presidential and congressional review through consolidating the financing and isolating the subsidy elements.

Even though the proposed coordination is mild, a greater consciousness of the need for planning is implicit. Housing and farm credit programs are likely to continue expanding, and new credit agencies have been proposed for such purposes as pollution control and aiding students and state and local governments.[53] The subsidies involved are increasingly a burden to the taxpayer: extensions of credit under federal programs in fiscal 1970 were estimated by the government to entail subsidies in excess of five billion dollars before the loans are repaid.[54] The next section considers the topic of planning and mixed enterprise more directly.

Planning and Mixed Enterprise

American planning, a government report states, "relies in diverse and 'unplanned' ways on governments, businesses, consumers, workers and voluntary and private organizations, large and small, to work within an environment of freedom to achieve social and economic objectives shared by all."[55] Though the statement ends with a euphemism, it has some merit as a description of the process of American planning. The management of aggregate demand is, as Jesse Burkhead has noted, "National economic planning—American style."[56]

Planning has made headway in the United States against a popular feeling that it is socialistic, if not communistic. The recent profusion of "five-year plans" in large American firms may be helping to remove the unfavorable connotation the term has had.[f] Some versions of planning have been more acceptable in the American environment than others. Manpower planning, for example, is generally accepted, and there have been various experiments with it in the national government since the second World War. Less fortunate until very recently, when ecology became a vital concern, was "resources planning." The National Resources Planning Board, created by executive order in 1939, soon aroused the jealousy of Congress and was abolished. Although the Employment Act of 1946 was a watered-down version of a liberal full-employment bill, the Council of Economic Advisers has been flexible in meeting emerging problems, moving from an original concern with maximum employment, production, and purchasing power to such matters as inflation, growth, balance of payments, and ways of increasing the opportunities for the poor.[58] Concern for even broader purposes has fostered efforts to declare "social accounting" a national goal, establish a Council of Social Advisers, require the President to submit an annual Social Report to Congress, and create a Joint Committee of Congress to examine the substance of the Social Report.[59] Stewart Udall has remarked on the existence of specific national program plans, such as the moon shot, the interstate highway program, and the G.I. Bill of Rights.[60] There are increasing experiments in regional and state developmental planning.[61]

The prominence of fiscal policies under Keynesianism makes the national budget a tool of informal planning. As compared with the coordination between

---

[f]"To a great degree, professional planning by big business is an answer to the socialist's major economic criticism of market capitalism: that it is wasteful because businessmen are free to use resources pretty much as they please without any rational plan."[57]

annual budget proposals and planning in countries with formal plans, "the practice in the United States stands in marked contrast to such efforts to relate the government budget to the overall economy, and both to national long-term objectives."[62] It should also be conceded that budgeting is more limited than planning, for it relates only to the public sector, covers a shorter time span, uses different classifications and measurements, and implies different kinds of responsibilities and different attitudes in leadership and staff.[63] Still, given the scale and diversity of government activities and their weight in the economy, it is apparent budgetary prescriptions can be influential far beyond the walls of a government office. Increasingly, there have been attempts to view the budget programmatically rather than in cold financial terms. Inspired by the efforts of the Department of Defense under Secretary Robert S. McNamara, President Lyndon Johnson ordered a governmentwide adoption of a Planning-Programming-Budgeting System (PPBS) in 1965, a step that has met only limited success.[64]

A feature of aggregate economics are national income accounts, which "depict in quantitative summary fashion the manner in which the various economic units within a nation are interrelated in the production, distribution, and utilization of goods and services."[65] There are several technical problems in classifying public enterprise which may be noted in passing. According to Gerhard Colm, public enterprises "could be included in a broad enterprise sector, which would then be subdivided into private and public enterprises. Or they could be included in the government sector, which then would be subdivided into government enterprises and administrative agencies. For most questions, the first alternative appears preferable."[66] A second classification question carries the implication that the national income accounts understate the contribution of government and government enterprise to the nation's total economic efforts. It is pointed out that "in calculating the output of the private sector, national income analysts always take into account the capital used in producing the goods and services that are eventually sold. No account is taken, however, of rent paid, supplies used, or capital depreciated in producing the government's output." More specifically, "the accounts show only the net balance between the subsidies advanced and the net surpluses earned by various government enterprises."[67]

The uncertainties of fiscal planning when privately-owned bodies are involved influenced the President's Commission on Budget Concepts in recommending, as noted above, the exclusion of the credit mixed enterprises from budget receipts and expenditures. The commission observed that "the absence of budgetary review means that only rough estimates can be entered in the budget document for forward periods, and the difference between estimated and actual results . . . has introduced significant estimating errors. . . ."[68] In a staff paper for the commission, Comptroller General Elmer B. Staats suggested going further. He would not have waited for full private ownership to be achieved but would have excluded units in process of transition to this status at that point when ownership becomes more than 50 percent private.[69] As implied in the preceding section, however, an emphasis on ownership as the criterion for governmental direction appears to be giving way to recognition of the enormous economic leverage which the credit agencies have in shaping the economy.

This was recognized, to a degree, long before the recent huge expansion in credit programs and the President's statements in his budget message. The borrowing programs of all of the mixed enterprises are subject to federal supervision, and, either by law or custom, all consult the Treasury Department in planning their offerings.[70] Beyond consultation with the Treasury, there have been several actions that partially anticipated the coordination attempts of the Nixon administration. The Participation Sales Act of 1966 authorized the Federal National Mortgage Association to sell beneficial interests, or participations, in mortgages or other types of obligations in which a half-dozen federal agencies have a financial interest. Though the major political motivation was undoubtedly the favorable effect upon the budgetary deficit,[g] there were benefits for fiscal coordination. A legislative committee noted among the advantages "the effective coordination of these offerings, not only with one another but also with the Treasury's own debt management operations."[72] In 1970, a commission appointed to study the farm credit system recommended a consideration of the feasibility of replacing the numerous bonds and debentures of the three groups of banks with a single farm credit action.[73] A staff paper for the commission found that the impact of the credit programs on the economy and financial markets "is becoming much too large to allow them to function independently of the Government's overall economic policies. Now is the time for Farm Credit Agencies to think through what their own priorities are and how they might fit into broader national objectives."[74] A joint Treasury-Federal Reserve study of 1966-1970 argued for a single marketing unit for all federal agencies as a way of making agency issues available "in larger and more tradeable blocks."[75] In urging the same course of action, a former member of the Council of Economic Advisers put the case in language closer to economic planning: "... we need effective control over such loan programs *if the objectives of public policy are to be realized.*"[76]

The political clout of interest groups behind the credit mixed enterprises and the loose government structure constitute formidable (and related) obstacles to integrated government direction of the credit mixed enterprises beyond the steps noted. These points can be briefly illustrated with examples from recent history.

As to the first barrier, rising interest rates led the Johnson administration, in 1966, to restrict new issues of agency securities in the markets to amounts

---

[g]Under the administrative budget then in use, loan transactions were counted as a part of the national debt. In selling the rights of assets instead of title to the paper itself, the receipt would be counted in the administrative budget as a "negative expenditure," thereby reducing the total expenditures and hence the budget deficit.[71]

necessary to refund maturing issues. The farm credit corporations cooperated fully in this request. By April 1967, nevertheless, when the inflationary trend had receded somewhat, farm groups and their spokesmen in Congress became restless over the fact that the President's temporary order had not yet been rescinded. A congressman worried that "the administration is using the [farm credit system] to regulate the economy," and a spokesman for the American Farm Bureau Federation detected "indications that the issue at stake here is not economic, but political, and involves the independence of the farmer-owned farm credit system."[77] During the same period, the Johnson Administration also moved to expand the authority of the Federal Home Loan Bank Board over the dividend rates paid by federal savings and loan associations. The Interstate Rate Control Act, which granted authority to the board to set maximum dividend rates, was passed by Congress in 1966, after an appeal by the Administration. The savings and loan associations, which had strongly resisted the move as late as Spring 1966, were prompted to accept it because they needed congressional action to protect them against competition from banks during the monetary crisis of 1966.[78]

Housing credit can be taken as an example of the second obstacle. Though housing shortages tend to activate the political branches of government, there is sharp disagreement on the effectiveness and even the feasibility of overall government direction in this field. In 1966, in response to one of the frequent crises in the highly volatile housing construction industry, Congress enacted a statute (Public Law 89-597) empowering the Federal Reserve Board to purchase obligations of the Federal National Mortgage Association and the Federal Home Loan Banks for a one-year period in order to bring about a reduction of interest rates on home mortgages. The board, however, did not see fit to take such action. Noting this with disapproval, the Joint Economic Committee of Congress recommended renewal of the legislation and strongly urged the board to "use this authority consistent with congressional intent."[79] The Commission on Mortgage Interest Rates, established by Congress, not only reiterated the recommendation for action by the Federal Reserve Board but urged that various other steps be taken to increase investments in housing-type obligations.[80] Then and subsequently, the Federal Reserve and the Treasury have tended to throw cold water on proposals that would force more money into the housing market at a time when the government was conducting a fight against inflation.[81] Another incident related to housing also showed policy decisions. The experience of the Federal Home Loan Bank Board (FHLBB) in yielding to the White House's request in 1962 to advance mortgage money to stimulate the mildly recessive economy led eventually to the board's decision to follow its own counsel. The idea of advancing funds was enthusiastically backed by the savings and loan industry, but when tight money days came in 1966, there were not enough funds to meet the demand for mortgage money. According to a historian of the board, it delcared its "freedom" from the rest of the government, and

"...now, the FHLBB will limit advances when home-financing money is plentiful even though the economy is lagging and it will expand advances (if it can) in periods like 1966 when the economy is overheating."[82]

Despite the existence of these familiar, antiplanning features of the American government scene, there is reason to think that the inclusion of federally-assisted credit programs in the national budget will become more of an issue in the future than at present. Increased reliance on fiscal and monetary planning makes huge, subsidized programs that are outside the budget appear progressively more anomalous.

The difficulties of bringing such programs under the budget should not be minimized, as spokesmen for the credit mixed enterprises emphasize.[83] First, the budget cycle is slow and uncertain, especially in its congressional appropriations phase. To require federally-assisted credit to run the risk of delay might well turn countercyclical intent into procyclical reality. In addition, the size and timing of mixed enterprise borrowings are already coordinated by the Treasury. Finally, though the Treasury is the statutory lender of last resort for some of the mixed enterprises, they have not actually used these standby lines of credit.

To these practical objections, some would add a theoretical disagreement. Economists do not agree as to the precise effect upon national policy goals (under Keynesianism) of the actions of the credit agencies. Does their borrowing in the private capital markets result in smaller credit formation elsewhere, or does it add to the flow of total credit and total spending on goods and services?[84] Can secondary market operations in home mortgages be manipulated successfully for stabilization purposes?[h]

The case for inclusion of federally-assisted credit programs in the national budget has been made by a former official of the Nixon administration who worked closely with the problem.[86] His reasoning deserves summarization as an example of an emerging view on an important issue. Federal credit programs are not mere financing instruments but involve the allocation of national resources. At present, this allocation of resources takes place outside the discipline of the budget and without reference to the broad economic plan outlined in it. Subsidized borrowers tend to be insulated from both monetary and fiscal restraints. As most loans outside the budget require direct federal payment of interest or other debt service subsidies, the flexibility of future economic decisions is limited. Inclusion in the budget would force federally-assisted credit programs to be justified on their merits and in the light of program priorities.

This reasoning suggests that a planning perspective may be entering into the consideration of federally-assisted credit, of which the credit mixed enterprises

---

[h]"The extent to which secondary market operations in home mortgages should be manipulated by the government for stabilization purposes, then, depends primarily on the nature of the cyclical interactions among different parts of the construction industry. Since these cannot be foreseen with perfect accuracy, federal lending policies in this area, as in most others, should not be laid down in advance but should vary with the specific circumstances prevailing at the time."[85]

are a part. Such thinking is apparently far from making itself felt in structural arrangements, but it may indicate the dawn of a shift away from the view that makes inclusion and exclusion in the budget dependent upon the public-private dichotomy.

Conclusion

The discussion of obstacles to a clear articulation of the government role in American mixed enterprise can be summarized as follows:

1. The expected strength of the private sector and a corresponding weakness of the government partner appear to be a reality.
2. This imbalance complicates the responsibility government bears for its participation. Even the form of participation has been progressively affected: capital shares are no longer employed and, by itself, government membership on boards of mixed enterprises is of inconclusive significance and tends toward symbolism.
3. The indistinctness of the mixed-enterprise image mirrors the blurring of differences in the society at large between entities called public or private, profit or nonprofit. By definition, a partnership or mixed enterprise in the United States is shaped strongly by the pluralist pattern of gaining broad freedom for the private partners while enjoying reassuring support from the government.
4. Passage into private ownership has capped this political process for mixed enterprises, aided by the government's wish to remove items from the budget whenever possible.
5. Ownership as a criterion for treatment, which was challenged by the government's financial agencies some years ago, is now encountering a stiffer challenge on grounds closer to planning. Even while extrabudgetary credit, which heavily involves mixed enterprises, continues to expand swiftly, there are second thoughts about the extent to which the government can permit it without review and coordination.

Under the conditions described in this chapter, the conjunction of weak national economic planning and private-dominated mixed enterprise is bound to be rather tenuous. There may even be conflicting trends in that mixed enterprise's passage into private ownership has occurred in an era of closer government coordination of the economy. Still, the surge of the latter trend means that the government is increasingly unlikely to overlook possible ways of shaping private action; mixed enterprises, by definition, stand on the border areas between the two sectors.

5 Contrasts and Convergences: India and Pakistan

Treating these volatile nations together may seem somewhat incongruous. In their quarter-century as independent nations, they have had numerous quarrels and several open conflicts, culminating in the savage fourteen-day war of late 1971 that resulted in the dismemberment of Pakistan and the birth of Bangla Desh.

Yet, there is logic in grouping them for discussion in this volume. In general, their proximity to each other, their common history of British rule, and their simultaneous birth as new states suggest it. There are other similarities closer to the present topic. Both nations have vigorously sought to industrialize. Both have taken economic planning more seriously than their neighbors have, according to Gunnar Myrdal, but economic inequalities have also increased more in these countries than nearby.[1] Both have therefore had to face the sharp challenge of redefining development goals.

Such similarities can, of course, be matched with differences, some of which contribute to the recurrent tensions between these nations. Though the respective industrialization paths followed by each are not in the tension-producing category, they are of interest here for their influence upon the use of mixed enterprise.

Concededly, the dismemberment of Pakistan renders the information on that country primarily of historical significance. Yet, the account given here should have value in picturing the problems faced by new nations employing mixed enterprise in circumstances of divided territory and differing economic conditions. It should also be a basis for perceiving some of the problems facing Pakistan in the future.

India

India has attracted worldwide attention because of its size, its experimentation with democracy, and its rivalry with Communist China. Also part of the picture is India's attempt to mesh public and private ownership in a way which will eventuate in a viable economy. Though mixed enterprise has not been crucial to this experiment, it has had a part to play. That role has been stronger in the financing of industrial and commercial development than in its operation.

The relevant historical background of mixed enterprise, which applies at least in part to Pakistan as well as India, can be briefly traced. Although the nineteenth-century government of India was primarily guided by the laissez-faire attitudes prevalent in Great Britain, it was not totally inactive in public enterprise. In 1860, it established a harness and saddlery factory, and over a period of time, it created ordnance factories.[2] In rail transportation, the government flirted with every form of ownership and control. Between 1850 and 1868, the government "guaranteed the rate of return on bonds and participated in the profits, if any. The management was in the hands of the company, but the Government reserved certain powers of control and supervision in important matters."[3] State ownership flourished from 1869 to 1882, when, after opinion in England had crystallized against this form, a return to the guarantee system occurred. This time, the government was to have a larger share of any profits, and the lines constructed were to be its property. By the early twentieth century, India's railroad system was a mélange of thirty-three separate administrations. Private companies ran twenty-four of these, native states managed five, and government agents ran four.[4] Because the railroads almost invariably lost money, and the government had to pay the guarantees, the British Parliament investigated the situation several times.[5] The Acworth Committee in 1920 finally recommended state ownership of the entire system, and three years later, the Indian government began acquisition of the roads, although the process took more than twenty years. Before independence, the Indian government had also undertaken a limited number of other public ownership ventures, including the generation and distribution of electricity and the construction of irrigation works.[6]

However the railroad situation is analyzed, a truer precedent for mixed enterprise in modern India was found in certain of the more progressive princely states. Mysore, it has been said, "established the pattern for state and mixed enterprises which characterizes modern India."[7] The Mysore government began its developmental activities as early as 1870, and, aside from total or partial ownership of enterprises, these included making loans, giving guarantees, and providing research and technical assistance. Wholly-owned factories included iron and steel, sandalwood, soap, silk weaving, buttons, and sugar, the last-named on an experimental basis. Mixed enterprises were begun chiefly to encourage private capital to venture its money in projects regarded as worthwhile. Especially in the 1930s, and for paper, and silk, the government undertook preliminary surveys, floated issues of stock, subscribed to a portion of the share capital, and placed its representatives (usually a minority) on the board of directors. Hyderabad, Baroda, Gwalior, and Travancore also had substantial records of investing in and sponsoring industry. The Indian provincial governments, as distinguished from the princely states, were much slower to begin mixed enterprises, but they did after 1918. After independence in 1947, mixed enterprise was a fairly common phenomenon in the states.

The mixed enterprise activity of some of the princely states was encouraged after 1918 by the publication of a report of the Indian Industrial Commission.

In urging an active policy of governmental encouragement of industry, the report suggested the possibility of contributions to share capital along with such other suggestions for financial aids as loans, guarantees of dividends, and purchasing output. Though there were other pronouncements by the Indian government in later years, including a statement of industrial policy in 1945, action by the central government awaited the coming of independence in 1947.

Since independence, industrial activity in the public sector has been in the contrasting shadows of ideological drive and empirical necessity. The socialist inclinations of the Congress party antedated 1947 by many years. As early as 1931, the party passed a resolution that the "State shall own or control key industries and services, mineral resources, railways, waterways, shipping, and other means of public transport."[8] A statement by the Congress in 1948 appeared to be more sweeping: "In respect of existing undertakings, the process of transfer from private to public ownership should commence after a period of five years."[9] New undertakings in key industries or in the nature of monopolies were also to be in the public sphere.

An Industrial Policy Resolution of the same year was more specific, though perhaps no clearer. Munitions, atomic energy, and railroads were to be exclusively governmental, and in any emergency, the government would have authority to take over "any industry vital to national defense." A more controversial portion made the government responsible for new undertakings in coal, iron and steel, oils, aircraft manufacture, shipbuilding, and communications equipment except for radio-receiving sets. While asserting its "inherent right" to acquire any existing industrial undertaking, the government promised "to let existing undertakings in these fields develop for a period of ten years, during which they will be allowed all facilities for efficient working and reasonable expansion."[10]

In 1956, a Second Industrial Policy Resolution, which has not been superseded to date, gave some indication of where mixed enterprise might fit into the picture. Three categories of industry were established. The future development of the first, which consisted roughly of industries named in the 1948 Resolution plus electricity production and equipment, rail and air transport, and most mining, was made "the exclusive responsibility of the state." Nevertheless, except for rail and air transport, arms and ammunition, and atomic energy, which were to be government monopolies, some private participation was to be possible. Aside from the expansion of the existing privately-owned units, the state might endeavor to secure "the cooperation of private enterprise in the establishment of new units when the national interests so require." If so, the state would ensure, "either through majority participation in the capital or otherwise," that it had the required means of control.[11] Mixed enterprise was also envisaged as a definite possibility in the second category of industries (some mining, aluminum, machine tools, ferroalloys and tool steels, heavy chemicals, essential drugs, fertilizers, synthetic rubber, and road and sea transport). These would be industries "in which the state would 'increasingly establish new undertakings,' without denying private enterprise its opportunities 'either on its own or with State participation.' "[12] The residual category of industries would in general be left to the private sector, though the government did not eliminate the possibility of its participation.

Various factors modified the picture conjured up by these statements. Reading them closely has convinced at least one qualified observer that the government hedged the language so as to allow for deliberate ambiguity.[13] Such ambiguity recognized the fact that the socialist faction of the Congress had to contend with a private enterprise group. Also, officialdom learned some lessons during the Second Plan (1956-1961). These included, according to John P. Lewis, surprise at the "buoyancy of private industrial investment," an enhanced appreciation of joint ventures involving foreign firms, and a far greater realization of the complexities of public-enterprise management.[14] By the time the Fourth Plan was reached, the volume of assistance given private development efforts and the attempts to improve incentives for private entrepreneurship had both increased.[15] In considering the direct governmental role in industries, a judgment made as long ago as 1957 appears to be not far off the mark: "The basic motivation comes not from a socialist determination to dominate the economy for ideological reasons (though that motive is present); the primary driving force is a determination to prime the pump of economic growth."[16]

For both joint enterprise and mixed enterprise, the limited or joint-stock company has been employed. The other forms, departmental management and the public corporation, are not ordinarily well suited to joint ownership. The company form apparently won a contest of popularity with the public corporation on more general grounds than this, however. Despite some feeling after independence that the public corporation was particularly appropriate to socialism, objections were soon raised about the amount of parliamentary time involved in passing separate statutes if there were to be many enterprises, and about the amount of flexibility inherent in the corporate form.[17] The company form was familiar, having been used even before independence, mainly in the private sphere but in the public sector as well. With government as the sole or predominant shareholder, the company form offered sufficient flexibility for changes, for partnership with private business, Indian or foreign, and for preventing a too independent attitude on the part of the enterprise. By 1963, at the central government level, there were more than fifty companies as against four departmental undertakings and eight statutory corporations, all in the finance and public utilities field.[18] This trend ran against the recommendation of the Estimates Committee in Parliament. It favored restricting the use of the company form to emergency takeover by government, to mixed enterprise, and to enterprises which the government intended to transfer to the private sphere.[19] This view had little apparent effect. At the end of the 1967-1968 fiscal year, of the eighty-three industrial and commercial undertakings (other than departmental projects) of the central government, seventy-seven were "government companies," (that is, companies in which the government's participation was at least 51 percent), as against only six statutory corporations.[a] When companies established by state governments are included, the total of government companies at the end of 1967-1968 stood at two hundred forty-one.[21]

Commendably, public enterprise forms have been regarded as secondary in India to the achieving of public purposes, especially the participation of private sources. Thus, whereas a public corporation ordinarily has no shares or shareholders, in India, some have both. These are primarily the financial group of corporations, which are, or have been, or are destined to be, mixed-ownership bodies. Such corporations as the Damodar Valley Corporation and the Air India International Corporation, which are intended to be wholly government-owned, have no stock. As to mixed corporations, the state generally retains the majority interest in shareholding, although even this is not an inflexible rule. There are, however, restrictions on private shareholding.[b] Under the Companies Act of 1956, the basic statute under which both business and government establish firms, there is provision for both private companies and public companies. The former category is suitable for a closely-held, family-type firm, and the statute recognizes this by limiting the number of members to fifty, excluding employees; by restricting the right to transfer shares, if any; and by prohibiting any invitation to the public to subscribe to shares or debentures. In addition, a private company does not require a certificate to start business, and it need not publish a report nor hold an annual meeting. These qualities led the government to consider the private company form suitable for its wholly-owned ventures. The public company form, originally designed for larger private companies offering shares on the market, has been used by the government for its mixed enterprises and joint enterprises. The splitting of ownership, the use of share capital, the necessity of issuing a prospectus are all factors compelling the use of the public company form in such cases.

Mixed Enterprises in Industry and Commerce. The modest place occupied by industrial and commercial mixed enterprise in the Indian economy becomes clearer when statistics on investments of the central government are examined. In 1968, for its eighty-three industrial and commercial undertakings (noted above), the central government's contribution (in the form of equity and long-term loans) amounted to 91 percent of the total.[23] (The government has

---

[a]Confusion was engendered because a number of the seventy companies had "corporation" in their titles, even though they were companies and not statutory corporations.[20]

[b]Shareholding may be restricted to institutions (scheduled banks, investment trusts, and cooperative societies); individuals or institutions may be restricted to the purchase of a certain number of shares; the transfer of shares may be restricted so as to prevent domination by a private individual or institution; or large shareholdings may be rendered ineffective by restrictions on the exercise of voting power and the right to receive dividends.[22]

sought to keep equity and loans in rough balance.[24]) Not only were the contributions of state governments and private parties, both foreign and domestic, vastly overshadowed, but less than one-tenth of their relatively small investment was in equity in twenty-one undertakings.[25] Of these twenty-one, only nine fulfilled the mixed-enterprise requirement of equity investment by the central government and private domestic capital. The equity investment profile of these nine on March 31, 1968 is shown in Table 5-1. It will be observed that in only one unit, Goa Shipyard Ltd., did the private domestic investment outweigh that of the central government. In the others, the private domestic contribution was under (sometimes far under) one-third of the central government's, and in only one case did it approach one-fourth of the total investment.[c]

The lukewarm attitude of the government toward private participation in the form of "people's shares" may have been a factor, though probably a minor one,

Table 5-1

Equity Investments in Industrial or Commercial Mixed or Composite Enterprises of the Indian Central Government (Figures: Rs in lakhs)*

Name	Central Govt.	State Govts.	Private Parties (India)	Private Parties (foreign)	Total Investment
Praga Tools Ltd.	178.6	47.6	19.3		245.5
Central Warehousing Corp.	745.9		194.7		940.6
National Newsprint & Paper Mills Ltd.	255.0	169.7	68.8	1.0	494.5
Rehabilitation Housing Corp.	5.0		1.3		6.3
Cochin Refineries Ltd.	369.8	50.0	95.2	185.0	700.0
Fertilizers & Chemicals (Travancore) Ltd.	1,065.0	258.5	86.0	1.5	1,411.0
Goa Shipyard Ltd.	13.5		46.6		60.1
Mogul Lines Ltd.	80.5		1.4	19.3	101.2
Ashoka Hotels Ltd.	234.1		15.9		250.0

Source: Adapted from Bureau of Public Enterprise, Ministry of Finance, Government of India, *Annual Report on the Working of Industrial and Commercial Undertakings of the Central Government: 1968-69* (New Delhi, 1969), pp. 142-144.

*According to another source, in March 1969, there were seven companies owned by the central government and private parties and another eight owned by the central and state governments and private parties; but the instances in which the private parties are domestic—thereby making the companies mixed or composite enterprises—are not identified. See Government of India, Ministry of Information and Broadcasting, *India: A Reference Annual*, 1970 (New Delhi, 1970), p. 204.

[c]In addition to the eighty-three units surveyed above, the central government has invested funds in twelve others, the best-known of which is the Damodar Valley Corporation, where it has no responsibility for day-to-day management. Some of these have investments by private capital, but available information does not indicate whether it is foreign or domestic.[26]

in accounting for the limited use of mixed enterprise. In the mid-fifties, the Estimates Committee of Parliament recommended that at least 25 percent of the capital investment in joint-stock companies should, with safeguards against abuse, be made available for public subscription. The suggestion was rebuffed by the government but pressed again by the committee a few years later. The pressure led the government to set up its own study group in 1960. The group's report stressed the desirability of participation by the general public, if feasible methods could be found, partly because it might "generate better understanding and appreciation of the processes involved in the industrialization of the country and to that extent help promote and speed industrial development."[27] To aid in this process, the study group suggested share denominations of not more than Rs. 100 each, restrictions on the transfer of shares to undesirable persons, and inauguration of the experiment in a few undertakings that had already started earning profits.[28] The proposal did not find favor with the government, mainly, one commentator has suggested, "because it did not wish to complicate matters by introducing a private sector segment, howsoever small, into a State undertaking."[29] Two of the complications that critics of the scheme apparently had in mind were the possibility that shareholders might obstruct the normal functioning of a public undertaking; and that failure of the scheme because of a poor response from the public might damage the prestige of public enterprise.[30] More generally, there may also have been skepticism about the existence of an investable surplus in the hands of the public, or at least, the separability of any pool of resources, if it did exist, into its public and private compartments.[31] Rivalry between the two sectors was also seen as a hazard because of doubt that mixed enterprise could compete with wholly private undertakings in attracting financing by the public.[32]

Use of the corporate form rather than companies was revived as a recommendation by the Administrative Reforms Commission in 1967. Its reasons included the opportunity for debate in Parliament when a statutory corporation is created, a resulting clarity of objectives and demarcation of powers, and the assurance of greater autonomy because Parliament would guard against executive encroachment. The company form, nevertheless, was preferred for "undertakings which have an element of private participation" as well as for certain other special circumstances.[33]

The circumstances of participation by private companies, as distinguished from the general public, do not suggest great enthusiasm for mixed enterprise on the part of either these companies or the government. In some cases, "private parties continue as shareholders because of the fact that the project was originally undertaken in the private sector and the State had to come in because the private parties could not find enough capital to go on with the project."[34] In several other instances, mixed companies were transformed into wholly-owned government companies after only a half-decade or so. Thus, the government bought out the Scindia Steam Navigation Company's investment in

Hindustan Shipyard Ltd. and then spent a considerable sum in developing the yard.[35] Another company in which the government shared ownership with Scindia was Eastern Shipping Corporation, and here again, the government took over sole ownership. It merged the corporation with the wholly-owned Western Shipping Corporation Ltd. to form the Shipping Corporation of India Ltd. In short, the comment of an observer in 1963 still seems justified: "There is an almost uninterrupted trend leading to the flotation of Private Companies as Central Government Companies."[36]

Mixed Enterprises in Finance. To help industries obtain long-term financing, the government established special financial institutions. Especially before 1964, less so since then, mixed enterprise has been more prominent in finance than in industry and commerce. The reasons are not hard to find. Government initiative in long-term financing was necessary because commercial banks extended only short-term credit, usually for working capital.[37] At the same time, "when a financial concern serves both the public and the private sector, or especially the latter, it is thought worthwhile to have representation of that sector on the managing board through such a partnership."[38]

A considerable array of agencies was established to supplement the work of the Reserve Bank in regulating the supply of credit to the banking system as a whole and the work of the State Bank in aiding rural, agricultural, and small-scale industrial finance. The Industrial Finance Corporation (1948) was to provide long-term loans to large-scale industry. Long-term loans to medium and small industries both publicly- and privately-owned were furnished by state financial corporations set up under the State Financial Corporations Act of 1951. Small industries are also aided by the National Small Industries Corporation (1955). The National Industrial Development Corporation (1954) was intended to provide assistance through equity participation.[39] In practice, it "has become an agency very different from that originally envisaged. It is still a 'gap-filler,' to the extent that it investigates and pioneers new projects, but no longer a means of stimulating private sector activities, except insofar as it retains its original responsibilities towards the jute and cotton textile industries."[40] The Industrial Credit and Investment Corporation (1955) was established partly to show the government's regard for private enterprise;[41] it provides both rupee finance and foreign exchange. The Refinance Corporation (1958) was created to supplement the efforts of the hard-pressed commercial banks by refinancing medium-term loans granted to industry by these banks.

The special financial institutions have had a powerful means of influencing the actions of industrial units to which they lend money. When the Industrial Finance Corporation makes a loan, it "reserves to itself the right to appoint and remove from time to time two directors on the Board of Directors of the concern, such directors being nonrotating and not liable to hold any qualification shares."[42] The Industrial Credit and Investment Corporation has a somewhat similar, but less stringent requirement.[43] The regulation for the wholly government-owned National Industrial Development Corporation resembles the IFC's but stipulates only a single director.[44]

In 1964, the special industrial financing institutions were considerably reorganized to provide a stronger, more hierarchical structure.[45] The Industrial Development Bank of India (IDBI) was established as a wholly-owned subsidiary of the Reserve Bank of India. Though legally an autonomous statutory corporation, it has the same board of directors as the Reserve Bank.[d] The Industrial Finance Corporation in turn was made a subsidiary of IDBI, which took over the IFC shares held by the central government and the Reserve Bank. The IDBI also took over the work of the Refinance Corporation in 1964 and broadened its refinancing of loans to include loans made by the Industrial Credit and Investment Corporation and the Industrial Finance Corporation. As an apex institution, the IDBI also fills gaps in direct financing left by the other institutions and has a special responsibility to aid the development of such strategic sectors as fertilizers, alloy and special steels, and petrochemicals.

Private participation in financial mixed enterprises has been substantially reduced by the 1964 changes that brought the IDBI into prominence, as well as by the nationalization of insurance in 1956 and of fourteen commercial banks in 1969. When they began operations, the Industrial Finance Corporation (and its state counterparts), the Industrial Credit and Investment Corporation, and the Refinance Corporation all had stronger elements of private participation, as a brief review will indicate.

When the Industrial Finance Corporation was established, only 20 percent of its share capital was held by the government. At the beginning of 1949, this holding was doubled when the Reserve Bank, which held another 20 percent, was transformed from a mixed body to a wholly-owned government corporation.[47] After the nationalization of life insurance in 1956, the government's portion of the Industrial Finance Corporation again escalated. Originally, banks, insurance companies, and institutional trusts had held 60 percent of the share capital, but after the insurance nationalization, it was the government which controlled roughly that proportion (64 percent).[48] Private individuals were not allowed to become shareholders, but it is extremely dubious whether they would have been attracted in any case because the top dividend rate was fixed at 2¼ percent.[49] The government guaranteed the payment of the annual dividends.[50] The ways in which members of the board of directors—aside from the chairman, who was appointed by the government after consultations with the board—were chosen reflected the complexity of IFC's ownership. Some directors were

---

[d]"The object of placing the IDBI within the Reserve Bank set-up is essentially two-fold. Firstly, such an arrangement inspires confidence with the public; . . . Secondly, since so much of central bank credit is made available to the private sector . . . the Indian view has been that the Reserve Bank should be continually in a position to . . . lay down the broad guidelines for its allocation."[46]

"nominated" by the government (four) and the Reserve Bank (two) and others were "elected" by the Scheduled Banks (two), the insurance companies (two), and the Co-operative Banks (two).[51] Nominated members served at the pleasure of the appointing authority, whereas elected directors served for four years and could be reelected twice. This arrangement allowed for the necessary differences in the selection process between public and private spheres and provided for an even balance between them. The chair, however, was held by an additional government director.[52] The IFC had liaison with its counterpart organizations in each state through its "right to appoint a director to each state corporation board and by the fact that the state corporation often acts as the central Corporation's agent for the disbursement of assistance."[53] Public subscription of up to 25 percent of a state corporation's capital was permissible, but the nomination of a majority of directors by governmental and quasigovernmental financial institutions assured government control.[54]

The Industrial Credit and Investment Corporation (ICIC) also had a rich ownership mixture. Of its issued share capital, 30 percent was subscribed by British and American private enterprise and 70 percent came from Indian banks, insurance companies, and the general public. The government of India provided working funds, for which it "received special stock, not having rights to vote or receive dividends but having representation on the board of directors."[55] More specifically, "of the eleven directors, the Indian government appointed only one. Seven represented Indian shareholders, while the British shareholding interest was sustained by two and the American by one."[56] Although the mixture thus began as heavily private, the nationalization of life insurance made the government the corporation's largest shareholder (18 percent of share capital).[57] Probably, this change did not seriously diminish the ICIC's status as living evidence of Indian interest in the private sector. Not only was its task private sector stimulation, but it drew its strength, as noted above, largely from private capital. Foreign private capital was invited to play so large a role partly in order to reassure foreign investors about the Indian government's policy toward the domestic private sector, according to the ICIC's first chairman.[58] In addition, the chairman believed that it was "an advantage to have such participation both in the share capital and consequently in the management of the Corporation."[59]

One-fifth of the paid-up capital of the Refinance Corporation was subscribed by fourteen commercial banks, but the rest came from the Reserve Bank, the State Bank, and the Life Insurance Corporation.[60] Originally, the corporation's refinancing facilities were confined to the shareholder banks, but these facilities were later extended to all the licensed commercial banks in the country.[61] Substantial credits were placed at the disposal of the corporation by the government.

Planning and Mixed Enterprise

Though evidence of any special treatment for mixed enterprise is lacking, economic planning in India, accompanied as it is by extensive control of private business activity, is as elaborate as can be found in the non-Communist world. From the formulation of the broad strategy and aims to parliamentary debate on the outlines, one writer has counted fifteen important steps in the development of Five-Year Plans in India.[62] A glance at the fifth step, which consists of establishing targets for the private as well as the public sectors, may suggest the extent of planning. Discussion with industry representatives is facilitated by the existence of development councils established under the Industries (Development and Regulation) Act of 1951. These councils consist of representatives of employers, employees, and consumers as well as persons with knowledge of technical aspects of the industries concerned. During discussions with government officials, the targets, the expenditure needed, and sources of supply of funds are estimated. The number of industries studied in this intensive manner has steadily increased, from forty-two industries in the First Plan, to fifty-one in the Second, and to seventy-six in the Third.[63]

The planning road has been rocky for India. In December 1967, the Fourth Five-Year Plan, begun only twenty months earlier, was suspended because it was out of step with realities. Recession, inflation, high military expenditures arising from conflicts with Pakistan and China, and uncertainties about foreign aid were among the contributing causes.[64] In various economists' judgment, the industrial achievement had been significant, but the record was below what was planned.[65] A revised draft of the Fourth Plan, now for the years 1969 to 1974, was presented to Parliament in 1969. The revision recognized that providing a certain rate of economic growth would not alone take care of social problems.[66] Events subsequent to 1969, especially the costs of caring for millions of refugees from East Pakistan and of the 1971 war with Pakistan, made even a revised Fourth Plan more obsolete than the original at the time of its suspension.

Even the machinery of planning has been in dispute from time to time. The Planning Commission began as a nonpolitical advisory body with a linkage to the government through the chairmanship of Prime Minister Nehru. By the middle 1960s, various cabinet ministers had become commission members and even gained a majority.[67] The change in membership without official change in duties created confusion. In 1967, the Administrative Reforms Commission, which had been appointed by the government a year earlier, proposed that the Planning Commission be made a wholly technocratic body through the elimination of its minister-members, including the Prime Minister.[68] The government did not accept this recommendation, and, in 1971, Prime Minister Indira Gandhi moved strongly in the other direction. She assigned the most important tasks of the Planning Commission to the Ministry of Planning and named a trusted friend as head of both units.[69]

In obtaining adherence to development plans, the Indian government has rather far-reaching powers over the private sector. A particularly interesting example is found in an amendment to the Companies Act of 1956. The government is authorized, at its discretion, to nominate two directors to protect minority interests or to advance the public interest.[70] Under the same statute, the government has exercised its authority to investigate the long-used but declining managing agency system and to dismiss managing agents in certain companies.[71]

The importance of the Industries (Development and Regulation) Act in providing the means for implementing the industrial policy set forth in the Industrial Policy Resolutions of 1948 and 1956 can scarcely be exaggerated. The act gives the government four powerful tools. First, licensing of industrial enterprises is used to "control and regulate the flow of resources into the industrial sector vis-a-vis other sectors, and to allocate resources within this sector among various industries in an assigned order of priority."[72] Licensing is intended "to ensure that the development of industries proceeds according to the pattern envisaged in the Plans."[73] Next, if volume or quality of goods decline, or prices rise sharply, or there is mismanagement, the government can investigate the operation of any private industrial enterprise and issue directives which must be heeded. Third, if there is no adequate response to the directives, the government can take over management of the enterprise for five years, or longer if the public interest requires. Finally, the government can exercise control over the supply, distribution, and price of goods produced in scheduled industries. In practice, the third and fourth powers have been little used, but the first has been rather hampering both to domestic and foreign private industry.[74] To an Australian observer, the licensing system has even contributed to "the mentality of the harem: each industrialist wants to get over his competitors not by increasing efficiency or reducing cost, but by securing preferential treatment and perpetuating scarcities in the particular goods he is producing . . . a negation of a true planned economy . . ."[75]

In the late 1960s, the stresses of this system and the need to stimulate the economy, especially with foreign investments, led to a considerable relaxation of regulation.[76] Trust may still be lacking, however; there are complaints that the private sector, which originates about 90 percent of the gross national product, is "not taken into the confidence of the government or the Planning Commission in important national matters."[77]

Since the mid-1960s, there has also been considerable debate and policy fluctuation over the extent to which public enterprise (including mixed and composite enterprise) needs to be integrated into developmental efforts in order to obtain planning objectives. The Industrial Policy Resolution of 1956 had stated that "it is to be expected that public enterprises will augment the revenue of the State and provide resources for further development in fresh fields."[78] Nevertheless, there had been considerable doubt about the seriousness of this approach. In the original version of the Fourth Plan, it became official policy that government-run enterprises should earn a 12 percent rate of return on capital. This figure was chosen, it has been suggested, because: "The planners know the rate of output it is desired to achieve from a given state enterprise, as well as the wage level and the marginal capital-output ratio. . . . The condition is then added that the public enterprise should become self-financing."[e] The 12 percent figure would be reduced in proportion to the amount of funds scheduled to come from the government budget. The Administrative Reforms Commission was broadly supportive of this approach. It recommended that public enterprises "should aim at earning surpluses to make a substantial contribution to capital development out of their earnings besides making a contribution to the Exchequer."[80]

The commission's main concern was with the organizational aspect of integrating the performance of "public sector undertakings" into India's developmental effort. It recommended that many of the undertakings be grouped according to activities and that "sector corporations" be created to supervise the undertakings for iron and steel, coal and lignite, mining, engineering, electricity, oil, fertilizer, chemicals and drugs, shipping, airlines, and hotels and tourism.[81] The respective sector corporations were not to engage in detailed administrative control but were to help the units under them in such staff functions as budgeting, personnel, information and reporting, performance appraisal, and grievance handling. The commission thought the sector corporations would "avoid the fragmentation of the industrial effort in the public sector," and "make Government control more effective by keeping it confined to a few vital and strategic points."[82]

Although the government failed to act on the commission's recommendations, the latter's reasoning is worth reporting here because of references to mixed enterprise and to the Italian system as a possible model. In envisaging the structure below the proposed sector corporations, the commission listed three possibilities: (1) if independent legal status were given to the constituent units, a multitiered system, such as that for IRI and ENI in Italy, would be achieved; (2) the statute establishing a sector corporation might specify the organizational structure underneath it; and (3) finally, the organizational structure below a sector corporation could be determined in conferences between it and the government. The commission believed circumstances should determine preferences among these alternatives, and that one relevant circumstance was private participation. Where this was involved, the company form should continue to be used, but it would no longer be necessary to have government representatives on the board of directors. Instead, "the State-owned shares in an undertaking in which there is private participation should be transferred to the sector corporation," and it "should nominate its representatives from among its directors and the executive heads of departments to serve as part-time members on the boards of such companies."[83]

The recommendations of the commission were also designed to strengthen

---

[e]In 1964, a Planning Commission document had noted "general agreement that public enterprises should yield adequate profits" and "a general consensus that this rate should not generally be less than 10 percent."[79]

financial planning within the public undertakings. The absence of performance budgeting was noted and its installation urged. The commission also recommended that a new procedure be adopted to overcome the absence of "a five-year perspective in the latter years of the Plan."[84] Following the British model, the government should annually approve, after discussions, each enterprise's plans for development and capital expenditure for the next five years.

Industrial and commercial undertakings, the target of the Administrative Reform Commission, were not alone in finding it difficult to fit their activities into national plans. Early in its history, the Industrial Finance Corporation also had problems. Its reluctance to gear activities to the requirements of the plans and its inclination to favor large and well-established concerns helped to account for the appointment of an Inquiry Commission in 1952. The IFC, as A.H. Hanson has noted, has always faced a special kind of dilemma: "When, on the orders of the government, it behaves 'uncommercially' it is condemned for wasting public money in 'infructuous' investments; when it allows commercial considerations to guide its investment policy it is accused of neglecting plan priorities."[85] Under these conflicting pressures, the corporation exhibited a certain amount of operational rigidity, a circumstance which one Indian writer had laid to "the control exercised by the Government on its policies."[86] This control took the form of an injunction to the IFC to follow government policy and to refer disputes to the government; the government made it clear that it would supersede the board of directors at any time it failed to carry out instructions.[87] The advent of planning did, however, change the conception of the industrial financing problem. Instead of simply aiding small- and medium-sized enterprises, the aim of the special financial institutions was to obtain a rising share of the savings-flow for industrial development and to ensure its allocation according to planned priorities within the industrial sector.[88] In addition to loans, the special financial institutions have often been empowered to invest in industry, but they do not exercise any management functions through their share ownership.[89]

It is conceivable that governmental direction of the economy is tending toward more public enterprise autonomy but with higher performance standards than previously. For example, the position taken by the government in a 1969 memorandum on public undertakings appears to give more freedom to enterprises than the Administrative Reforms Commission had recommended.[90] The memorandum summarized recent government decisions to this effect. Thus, one required the government to put into writing any directive that requested an enterprise "to act in a manner dictated by the economic considerations." Another sought to end the much-criticized practice of temporarily assigning civil servants to enterprises for brief periods. Assignees are now to be required to choose between a return to the civil service or permanent attachment to the enterprise within one to three years, depending on the level of service. Thirdly, ministry officials are not to be chairmen of public undertakings, the Secretary is not to be a board member, and selection of top management posts is to be made from the private sector as well as from the government and public enterprise. Although the memorandum gave no endorsement to the commission's notion of creating sector corporations to oversee the operations of the public enterprises, it suggested steps to be taken to improve "the working and profitability" of these undertakings in light of an overall net loss.

Concern for the spotty performance of the public undertakings has stimulated little discussion of mixed enterprise as a possible solution. A 1968 article in the *Indian Journal of Public Administration* was an exception. It proposed that existing units should be converted to mixed enterprise, new ones begun as such, private monopolies given competition by mixed companies, and mixed enterprises given private sector competition.[91] This appeal to intersector competition was answered in a later issue of the *Journal* with the complaint that it confused ownership with management.[92] It is worthy of note that in this exchange of views, neither the defense nor the criticism of the idea revolved around India's experience with mixed enterprise but with an abstraction. This is probably an effective commentary on the somewhat marginal character of Indian mixed enterprise at the central government level.

Pakistan

Pakistan's use of mixed enterprise is interesting for several reasons. First and foremost, it is probably the leading example of an attempt to use the Japanese method of developing industries in the public sphere with the intention of turning them over to private enterprise. Secondly, the points of comparison and contrast with neighboring India which, like Pakistan, employs five-year plans, are intriguing.

From the beginning of independence in 1947, the Pakistan government conceived as its primary developmental role the provision of infrastructure for an intensive industrialization effort. Its industrial policy statement of 1948 emphasized public ownership and operation of the usual gamut of public utilities such as the mails, telegraph, telephone, radio, railroads, and air transport. The prospect of eventual nationalization for road transport, where public and private enterprise coexisted, and river transport, which was in private hands, was not ruled out.[93] Aside from these areas, public ownership was envisaged in arms and ammunition, the generation of hydroelectric power, and the manufacture and operation of railway, telephone, telegraph, and radio equipment. Otherwise, private enterprise was strongly encouraged, with the possible exception of two contingencies to be discussed shortly.

A restatement of industrial policy in 1959 largely confirmed the pronouncement of a decade earlier, but it gave even more encouragement to private enterprise. Arms and ammunition, railroads, air transport, telecommunications, and atomic energy were reserved for public enterprise. This time, river transport was assigned to private enterprise—with no threat of ultimate nationalization. Road transport continued as a field for both public and private enterprise. Under the restated policy, private enterprise was to receive maximum support within the framework of the five-year plans.

The second industrial policy statement also dropped one of the two 1948 reservations laid down by the government in backing private enterprise. No longer was it to be policy that "Government reserve their right to take over or participate in any industry vital to the security or well-being of the State."[94] The second reservation, which has persisted, is more relevant to the topic of mixed enterprise: "Government might find it necessary in the national interest, in the event of private capital not forthcoming in adequate measure for the development of any particular industry of national importance, to set up a limited number of *standard* units more as a means of attracting private enterprise than for any other object."[95] This reservation reinforces the idea of comparing Pakistan's development policy with that of Japan, as some have done,[96] for it suggests the hope of transferring various industrial enterprises to the private sphere as circumstances permit.

This emphasis on private sector development must be placed in context. No doubts were expressed about continuing government operations in basic utilities, such as water, power, and transport. After 1950, gross government investment more than doubled every five years, and the provision of infrastructure needed by industry enabled it to grow.[97] Public investment as a share of total industrial investment increased from less than 5 percent in 1949-1950 to almost 20 percent in 1964-1965.[98]

The chief instrument for executing the policy of beginning mixed and other enterprises and transferring them to the private sector was the Pakistan Industrial Development Corporation (PIDC), a wholly-owned government corporation which was created in 1952. It was divided in 1962 into the East Pakistan Industrial Development Corporation and the West Pakistan Industrial Development Corporation. Because of their importance in beginning and transferring mixed enterprise, it is useful to look at these corporations, even though they are not mixed enterprises themselves.

The PIDC began with great energy and flexibility under a dynamic leader, Ghylam Faruque, who has been compared to Enrico Mattei of Italy.[99] He was assisted by an unpaid board of private industrialists.[100] The corporation pioneered in industries and areas neglected by private investors during the early period of industrialization. At the beginning of the First Plan period (1955-1960), the PIDC undertook some thirty industrial projects, mainly in paper, jute mills, cement, fertilizers, shipyards, and a gas pipeline. Of the total expenditure of Rs. 560 million, the government's share was about 68 percent.[101] Its method of operations was described in the following manner in 1958: "The capital required for each project is normally offered for private subscription with the Central Government providing any amounts remaining unsubscribed. In practice, no offer of shares has been made in the market at the outset, but after a project has been developed to the state of operations, private participation is procured either through a public issue of shares or by partnership or other sharing arrangements negotiated with business groups."[102]

There seems to be considerable agreement that the PIDC achieved much quicker industrialization than if private enterprise had been left to do the job alone.[103] It was aided not only by its vigor and flexibility but also by its favorable treatment from the government as compared with private enterprise. "As a result, some private entrepreneurs were delighted to have the PIDC join them in a venture because this assured safe passage through the bureaucratic jungles."[104]

The PIDC record was better in beginning enterprises than in transferring them to the private sector. The very aggressiveness of the corporation in sponsoring enterprises led it into difficulties in disposing of them. Unpressured by economic circumstances that normally face a private enterprise and encouraged to invest in many sectors of the economy to advance economic development, it apparently made some costly mistakes.[105] The success of projects varied widely. The PIDC realized that it would be easy to sell its profitable ventures, but to be left with the rest was unacceptable. By 1959, the PIDC had transferred only slightly more than 10 percent of its total investment in completed industrial plants, an amount exceeded by continuing investment.[106] For its entire decade of life (1952-1962), the PIDC undertook fifty-four projects.[107] Thirty-three were in West Pakistan, but the twenty-one in East Pakistan involved a higher total outlay. The total disinvestment of government capital amounted to Rs. 44.10 million out of a total capital cost of Rs. 1286.75 million, of which Rs. 299.93 million had been contributed by the private sector.

The two provincial industrial development corporations thus were left with a difficult task. From 1962 to 1969, the West Pakistan organization completed twenty-one projects to add to the thirty-three it had inherited from the parent unit.[108] During the same period, WPIDC disinvested ten projects.[109] The East Pakistan agency's project completion record more than matched that of its western sister, but no transfers to private ownership were listed among its activities.[110] In commenting on the net loss suffered by EPIDC projects in 1968-1969, the Ministry of Finance commented ruefully, "investment funds plus something more is required for economic development."[111]

The slowness of disinvestment has various explanations. Private capital is not plentiful, especially in East Pakistan, where only about 22 percent of the total private investment was estimated, in 1968, to be taking place.[112] The procedure of transfer is cumbersome, as the agreement of a government committee must be secured in each case.[113]

Some Pakistani officials favor the explanation that the public is naturally reluctant to invest in enterprises whose purpose may not be exclusively profit-making when there are privately-owned enterprises in which to invest.[114] Even those PIDC projects with good commercial prospects, however, have not attracted private investors. The case of Sui-Northern Gas Pipe Lines was noted by one official: "In this enterprise, 33% of the capital was contributed by the Government, 33% by the BOC [Burmah Oil Company] and 33% was floated to the public for shareholding. This being a fairly attractive project, we had expected that the public would come in enthusiastically to contribute their share for this project. It was surprising that the public contributions came to only one-third of what we had set apart for them . . ."[115] (Yet, the same official noted that the public had invested in the Zeal-Pak Cement Factory, which had been yielding good profits and whose share value had almost doubled.[116]) The disappointment with the initial offering of the pipe-line company was attributed by another official partly to the large size of the stock offering in relation to the capacity of the stock market to handle it.[117]

Explanations of a nonfinancial character are more speculative. Suspicions of empire-building are occasionally voiced and quickly denied.[f] Does ideological suspicion of the private sector produce governmental foot-dragging? There is a hint of this in a Pakistani newspaper editor's complaint about the injustice of handing over enterprises begun with public money when they become profitable, leading to the "impairment of the public sector."[119]

Mixed Enterprises. The strategic financial area is, as in India, a favorite home of mixed enterprise. Pointing to a pattern of joint ownership and management, S. Russell Andrus wrote in 1958: "The first important institution of this kind was the central bank of the country, the Rs. 30-million State Bank of Pakistan, 49 percent of the capital of which was subscribed by the public. Next came the Rs. 30-million Pakistan Industrial Finance Corporation for meeting the medium-term and long-term capital needs of industry. In 1949, the National Bank of Pakistan, a quasicommercial banking institution, was established with 25 percent of its capital held by the State."[120] In 1961, the Pakistan Industrial Finance Corporation was replaced by the Industrial Development Bank of Pakistan (IDBP) with a mandate to broaden its lending to include medium-sized and smaller, as well as large, industrial units. The government subscribed 51 percent of the capital, and the rest came from banks, insurance companies, and other investors. In 1970, IDBP was given the task of administering an Equity Participation Fund designed to help entrepreneurs of moderate means in East Pakistan and the less-developed areas of West Pakistan.[121] Commercial banks, including the National Bank of Pakistan, were encouraged to hold shares in the

---

[f]The explanation of empire building was suggested to the present writer by a Pakistani civil servant. In the opinion of the finance director of WPIDC, however, "WPIDC has so many new projects in its portfolio that it is anxious to hand over many of its existing projects in order to be in a position to take up the new ones which are bigger and more sophisticated, involving huge investment."[118]

Fund and to participate in equity investments. The planned share capital was to be contributed by the central government (40 percent), the two provinces (20 percent), the State Bank of Pakistan (20 percent), and private institutional investors (20 percent). Despite administration by the IDBP, the Fund has its own board of directors.

Still other specialized, jointly-financed or jointly-managed credit agencies were created. Original intentions about mixing were not always completely realized. The Agricultural Development Bank of Pakistan, the IDBP's opposite number, secured its capital base from budgetary contributions made by the government,[122] although its charter was for a mixed corporation in which the government would hold a majority interest.[123] Of two provincial small industries corporations, East Pakistan was originally intended to have a mixed enterprise, as a minority of shares were reserved for public subscription.[124] The Pakistan Industrial Credit and Investment Corporation (PICIC) provides still another variant on the mixed enterprise theme. PICIC was launched in 1957 to make loans and equity investment in new or expanding enterprises; its capital was entirely private, but by 1967 it had Rs. 60 million of government advances "ranking below capital."[g] Limited as to resources, neither IDBP nor PICIC was adventuresome at first in aiding any but large investors, although PICIC was the more conservative, probably because of its private ownership.[126] A claimed consequence of the respective ownership profiles of these two corporations with similar lending tasks is that PICIC found it easier to acquire assistance from foreign aid agencies.[127] By the middle 1960s, both agencies were serving to reduce the concentration of economic control by supporting newcomers more effectively than they had done at the beginning.[128]

Concern about broadening the base of industrial shareholding and permitting opportunities for the small investor stimulated the creation of two other mixed enterprises in fields related to finance. The National Investment (Unit) Trust was created in 1962. The National Bank of Pakistan was given the task of custodian of the property of the mutual fund, and the National Investment Trust Limited was established to manage the investments. The latter is owned equally by a dozen public and private sponsors. Despite the creation of NIT, a 1965 government study found that 75 percent of the equities of most of the companies listed on the stock exchange were held by less than a score of individuals.[129] Institutional investors, including NIT, held 20 percent while the remaining 5 percent was held by small investors. As a consequence of these findings, the Investment Corporation of Pakistan was spawned in 1966 to bring greater depth to the capital market and maintain stability in share values. These ends are sought through such steps as originating, underwriting, and distributing new stock issues, underwriting the excess holdings of closely-held companies

[g]"A special feature of these advances is that until repaid, these are subordinated to all debts, liabilities and share capital of the Corporation and, therefore, counted as equity for the purposes of debt/equity ratio."[125]

that are going public, and buying and selling stocks and securities. To secure the interests of its shareholders, ICP customarily reserves the right, when it underwrites stock issues, to be represented on the board of directors so long as it holds a minimum number of company shares.[130] This has the effect of further intertwining the public and private sectors.

A second prominent field for mixed enterprise in Pakistan is transportation. The elite organization, and a highly successful one, is undoubtedly Pakistan International Airlines Corporation (PIAC). Its reserves are more than 60 to 70 percent of its capital, built up through a pricing structure based on commercial considerations. Commenting on a PIAC fare increase, an official of the Ministry of Finance noted in 1967: "This could not happen if the Government were entirely social minded because when an enterprise is already making a profit of, say, 20 to 25 percent on their equity capital, according to the public welfare concepts there is no reason why they should raise its fare structure."[131] The National Shipping Corporation is also run on commercial lines, though it "follows the Government directions on policy matters."[132] Dividends increased from 10 percent in 1964-1965 to 17.5 percent in 1967-1968; the government received its share, based on its one-fourth ownership status.[133] Provincial transportation units with stated intentions of becoming mixed enterprises include the East Pakistan Road Transport Corporation, and the East Pakistan Shipping Corporation.[134]

The remaining mixed enterprises are scattered among several fields. The Pakistan Insurance Corporation probably is the most prominent. It was created in 1953 in order to reduce the liability created when insurance companies remitted large amounts of foreign exchange to obtain reinsurance facilities in foreign countries. In addition to transacting all forms of reinsurance and promoting new insurance companies, the corporation underwrites the issue of stocks, bonds, or debentures of insurance companies. It also services and administers a scheme for handling government business through coinsurance with Pakistani companies. For the present study, the most interesting task is the launching and transfer of new insurance companies. The corporation "has actively assisted in establishing one insurance company in West Pakistan and two in East Pakistan by participating in capital, granting reinsurance treaties on favorable terms and after managing them initially, it has handed them over to private interests."[135]

Two companies formed for oil exploration are Pakistan Oilfields Limited and Pakistan Petroleum Limited. In the former company, at least, the 30 percent of issued and paid-up stock not held by the cooperating private oil company was taken up by the government to the extent that the public did not subscribe to shares reserved for it.[136] The Karachi Electric Supply Corporation Limited began as a privately-owned company in 1913 and became a mixed enterprise in 1952 when heavy demands for electricity expansion required the government to purchase a majority interest. The corporation supplies about 23 percent of West

Pakistan's electricity.[137] It is managed by a private limited company wholly owned by the government and operates under the overall supervision of the board of directors. The government has regularly taken its dividends, and, by 1968-1969, these, plus bonus shares, had reached the equivalent of 100 percent of the total share capital subscribed by government.[138]

Several additional ventures were begun with the intention, still unrealized, of becoming mixed enterprises. The Jute Trading Corporation Limited was to be jointly owned by the central government, the East Pakistan provincial government, the Pakistan Jute Association, the Jute Growers Association, and members of the public. Soon after the corporation's establishment in 1967, the Pakistan Jute Association withdrew from participation, and the shares of the growers and of the public had not been floated by mid-1969.[139] Similarly, in 1969, the government entertained the hope that the Karachi Steel Mill Project, an effort of the government-owned Pakistan Steel Mills Corporation, might be owned by private companies, members of the public, and foreigners, as well as the government itself.[140] A composite enterprise for which capital was authorized but not issued is Petroleum Development of Pakistan, which was established in 1956 to explore oil. Of the authorized capital, domestic private investors were to raise less than 2 percent, with the government and a foreign oil company contributing the rest.[141]

If this review suggests that mixed enterprise has frequently been employed for institutions important to economic development, Table 5-2 indicates that management arrangements have been carefully drawn to reflect realities extending beyond ownership data. Thus, despite a lack of equity, the government has directors on the board of PICIC to reflect the large loans it has made to the corporation.[142] Similarly, the government has a majority of the directors on the Investment Corporation of Pakistan's board, presumably on the basis of its annual appropriation of profits from the State Bank to ICP.[143] In general, the table suggests that the government has been more eager to retain control of boards than to reflect accurately the ownership percentages. One common device for assuming government influence has been government appointment of the managing director or chairman, or both.

Planning and Mixed Enterprise

A dialectic between planning and controls appears to have taken place in Pakistan. Although the industrial policy statements reviewed earlier left most manufacturing industries to the private sector, an elaborate system of administrative controls was instituted. There were direct controls on import licensing, control of foreign exchange, capital investment, credit institutions, prices, profit margins, manufacturing quantity and quality, and other areas.[144] Planning for private sector investment was primitive, however, and sanctions relatively

Table 5-2
Pakistan Mixed and Composite Enterprises*

	Paid-up Share Capital		Composition of Board of Directors	
	Subscribed by Central Government	Other Subscriptions	Appointed by Central Government	Elected by Shareholders
State Bank of Pakistan	51%	49% by the public	6+ Governor and 1 or more Deputy Governors	3 (1 from each registration area)
National Bank of Pakistan	25%	75% by the public	3+ managing director	9
Industrial Development Bank of Pakistan (IDBP)	51%	49% by insurance companies and private investors	6+ chairman and managing director	3
Pakistan Industrial Credit and Investment Corporation (PICIC)	none	60% domestic private, 40% International Finance Corp. and foreign private capital	3+ managing director	17
Investment Corporation of Pakistan	none	by 16 leading banks and insurance companies, including IDBP and PIC	5+ managing director	5
National Investment Trust Limited	8.5%	8.5% subscriptions each by 4 leading banks, 3 financial institutions, PIC, and 3 leading industrialists	managing director	12

Pakistan Insurance Corp. (PIC)	51%	49% domestic private, mainly insurance companies	5+ managing director	3
Pakistan International Airlines Corp. (PIAC)	89.5%	10.5% private	5+ chairman and managing director	2
National Shipping Corp.	25%	75% by the public in East and West Pakistan in equal proportion	5, including managing director, chairman and financial director	4
Karachi Electric Supply Corp.	54%	46% private	(12 members, unspecified affiliations)	
Pakistan Oilfields Limited	18%	70% by Attock Oil Company, 12% by the public	(6 members, unspecified affiliations)	
Pakistan Petroleum Limited	29.26%	70% by Burmah Oil Company, 0.74% by the public	2	4, including chairman, by Burmah Oil Co.

Sources: Economic Adviser to the Government of Pakistan, Ministry of Finance, *Government-Sponsored Corporations and Other Institutions, 1968-1969* (Islamabad, 1969), *Pakistan Economic Survey, 1969-70* (Islamabad, 1970), and *Central Government Corporations* (Rawalpindi, 1966); and Richard F. Myrop, et al., *Area Handbook for Pakistan* (Washington, D.C., 1971).

*The list is limited to units with central government participation. A possible addition to the list is the Karachi Port Trust. Information on its financial structure is lacking, but it has a mixed board. See Raymond C. Miller, "The Karachi Port Trust," in Guthrie S. Birkhead, ed., *Administrative Problems in Pakistan* (Syracuse, 1966), p. 155.

ineffective.[145] The spirit of planning became increasingly anticontrol, as the language of the plans suggest.

The Second Five-Year Plan (1960-1965) stated: "The Government intends to let the industrial pattern respond to market prices, not to trammel it by prescribing a rigid plan for industrial development. Nevertheless, it is important to establish what industries can best be developed, and to indicate where the national interest appears to lie."[146] A dozen criteria for the establishment of new industries and the expansion of certain of the old were then set forth.[147] Among the recommendations in the Plan were measures for the use of governmental regulation to encourage orderly industrial growth and the use of price control only as an exception.[148] In a revision of the Second Plan, it was noted: "The climate for economic development has definitely improved as a result of recent measures taken by the Government. The most significant development has been the progressive relaxation of government controls and restoration of market incentives."[149] The Third Five-Year Plan (1965-1970) continued this theme. After observing that the level of private investment activity had quadrupled during the Second Plan, the Third Plan document remarked: "This acceleration in private investment activity was intimately linked with the adoption of liberal economic policies recommended by the Plan and a gradual relaxation and withdrawal of direct controls on prices, distribution, imports and investment decisions."[150] Investment continued to be directed by an investment schedule and aided by the credit instruments previously noted.

Although a more relaxed form of planning was thus progressively adopted, part of the credit for the confidence of the private sector in the planning process may accrue to the development of sophisticated planning machinery. When the harshest control measures were adopted, there was no planning body. Its creation coincided with the beginning of the First Five-Year Plan (1955-1960), and in the ensuing decade, a high degree of skill was attained. Gustav Papanek lays the influence of the central planning agency and those for East and West Pakistan to their lack of executive responsibility, the strong backing they received from the highest political authorities, and their professional competence, which was augmented by the use of foreign technicians.[151] The influence of the Planning Commission was reinforced when it became the principal body to negotiate foreign aid, and this in turn "improved its leverage over the bureaucracy in promoting the decontrol of the private sector."[152] Increased foreign aid, in fact, has been credited with being the true cause of the liberalized economic measures that preceded a spurt in economic growth.[153]

With its enormous emphasis on economic growth, planning in Pakistan soon encountered criticism that it slighted social justice. As early as the time of the Second Plan, for instance, one critic observed that it showed "very little evidence of consumption planning," that is, "what consumer demand is likely to be, what rates of increase in per capita consumption are proposed for which commodities, and what policies will be followed to ensure a proper matching of consumer demand and supply in the market."[154] Another set of commentators said of the Third Plan: "The great and obvious shortcoming of the Plan is the inadequacy of its provision for the development of human resources."[155] The increasingly desperate plight of the East Pakistanis, the comparative prosperity of West Pakistan, expressed government concern about the concentration of wealth through industrialization, and other factors threw increasing doubt on the efficacy of the planning process. The Fourth Plan (1970-1975) was drafted in the uncertain period after the change of leadership from Ayub Khan to Yahya Khan, and its implementation was subsequently disrupted by the troubles in East Pakistan and the short war with India. Some of the events confirmed the proclaimed need, in the Fourth Plan, for a changed outlook on development. In commenting on the urgency of achieving social justice through planning, the Plan recognized the necessity of meeting the demands of the masses for a share in economic progress, and in East Pakistan to increase public-sector development expenditures greatly and those for social services even more.[156]

Whatever their merits or defects, the plans are useful in this study for their help in assessing the extent to which mixed enterprise has fit into a developmental perspective in Pakistan. In the planners' eyes, how did mixed enterprise relate to the priority given to private enterprise, to economic and social aims, and to the respective developmental stages of East and West Pakistan?

In suggesting a primary reliance on private enterprise, the Second Plan also foresaw direct participation by government "in those enterprises which are essential for overall development and where private capital is not forthcoming or high considerations of national security intervene."[157] The PIDC was seen as the primary medium of government action, but the Plan noted in the next breath that "The charter of the Corporation enjoins it to divest itself, at the opportune time, of its investment in the undertakings that it promotes."[158]

The Second Plan also spelled out a philosophy for mixed enterprise that meshed with the priority given to private enterprise and reinforced the emphasis upon economic growth. With reference to a "semi-public sector" consisting of "government-sponsored corporations which draw their finances both from the public and private sectors" and operating under "a board of directors which combines representation from the Government and from private enterprise," the Plan urged: "It is essential that the commercial nature of the corporations be greatly emphasized and their future policies be so framed as to promote maximum efficiency and growth; their price policy should, no doubt, be guided by considerations of social gain, but the need for financing their future expansion out of their own resources must also be given due weight."[159]

Although the Third Plan was still primarily growth-oriented, it gave more attention to the structure of the economy than the Second Plan did. In part, this may simply have reflected the fact that the economy's outlines were becoming clearer. Significantly, however, the marked disparity between economic progress in East and West Pakistan drew attention. According to the Plan, the absence of a substantial infrastructure and the lack of a strong private sector in East Pakistan required an expansion of the public sector.[160] As this regional disparity was especially evident in industry, "... about half of the [industrial] investment is to be managed by the East Pakistan Industrial Development Corporation as against just over one-fifth by its West Pakistani counterpart."[161] The mixed enterprises in the financial field were also to be part of the array of instruments for stimulating private enterprise in East Pakistan. These instruments were to include: "... differential fiscal incentives, distribution of foreign loans through PICIC and IDBP and ... the formulation of the industrial investment schedule for the private sector politics regarding foreign assistance licensing and location of industry."[162]

A second matter of social concern recognized in the Third Plan was "the tendency of income distribution to move in the direction of growing inequalities."[163] Explicitly recognizing that relatively few entrepreneurs "owned and controlled a substantial portion of the small industrial sector," the Plan expressed the hope of balancing economic dynamism and excessive concentration of economic power.[h] Harmony between social and economic goals of the society was to be achieved, *inter alia*, by a broad-based ownership of new industrial ventures; hence, "The PICIC and IDBP should be asked to sanction more loans to industrialists outside the big family groups."[165]

The Third Plan also ranged mixed enterprise with other governmental instruments in expressing a policy for areas "in which unhampered private enterprise is not appropriate."[166] Between governmental regulation at one end and the operations of public corporations at the other, as means to ensure the public interest, stood "public-private collaboration in management and ownership." The choice among these instruments was to depend "on the particulars of each situation." Another portion of the Third Plan, nevertheless, could be read as suggesting a lower priority for wholly-owned government enterprise than for joint or mixed enterprise: "Public industrial investment will be undertaken only in those cases where private capital is not forthcoming, where a joint venture cannot be organized or where considerations of national interest dictate public investment."[167] At the same time, the demands on the public sector in the Third Plan were huge. Public corporations were to undertake 55 percent of the total investment in the public sector,[168] and the proportion of government investment to private investment in manufacturing was actually to increase, as compared with the Second Plan.[169]

Although the Fourth Plan continued much of the emphasis of the Third— even repeating almost verbatim the last quoted sentence above—it expanded the role of government. This course of action was deemed necessary because of a

---

[h]The details, which became widely known in Pakistan, were obviously disquieting: "In 1968, an estimated 66 percent of the nation's industrial capital, 80 percent of all commercial banking and 97 percent of the insurance businesses were said to be owned or directly controlled by some twenty families in West Pakistan."[164]

shortfall in private industrial investments of more than 50 percent in East Pakistan and the less-developed areas of West Pakistan. One of the contemplated measures was an increase, as compared with the Third Plan, in the proportion of government investment to private investment in manufacturing industries.[170] It was anticipated that both the enlarged industrial tasks and greatly increased government activity in the field of social services would place a greater burden upon public corporations. "Under the Fourth Plan, they will be called upon to implement almost two thirds of the total public sector programme."[171] This assignment was made despite uneasiness, expressed in the Plan, about the capability of the public corporations to handle their responsibilities, given past performance. Reorganizing these bodies into public limited companies under the Company Law was recommended as a way of achieving greater effectiveness.[172]

Certain mixed enterprises were assigned developmental tasks in the Fourth Plan. The allocation of investment in semipublic transportation and communication agencies was increased by about 50 percent over the Third Plan allocation.[173] A policy package to accomplish a major acceleration of private investment in East Pakistan foresaw various activities by mixed enterprises.[174] The National Bank of Pakistan, along with private commercial banks, was to be "encouraged" to hold shares in the Equity Participation Fund and to participate in equity investment in less-developed regions. In making loans, IDBP and PICIC were to strive for a debt-equity ratio of 60:40 and as much as 70:30 in special cases. Financial institutions controlled by the government were assigned specific regional targets related to the stimulation of private investment in East Pakistan through granting credit. At the provincial level, the East Pakistan Industrial Development Corporation and the East Pakistan Small Industries Corporation were to accelerate the role of private investment in several ways. EPIDC was to spur disinvestment and to join with EPSIC in combining with private entrepreneurs in ventures.[175]

Conclusion

India and Pakistan illustrate well the triumph of necessity over intention, even ideological intention. Although socialist rhetoric was heard in India even before independence, private enterprise attained remarkable strength in the newly-independent country. When the nation began, industrial policy resolutions—in the interest of consensus—incorporated what was probably intentional ambiguity. Government controls over private industry were comprehensive, but later were relaxed somewhat to encourage the private sector. It showed a vigor surprising to the socialists, but the latter were encouraged by such measures as the nationalization of the banks. In Pakistan, there was markedly less zeal for establishing a huge public sector. Private enterprise expansion, in fact, was the principal goal and though this end was kept in view and great strides made toward it, the public sector grew apace through the need to provide an infrastructure and to inaugurate enterprises that could be transferred to the private sector.

As to mixed enterprise, there were also certain ironies. Few of the numerous companies in which the Indian government participated had private participation, even though government study groups urged it and the company form lends itself well to mixed enterprise. Pakistan, frankly seeking to transfer government-initiated undertakings as soon as possible, on the Japanese model, actually was able to transfer far fewer than anticipated.

A common element in the mixed enterprise of the two nations was the extent of reliance on financial institutions as a means of financing industrialization. Genuine cooperation between the public and private sectors was far easier to obtain for financial enterprises than for those in industry. Probably, it was easier for the private sector to agree to cooperate in units that strengthened its interests than in those that could be seen as potential or actual rivals in industrialization.

Though each country tended to view its mixed enterprise idiosyncratically, both also related their efforts to those of other countries, by implication, if not always directly. The Japanese government's well-known example of beginning enterprises and transferring them to the private sector was the apparent model for the similar—but markedly less successful—program of the Pakistan Industrial Commission. In proposing a grouping of public undertakings under "sector corporations" for the purpose of improving their integration into planning, India's Administrative Reforms Commission looked to Italy's IRI and ENI. Both in their respective plans and literature about development, India and Pakistan kept a somewhat wary eye on each other's development institutions, including mixed enterprise. Although planning was extensive in both countries, it was not sufficiently elaborate to separate mixed enterprise from public enterprise in public sector planning. There were, however, recurring debates about the obligations of public enterprises to development budgets.

Diverse Experimentation: Israel, Mexico, and Taiwan

It is perhaps difficult to conceive of three nations with more widely divergent backgrounds and cultures than—Israel, Mexico, and Taiwan. A basis for bringing them together here is their reputation for rapid economic development in the postwar years and their thoroughly mixed economies. More pertinently, the development literature has contained hints that each of these nations has made use of mixed enterprise in different but perhaps equally intriguing ways.

Israel

It has been well said that "along with Japan and perhaps one or two other nations such as Taiwan, Israel is one of the few countries outside of Europe and the English-speaking nations of North America and Oceania to have developed successfully."[1] There is a far-reaching intervention of the public sector in economic activity, owing partly to a socialistic tradition built up during the British mandate, but probably more to other factors. "The role of the government in the past," two scholars wrote in 1968, "has been determined more by economic factors, such as the size and composition of immigration and the flow of foreign capital, than by ideology."[2]

Perhaps the most intriguing aspect of the Israeli economy is the existence of three sectors—private, workers', and government—and the unusual amount of interaction among them. This structure evolved out of the exigencies of the thirty-year (1918-1948) mandate period when the workers' sector, in close cooperation with the "national institutions," such as the Jewish Agency and the World Zionist Organization, undertook many economic activities that "normally belong to the State Sector of any economy."[3] The workers' and government sectors, in particular, encompass various forms of economic initiative and ownership. Thus, the latter is composed of companies owned by the government, the local authorities, and the national institutions. The rationale for considering the last-named as part of the government sector is that, under the mandate, they performed many government functions.[4] Immediately after independence, in fact, the state sector grew rapidly because of the integration of the various subsectors that had existed under the mandate as well as because of the need to replace British capital, which had been withdrawn.[5] Even today, the national institutions engage in such activities as agricultural settlement, afforestation, and immigrant housing.[6] The workers' sector includes cooperatives, kibbutz-owned enterprises, and firms wholly owned by Hevrat Ovdim, the economic arm of Histadrut. The various forms of economic endeavors have differences in form of organization, methods of operation, and degree of attachment to Hevrat Ovdim.[7] Histadrut "has a dual structure, being a trade union organizing the large majority of workers (about 76 percent in 1965) and comprising a majority of the population at large (about 58 percent in 1965), as well as a center of economic, social, and general political activity."[8] Histadrut was established in 1921 and many of its leaders have become leaders of the state; it has even been said that Mapai, the ruling party, "determines both government policy and Histadrut policy."[9] The vast majority of industrial enterprises (93 percent) and the great majority of workers (76 percent) belong to the private sector. The other two sectors, however, on the average have larger, more capital-intensive enterprises.[10] In the 1950-1966 period, the private and public sectors gained in relative importance, while the Histadrut sector declined.[11]

The three sectors coexist and, in fact, cooperate with relatively little friction. A live-and-let-live attitude extends across the economy, aided perhaps by a natural division of functions: "The Public Economy [government and workers'] sectors account for about 45 percent of the Net Domestic Product, and dominate the most important large-scale enterprises. On the other hand, the Private Sector dominates real estate, industry, trade, finance, and services. It enjoys almost all the profits generated in the economy."[12] The government's flexibility about economic arrangements has undoubtedly been of major importance in preserving a relaxed atmosphere. Though "the public sector share in investment is higher in Israel than in any other non-Communist country for which data are available,"[13] a policy of nationalization has never existed. On the contrary, the government has been eager to use a variety of means to spur development. It uses its resources "to gain complete ownership, to enter into partnership with private capital, to make loans, and sometimes to give grants."[14] Both the government and Hevrat Ovdim have not hesitated to enter into ventures with each other and with the private sector. Use of the term "gap-filler" to describe the entry of the government into commercial activity appears to be accurate.[15] Thus, the Moses Committee, which studied the management of state enterprises in 1965, noted the rarity of nationalization and asserted, "Even in those cases where existing enterprises were transferred to State ownership, this was not done out of ideological motives, but for various practical reasons, the main one being lack of private capital for further development."[16] It has been suggested that the entrepreneurial vigor displayed by Histadrut, the Jewish Agency, and the municipalities may have contributed to the government's forbearance.[17]

This pragmatic attitude was not the product of a failure to achieve ideological aims but seems to have been arrived at deliberately. The Cabinet declared as basic policy, "The Government will consistently pursue accelerated development . . . where necessary, the Government will set up development projects on its own or in partnership with local and overseas private and cooperative capital."[a] As to intersectoral mixtures: "If necessary, the government will establish its own development enterprises in partnership with private or cooperative capital of local or foreign origin."[19]

Israel has the three usual forms of public enterprise—departmental units, public corporations (called statutory authorities), and joint-stock companies. The chronology of establishment of these forms also followed a typical pattern. Thus, most departmental enterprises, which include the Postal and Telephone Services, the Government Printer, and the Railways, were founded before the establishment of the state in 1948 and functioned as departments of the British Mandate. Statutory authorities, which include the National Insurance Authority, the Ports' Authority, the Bank of Israel, the Standards Institute and various production and marketing boards, were mostly constituted after 1948. Their missions expressed the bent of the new state toward development: "They were designed to fill a gap in the system of basic economic institutions and meet the new needs engendered by the development of the economy, especially those calling for the exercise of statutory powers."[20] Joint-stock companies, established according to a Companies Law dating from 1929, also were largely the product of the postindependence era. They are the most common form of public enterprise organization in Israel. Only 15 of 110 companies existing in 1965 antedated 1948; about 70 were established between 1956 and 1964 alone.[21] The number of companies was 115 in 1970, indicating that growth had slowed. Most of the companies are small. When subsidiaries and affiliates are included, over half of the companies in 1966 employed less than ten persons each, and only eleven had more than a thousand employees.[22]

In the great proportion of companies—all but eighteen in 1965—the government has partners.[23] The partners cover a wide range from public to private, but the most frequent partners are Hevrat Ovdim, the Jewish Agency, and the National Bank of Israel, with around a dozen partnerships each.[b] Not far behind are several banks and the municipality of Tel Aviv-Joffa.

The government's flexibility in combining with partners is shown by statistics on paid-up capital. In twenty-three companies, the government held 25 percent or less of the paid-up capital in 1966; in thirty-six companies, it held 76 percent or more; and in between these percentages, there were forty-two other companies. In terms of the percentage of the total paid-up capital held by the government, the statistics were, of course, quite different. Less than 5 percent of

[a]The lone dissenter to the report did, however, comment: "On not a few points, to be sure, pragmatic and practical factors were in play, but the repeated and virtually apologetic stress laid on the fact that ideological elements were kept out of this process does not conform with reality."[18]

[b]Inspection of statistics indicates only slight variation for 1964, 1966, and 1970.[24]

the total paid-up capital was invested in companies in which the government held 1 to 25 percent of the paid-up capital, whereas almost half of the total investment was in companies in which it owned 76 percent or more of the paid-up capital.[25]

Government capital has been invested in companies dealing with a wide range of economic activities. In terms of the total capital invested in 1965, 32 percent was invested in banks, 20 percent in buildings and public works, 15 percent in electricity and water, 11 percent in mines and minerals, 10 percent in transport and communications, 6 percent in industry, and 6 percent in agriculture, trade, and other branches of the economy.[26] Though government investment in industry was small, it should be noted that investment in banking was an indication of support for the other branches of the economy, as it was chiefly in a variety of banks connected with development.[27]

Though the government is often a minority shareholder, the companies in which it has a majority interest are often the largest in the land. In 1965, an official of the Government Companies Authority found "the 50 companies in which the government holds the majority of the paid-up share capital are the largest and most important in regard to investment, employment and output."[28]

Although precise information is lacking, it can be inferred that in most cases, the larger companies are mixtures of government and worker sector capital rather than private capital. Thus, in Zim (shipping), the minority partners are the Histadrut and the Jewish Agency, and in El-Al, they are the same two plus Zim itself.[29] In industry, the government is an equal partner with Hevrat Ovdim in a holding company with twenty subsidiaries known as Industrialization of Development Areas, Ltd.[30] Private partners in the larger enterprises do exist, however. For example, the government reduced its original 85 percent share in the Dead Sea Works to 35 percent in order to qualify for a loan from the World Bank.[31] The shares were sold to the public.[32]

The number of partnerships between government and private enterprise might be higher had a trend begun in the late 1950s and continued into the early years of the next decade achieved greater momentum. Mutual expectations apparently were not fulfilled in enough instances to disillusion both partners.[33] The government felt its development aims were not always met and that the private partners sometimes failed to furnish the expertise expected. The private partners chafed at the lack of freedom and at the financial conditions. In the mid-1960s, the government sold its holdings in various companies to private interests. In some instances, the success of a company produced favorable conditions for sale, whereas in other cases, the government was motivated by its inability to be an active partner in the business or the lack of success of a company.[34]

Planning and Mixed Enterprise

Although a situation in which a government strongly influences the economy might lead to expectations of centrally-coordinated government planning of a high order, such is not the case. Though plans have been drafted, they have not been systematically implemented.[35] It has been suggested that the government's hesitation in regard both to planning and to nationalization may be traced partly to its eagerness to attract private capital from abroad.[36] The government's influence in less formal ways is frequently demonstrated. "The most important institutional characteristic of the Israeli economy from our point of view," two commentators on Israeli planning have written, "is the predominance of the public sector and the determining role of governmental activities in economic life."[37] Benjamin Ahzin and Yehezkel Dror take account of the various portions of the public and semipublic sector that produce about 20 percent of the domestic product; direct governmental action in the form of subsidies, special loans, tax reductions, and part ownership; and, finally, indirect means of control, such as import controls and customs levies. The authors conclude, "Israel emerges as the country with the largest amount of governmental influence on the detailed operation of the economy among all Western-type democratic states."[38] The prevailing type of policy has been said to lie "somewhere between the use of macroeconomic variables to guide the economy, and planning on the microeconomic level."[39] Israel's relatively high share of public investment resembles that of countries with a much lower income per capita.[40]

There are, as suggested above, formal plans and planning machinery. An Economic Advisory Staff was established in the prime minister's office in 1953 but survived only two years, after encountering opposition from political decision-makers.[41] Subsequently, the environment for planning became somewhat more favorable, and facet planning progressed significantly, especially in agriculture, water resources, and, to a lesser degree, industry.[42] In 1962, a Cabinet decision created the Economic Planning Authority. Its mandate included: preparing a four- or five-year comprehensive development plan for submission to the Cabinet; within the multiyear plan, preparing an annual plan for submission to the legislature; coordinating development plans made by ministries; and giving advice in economic matters.[43] The negative reception given the multiyear plan efforts of the authority, however, indicated that the authority had not achieved much influence.[44] The tentative character of the authority's planning is perhaps best indicated by its own comment on its plan for industrial development, 1968-1971: "The plan presented here primarily constitutes only a framework, designed to point out the objectives and directions of industrial development, to indicate, in general, the added volume of production and export, and the needs for investment capital and manpower during the next few years, and also to indicate the Government policies necessary to realize this plan."[45]

Under the circumstances, the statement of the minister of commerce and industry in 1964, "The actual planning is done in the various ministries, which combine authority and responsibility," may not be far afield. The plans of his own ministry are " 'must' reading for every industrial enterprise, government or private."[46] The targets set for each branch and subbranch of industry, both for local consumption and export, become, according to the Minister, obligatory forecasts.[47] Interdepartmental coordination of development efforts has occurred through joint administration of various instruments, such as a supplementary budget called the development budget, the granting of tax and other benefits to approved businesses, the use of tariffs and quotas, and direct employment by the government.[48] Activities of this nature have led one commentator to state, despite the absence of formal plan implementation, that "the government may be thought of as having engaged in a type of indicative planning, foreseeing future requirements and encouraging investments in these projects."[49]

Given the vigor of the government in shaping development, the place of mixed enterprise becomes a particular object of curiosity. The 1968-1971 plan for industrial development referred to above contained no specific references to mixed enterprises (in accordance with its announced generality). Nor do the comprehensive development plans appear to make such references. This does not mean—given the alert activism of the government—an absence of government influence over mixed enterprise. There are indications, for instance, that even when the government has only a minority of the shares in a company, it is far from powerless. It has been noted that in such cases, "the Government may have a decisive say by invoking the support of board members who are representatives of other Government companies or other bodies, the Jewish Agency for example."[50] The government may have reason to believe that the fullest use of persuasion is advisable. When failures and defects have come to light in companies in which the government has had a minor share, the public has been quick to blame the government despite its disclaimers about having control.[51]

Government attitudes about the permanence and profitability of mixed enterprises are also relevant to this discussion. The minister of commerce and industry stated in 1964 that it was government policy to sell its shares in companies (except those which control natural monopolies) "whenever possible," and gave as the reason that the sale of assets was the best way of obtaining income when taxation rates were already high.[52] He took cognizance of a situation in which managers of the Pakistan Industrial Corporation were reported to be reluctant to make profits because the greater the profits, the greater the probability of being sold to private entrepreneurs, who would replace their staff with their own designees. Israeli managers, the Minister asserted, need not fear success in making profits because they know that successful managers stay on.[53] A more basic reason for profit-seeking, he claimed, rests with the operating methods employed. In order to provide an industrial center for an area in which the government wants to create a town, "we have an arrangement from the beginning whereby we give an option to purchase to the managers or to the workers, or to the partners whom we take."[54] This technique has been used most successfully with small companies, which, as noted above, are the most numerous. Other methods employed have involved selling shares to the public, initiating a factory and selling it even before it begins operations, and transferring some of the shares of profitable companies to an investment trust and selling the shares to the public as a mutual fund.[55] In short, there seems to be considerable evidence that, as the Minister said on another occasion, "the State is interested not in ownership but in development."[56]

Despite what has been said, it is almost inevitable that a goal of profitability and sales will conflict with the need of a development-minded state to be concerned about other objectives. Israel has not escaped this dilemma. According to a government official, companies with government capital have at times been "obliged to submit themselves to a greater degree of government direction than firms in other sectors," and this affected their profitability.[57]

In discussing profitability of government companies, several matters must be considered. Far from all of the government investment—72 percent in 1963-1964—goes into companies intended to make a profit; the other companies are often set up for reasons of legal or administrative convenience.[58] This fact reduced the ratio of gross profit to equity capital to about 3 percent in 1962-1963, but even when such companies were excluded from the calculations, the average rate of profit on equity was only 5 or 6 percent.[59] Extenuating reasons were that the companies have expanded rapidly, resulting in a large increase in equity without an immediate rise in profits, and that many have competed in world markets and have not been able to fall back on a sheltered local market.

Until recently, government investment in a company undertaking nonprofitable tasks was regarded as a reward to the company and a substitute for subsidization. In such cases, there was a tacit agreement that the company would not pay dividends on the government shares.[60] In the mid-1960s, this practice was largely abandoned on the ground that subsidies ought to be openly granted. Because of a feeling that share capital should show a return even if the owner is the government, efforts were also made to prevent the establishment of joint-stock companies not intended to show a profit.[61]

There has been a degree of friction between the government and the companies as to whether profits should be plowed back into the companies for their long-term development or paid to shareholders, including the government, in the form of dividends. The Government Companies Authority, a unit of the Ministry of Finance charged with bringing order to the financial affairs of companies, issued a circular in 1964 instructing all companies that made profits to consult on their disposition with the ministry concerned and with the Authority. The claimed result was an increase in dividend payments by government companies.[62]

In closing this sketch of the intricate and fascinating Israeli scene, it is worth mentioning Israel's use of joint-stock companies, including mixed enterprises, to provide technical assistance abroad.[63] Some of its largest companies have formed joint ventures with foreign governments for development purposes.

Mexico

Mexico serves as a particularly appropriate country for inclusion in this survey. Both its public and private sectors are vigorous. A leader of economic thought in Latin America, especially for its stress on the "Mexicanization" of industry, Mexico has also maintained friendly and fruitful relationships with the Colossus of the North. As a student of the Mexican economy has said: "The comparatively advanced state of Mexico's development, the experience and eclectic character of Mexico's use of the two sectors, the vigor with which both sectors have operated—all these commend the Mexican case for study."[64] What makes it especially suitable for the present volume is the imaginative use of mixed enterprise. As in Israel's case, the Mexican example reveals a high regard for mixed enterprise as an important factor in development.

Even though "there are few programs of the Mexican Revolution for which historic precedent cannot be found,"[65] the watershed for modern Mexico remains the Revolution of 1910. One writer sees Mexico's revolutionary creed as consisting of the following interrelated components: (1) Mexicanism and constitutionalism; (2) racial tolerance, religious tolerance, intellectual freedom, and public education; (3) social justice; (4) political liberalism; (5) economic development; and (6) a share in world leadership and international prestige.[66] The Revolution marked a changed pattern of development. William P. Glade, Jr., has summarized the elements of this discontinuity as follows: (1) a rise in internally-accumulated capital from about 34 percent of total national investment to about 90 percent or more; (2) a recasting of fiscal policy so that public expenditures for basic development rose from 26 percent or less of total public expenditures to 82 percent; (3) transformations related to broader production possibilities and the use of more human resources in the economic process; and (4) increased national motivation and striving for innovation in technology and social organization.[67]

As to economic development, it seems to have followed two phases, with 1940 as the approximate dividing line, but the phases have been in the reverse order found so often in the postwar developing nations. Instead of opting for economic growth and then trimming this aim to accommodate a clamor for social progress, the Mexican revolution appears to have sought social goals first and then turned to a development strategy which benefited the upper and middle classes.[68] Inequitable income distribution developed during World War II because of the diminishing relative share of salaries and wages. The inequities increased in the 1950s and 1960s with inflation and an elastic labor supply resulting from migration from rural to urban areas.[69] How income distribution could become more inequitable under the aegis of a revolutionary party has been the subject of considerable controversy centering on the nature of the official party, the Partido Revolucionario Institucional (PRI). Most American scholars have emphasized the competition for power among the agrarian, labor, and popular (i.e., middle-class) sectors of the party, but a minority of scholars visualize domination by a small elite led by the incumbent president and his predecessors.[70] The latter school, its arguments reinforced by the existence of obvious income distortions, has sometimes even insisted that the government's ability to concentrate public sector resources on the promotion of rapid economic growth has been possible *"precisely because it has not had to respond to the demands of all the groups within the PRI."*[c] Whatever criticisms may be made of the equitable distribution of benefits from economic development, there is broad agreement on the adroit and flexible use of the public and private sectors in industrialization.[72] Public investment spending has been counter-cyclical in nature vis-a-vis private investment outlays and hence has fluctuated between one-third and two-thirds of total investment since 1930.[73]

The public sector appears to be remarkably influential, considering that the activities of government enterprises plus those of proper governmental institutions account for just under one-tenth of the gross national product, appreciably less than in some well-developed countries of Western Europe.[74] Part of the reason for the public sector's influence seems to be its concentration on ownership of the largest enterprises in Mexico. A 1964 survey found a government equity in nineteen of the largest thirty enterprises. Of these nineteen, the state owned fourteen outright (including the largest eleven in the country), and shared ownership of the other five with private parties.[75] Government investment was heavy in the infrastructure base of transportation and communications, electricity, oil, chemicals, iron and steel, and banking and finance. Government equity was also represented in a host of other industries, including the manufacturing of railroad cars, automobiles, electrical products, wood products, ships, newsprint, and textiles.[76]

If the relatively small percentage of public sector investment is deceptive, the public sector's ownership of essential industries may also be misleading. There is an unusually subtle relationship between the public and private sectors. Part of the subtlety derives from the fact that the Mexican "is accustomed to multiple ownership patterns, to public, private, mixed public and private, cooperative and communal enterprises."[77] Another part of it comes from the willingness of the government to step into any sector in the public interest and the fact that "the public sector is in a position to make or break any private firm,"[78] even though

---

[c]The reasons given are "first, the program of agrarian reform eventually produced a state of political quiescence in rural Mexico. Second, the increasing opportunities for socio-economic mobility offered by the turnover of political offices within the PRI and by the rapid pace of industrialization eased the traditional Mexican political problem of managing discontent among the educated mestizo segment of the society. Third, the development within the official party of the capacity to smother elite competition for political office perceptibly slowed the mobilization of large segments of Mexican society into active participation in political life. And fourth, the traditional cultural and psychological barriers to political participation continued to limit both the extent and the nature of political demands coming from Mexico's parochial and subject groups, which together comprise close to 90 percent of Mexico's total population."[71]

"private property is respected within a special social context...."[79] "Since 1940," another observer has written, "it has been common for careful observers to state that the Mexican government apparently is committed to wide direction and stimulation of, and intervention in, the economy, without an intent to destroy private enterprise."[80] Blunting the effect of direct governmental investment is the frequent case where "the government supplied some critical ingredient for the expansion of the private domestic sector: a riskless contract, a subsidized loan, an extension of the electric power or transportation system, a prohibition on imports, a curb on the operations of foreign-owned competition producing inside the country."[81] At the same time, and further adding to the complexity, representatives of public-sector entities may be directors of private firms.[82] Finally, despite all the potentialities for clashes, the political style tends toward accommodation. In the opinion of one observer, this traces to "a mutual fear of the consequences of open conflict" and to the fact that "an unending concern to detect and conciliate opposition from every quarter became the hallmark of the Mexican presidency."[83] Although successive presidents have differed in their developmental emphases and techniques,[84] they have been relatively consistent spokesmen for entrepreneur-oriented development under the guidance of the powerful PRI.[85]

Mixed Enterprise

As remarked above, the complexity of relationships between the public and private sectors extends to mixed enterprise. Mixed enterprise is thus part of a resourceful pattern. "While there are no serious suggestions of extensive outright nationalization," an observer has noted, "a government industrial policy is not at all constrained by a reluctance or a political inability to influence directly private-sector decisions in order to carry out its economic objectives, even if this means discriminating between firms or acquiring whole or partial ownership."[86] The subtlety extends to the operations of mixed enterprises. "Enterprises owned jointly by government and private interests," it has been said, "behave in some cases as if they were altogether public, and in other cases as if they were altogether private."[87] Faced with this situation, a student of the Mexican banking system evolved the rule that "an enterprise is presumed to belong to the private sector unless there is clear evidence of public dominance in its important policy decisions."[88] Another writer who found it "impractical to separate the public and private sectors of the economy in the respect to the legal ownership of capital," decided, more cautiously, to employ the government's own breakdown,[89] which assigns to the public sector the official enterprises or enterprises with state participation that are managed by the federal government.

Despite the difficulty of identifying mixed enterprises, it is apparent that they run the gamut of size. The largest, as stated above, rank among the top thirty Mexican corporate giants. The details are set forth in Table 6-1. It will be observed that there is no particular pattern of investment in this small but important array: two firms have a substantial majority of government capital, the remainder a minority, in one case only a trace. All but one company are composite, rather than mixed, enterprises.

Information on the total mixed-enterprise pattern is spotty. In 1963, it was reported that nearly 400 industrial undertakings were government or mixed enterprises.[90] In the same year, another writer found some seventy "state participation enterprises," which, according to law, "are created in the usual form of a private corporation, but are controlled by the state either through majority stock ownership, by a charter which establishes a series of stock to which only government can subscribe, or by a requirement that government select a majority of the board of directors."[91] A government compilation of 1964 listed forty-five state participation enterprises.[92] The list included Altos Hornos and the development banks. Even a decade ago, the most prominent development bank, Nacional Financiera (NAFIN), a mixed enterprise itself, "was creditor, investor, or guarantor for 533 business enterprises of all kinds; it held stocks in 60 industrial firms; and it was majority stockholder in 13 firms producing steel, textiles, motion pictures, plywood, paper, fertilizers, electrical energy, sugar, lumber, and refrigerated meats."[93] At the end of 1968, 5 percent of NAFIN's total financing of industry, amounting to 8,606.5 million persos, was invested in shares of industrial firms.[94]

The origins of mixed enterprise in Mexico are even more difficult to trace than its precise extent. The chief landmarks date from the 1940s. In 1941, and again in 1944, the government established funds for the purpose of promoting industries deemed essential to development but unable to attract sufficient

Table 6-1
Mixed Enterprises Among the Thirty Largest Mexican Firms

| Rank by Size | Name of Enterprise | Activity | Percent of Ownership | | |
			Government	Private Mexican	Private Foreign
12	Teléphonos de Mexico	telephone	20	71	9
13	Altos Hornos de México	steel	66.8	33.2	–
14	Celanese Mexicana	textiles	0.5	51.3	48.2
16	Sociedad Mexicana de Credito Industrial	finance	83	12	5
22	Tubos de Acero de México (TAMSA)	steel pipe	13.5	35.5	51

Source: Adapted from Frank Brandenburg, *The Development of Latin American Private Enterprise*, National Planning Association Planning Pamphlet 121 (Washington, D.C., 1964), p. 63.

private capital. Public ownership and operation were to continue only until private entrepreneurs were willing to take over. Although this arrangement did not allay the apprehensions of local and foreign businessmen, a lack of funds prevented both the 1941 and 1944 schemes from attaining even partial success.[95] Other efforts in this decade were more successful. Though the Nacional Financiera (as well as most of other development banks) was created in the early 1930s, it was not until 1945 that its duties were expanded from developing an organized capital market for public bonds and private securities to investing in industry.[96] Today, "it takes on private capitalists as its partners, frequently rescues a mismanaged private venture, and regularly lends money to private and public firms in the same industry."[97] The legal definition of "state participation enterprises," summarized above, dates from 1947. Mixed enterprise undoubtedly received a boost from the stress on the Mexicanization of industry. A presidential decree of 1944, for example, gave the government discretionary authority to require 51 percent Mexican ownership in all Mexican companies.[98] A 1960 law requires future mining concessions to be granted only to government enterprises, mixed public-private corporations, or Mexican corporations which have a majority of their capital subscribed by Mexican nationals.[99]

The structure of Mexican mixed enterprise reveals disparities between intent and practice. The intent was to have considerable participation in both capital and board membership on the part of the private sector. It does not appear to have lived up to these expectations. Though there were provisions for capital subscription from sources other than the government or its instrumentalities, government capital has had to step into the breach. Charles W. Anderson found, for example, that the bulk of the stock the banking community was to invest in Mexican development banks was actually subscribed by government banks. Furthermore, "this pattern is characteristic not only of the development banks, but of the entire structure of the decentralized agencies."[100] A lack of receptivity in the private sector concerning government plans for its participation appears to be the explanation. Yet, it must be said that, in backing mixed enterprise, the government assigned less importance to the mobilization of private capital than to such purposes as enhancing legitimacy through obtaining clientele participation, satisfying aspirations for more democratic forms, and providing a form of tutelage for marginal investment groups.[101]

Had the private sector participated fully in the development banks, it apparently would still not have reached a position of parity with the government. Although it was provided that private capital should have more than its proportionate share of representatives on the bank boards, the government representatives (from the work-related executive departments) have the authority, under most of the charters, to veto decisions.[102] At most, private interests can be said to have "structured access for consultation and advice in the banks," but not decision-making power.[103]

Planning and Mixed Enterprise

The Mexican government's concern for promoting economic development raises the question of its commitment to planning. Here again, a remarkable subtlety appears to exist. It is true that "most of what has been termed 'planning' in Mexico is far from the normally accepted concept of economic planning."[104] Yet, despite a long obituary list of central planning organs dating back to 1928, planning in the sense of guidance of national economic growth by the national government has long been a reality.[105] Bertram Gross argues that it is more realistic, in assessing Mexican planning, to consider together a "central guidance cluster" of four powerful institutions: the Presidency, the Ministry of Finance, the Bank of Mexico, and Nacional Financiera.[106] Robert Jones Shafer has encapsulated Mexican national planning as "diffused or mutual adjustment decision-making..."[107] He concedes, however, that there are obstacles to coordinating private and public efforts. These include: (1) the lack of inducements for coordination (at least in the 1962 plan); (2) the secretiveness of the government; (3) resistance from those elements of the business community that fear the advancement of socialism; (4) the antibusiness tradition of the Mexican Revolution; and (5) the lack of adequate theory and mechanisms for coordination of the public and private sectors.[108] Whatever the obstacles, Mexican economic growth soared in the 1960s, with real GNP expanding annually about 3 percent faster than the population.[109]

Increased sectoral and regional planning accompanied the drive for industrialization after 1940. Broader national planning has increasingly come to the fore in recent years, "spurred by the asserted need for better coordination of the multiplying facets of public socioeconomic development, and of integrating them with the activities of private enterprise."[110] Though the form of this planning is still extremely vague, an informed observer believes that the government consistently accepts the responsibility for at least three major courses of action which bear on national development: (1) the improvement of the education, health, and general well-being of the ordinary citizen; (2) the provision of the basic industrial overhead facilities; and (3) the stimulation of the necessary domestic investments in order to eliminate as many imports as possible.[111] At the same time, there is reason to think that formal and comprehensive planning will not come about easily. Neither the 1962-1964 nor the 1966-1970 plans were published nor even widely circulated within the government; also, "outside the planning of public investment, there is very little interministerial cooperation and a great deal of political rivalry between ministries."[112]

Planning of a sectoral nature is closely associated with public enterprise in Mexico. Electric power, petroleum, transportation, and irrigation have heavy government ownership and strong sectoral planning as well.[113] These fields also account for the bulk of investment from the federal budget in economic development; investment is the area "in which the nearest approach to national planning is achieved."[114] State enterprises make investments from their own revenues, and the federal treasury contributes heavily.[115] The government's reliance on decentralized agencies and enterprises for public investment increased greatly in the years after World War II; by 1958-1963, 60.2 percent of all public investments in Mexico was being undertaken by these units, though relatively few were large and directly productive.[116] The decentralized agencies and enterprises, numbering more than 300, ranged from electrical and petroleum companies to clinics for child care.

No better symbol of mixed enterprise involvement with Mexican development can be found than Nacional Financiera, whose nature and activities will be discussed at some length. Its importance in the financial structure of the country is suggested by a few statistics.[117] Its assets amount to one-eighth of those of all financial institutions, about one-half of all government financial institutions excluding the Bank of Mexico, and about four-fifths of those of the 100-odd private development banks. Although its shareholdings probably represent less than 1 percent of the total capitalization of all Mexican corporations, these shareholdings probably carry disproportionate influence because they are mainly concentrated in a relatively few large corporations in such important industries as steel, electricity, and fertilizers.

As previously noted, it took some time for NAFIN to reach the status of "the central promotional agency," as Calvin P. Blair labeled it in 1964.[118] Several of Blair's points about the unfolding of this developmental role are relevant to a discussion of mixed enterprise. The first is that World War II appears to have furnished an occasion for a strong industrialization effort, and mixed enterprise became the natural vehicle. Though private enterprise initiated numerous projects, it needed help. "NAFIN, for its part, was more concerned with activity than with property right; and practically every promotion was a joint venture in some degree."[119] After major purchases in iron and steel, electrical appliances, sugar, paper, and fertilizers, and less major investments in firms producing electricity, coal, laboratory glassware, electrolytic copper, cement, and many other products, it found itself, at the end of 1945, a stockholder in thirty-five corporations and majority owner of five.[120] The second point to be noted is that NAFIN's vigor produced apprehension in the private sector and resulted in a law which attempted to strengthen the private side of mixed enterprise.[d] In 1947, following the election of the probusiness Miguel Alemán as president, NAFIN's organic law was amended to insert "the explicit assurance that NAFIN

---

[d]At times, it also produced apprehension among the public. Speaking of the mingling of private American capital, private Mexican capital, and NAFIN capital in two big rayon yarn corporations, Celanese Mexicana and Viscosa Mexicana, Sanford Mosk noted in 1950, "Many Mexicans are troubled by such close association between their government and large American firms."[121]

would make every effort to obtain private cooperation in any promotions which it might undertake and, before offering finance, would see that private promoters put up as much capital as could reasonably be expected under the circumstances."[122] Because Nacional Financiera's powers were simultaneously broadened, the legal provision had more symbolic meaning than practical effect on its activities. Thirdly, although NAFIN's postwar investment was heavily in infrastructure—a reflection of the Mexican government's recognition of a basic need and the usefulness of the mixed enterprise in fulfilling it—the organization continued its industrial promotion activity. NAFIN's purposes included: replacing imports; financing projects whose capital requirements discouraged private industry; increasing the public sector's participation in important industries; and strengthening its own power position.[123]

Nacional Financiera's organization and operating methods bear the stamp of the Mexican economic and political environment. NAFIN itself is far from being a nearly equal venture by public and private capital. In 1961, for instance, the shares in the hands of the "general public" amounted to only 9 percent rather than the legally-permitted 49; of the 9 percent, only a small fraction was actually in the hands of private investors, the remainder being held by official investors (such as the Bank of Mexico) who were legally included in the "general public" category.[124] Even the small amount of true private participation was partly mandated by legal requirements that many private financial institutions invest in NAFIN. In 1964, the government was even listed as holding almost half as many "general public" shares as the Bank of Mexico; all other shareholders together held less than either.[125] Further paradoxes are that the private sector has representation on the board of directors far in excess of the amount suggested by its financial participation and that "general public" shareholders are legally entitled to choose a majority of the seven-member board. This arrangement becomes less surprising in practice. In 1963, two of the four "general public" board members came from the ranks of private sector giants, while the other two, respectively, were president and general manager of the Bank of Mexico and advisor to the finance minister. Three cabinet ministers voted the federal government's stock.[126] Membership on the NAFIN board naturally is valued by the private sector. In addition to the influence it obtains through board membership, the private sector also exercises some influence over NAFIN "through majority ownership in ventures with NAFIN participation, through the press, and through political pressure."[127] In toto, however, the influence of the chief executive and his cabinet, and, to a lesser extent, that of the central bank, would have to be weighed heavily.

Though NAFIN has sometimes been described as the Mexican government's "entrepreneurial arm,"[128] there is broad agreement that it is not usually the initiator of projects but a screener of those proposed elsewhere.[129] "Under the combined restraints imposed by the hostility of the private sector," Blair has written, "the diffusion of public development decision-making, an antiinflationary policy, a reliance upon conservative foreign lending, a poor internal market for risky equity shares, a fear of concentrated stock ownership, and a conformity to the fixed-income securities market, Nacional Financiera has had relatively little freedom to act as a bold entrepreneurial agent.[130] NAFIN has been more aggressive financially, having not failed to make a profit since its origin.[131] After a brief initial period of embarrassment about its profits, it rationalized them as "profits for growth," growth both for itself and the Mexican economy.[132] Relatively little has been paid out in dividends.[133] While the government successively increased NAFIN's authorized capital, the development bank provided a much greater share of the funds. It successfully sought direct credits from institutions abroad and borrowed on the home front through the issuance of nonequity securities, through credit from other banks, and through a variety of demand and time liabilities.[134]

Mention of NAFIN's powerful financial thrust naturally raises the question of whether investment is control. This question was answered in the negative by Charles W. Anderson, speaking of the entire group of development banks.[135] At the general policy level, he found a conformance with political (i.e., presidential) decisions on investment, even to the point of occasionally offsetting "obligatory losses in 'political' investments by stricter requirements and higher interest rates in other areas."[136] At a lower level, technical advice and investigation carried out by NAFIN and the Bank of Mexico might, he thought, have some influence. Nacional Financiera's majority control of certain industries, in his opinion, did not "seem to constitute a basis for the day-to-day control of these enterprises by the bank."[137] On the contrary, NAFIN's practice of giving the top managerial personnel of these industries considerable autonomy might explain, he thought, the complaints from officials about excessive freedom of action.

Through Nacional Financiera, Mexico offers an intriguing example of the use of mixed enterprise in the service of economic regulation. NAFIN's investments in firms apparently have at times been influenced by the competitive situations in the respective industries of which the firms are a part. Railroad car construction in Mexico can be satisfied through the existence of a single firm. Because of the natural monopoly such a firm would have, the Mexican government may have found it plausible—proof is lacking—to have NAFIN own the majority of the stock.[138] NAFIN's partial ownership of Diesel Nacional has been on somewhat different regulatory grounds. It 'enabled' the federal government to regulate private producers [of automobiles] through direct price and quality competition and to use its power as buyer of component parts to generate some integration of the national automotive industry."[139]

It is in the iron and steel industry that economic regulation perhaps has drawn the most attention. By combining regulation with its roles as purchaser and owner, the government has greatly influenced the course of the industry.[140] Import restrictions and tax concessions have protected the industry against foreign competition. On the domestic front, government has had authority to control maximum prices, has had the leverage of large purchase orders, and has also been able to exercise power through partial ownership of large firms. Its majority ownership of the largest steel company, Altos Hornos de México, has been especially significant. Norman Schneider has argued that the "exceptionally good" performance of the Mexican steel industry in the two decades after NAFIN promoted the creation of this integrated steel producer in 1941 can be attributed at least in part to the presence of the government-dominated firm.[141] In general, his argument is that a vigorous and expansion-minded government firm operating without subsidies can have "growth leverage" upon the privately-owned segment of the industry. If his contention is accurate, NAFIN-Altos Hornos may be said to serve as an outstanding example of promotional regulation. Blair, however, gives less weight to the regulation effects of partial government ownership. Unlike Schneider, Blair believes that oligopoly theory has only limited applicability to the situation in steel and textiles. Not only do the private sector firms know that restraining influences can be brought to bear through political channels, but the mixed enterprises (and NAFIN) know that "their behavior must reflect the general concern of the Mexican government for preserving alternative producers, for maintaining employment in various geographical regions, and for retaining the support of the private sector by demonstrating that the party and the administration are not dedicated to the proposition of public in preference to private ownership."[142]

Finally, the example of Nacional Financiera illustrates the likelihood that mixed enterprise is more than a passing phenomenon in Mexico. In 1955, NAFIN announced as an article of policy that it would turn its holdings over to private enterprise "once their economy is absolutely healthy."[143] In Charles W. Anderson's view, NAFIN's practices have been quite different: "It has played from its particular source of strength among the economic elites, which consider Nacional Financiera securities extremely attractive, and has promoted the idea of mixed enterprise."[144] In his study of Mexican planning, Robert Jones Shafer exhibited similar skepticism: "It is a moot question whether the long-term tendency of Nacional Financiera's operations will be to increase the government's share in ownership of economic enterprise, and unclear how much of its ownership the state ever will relinquish."[145] The basis for NAFIN's failure to make progress in transferring firms to the private sector has been articulated by Blair as follows: "Poor ones find no buyers, and NAFIN keeps its good ones to finance increases in its own capital, to serve as common funds to guarantee its own nonequity issues, and to carry the burden of bad investments. NAFIN has also been motivated in part by a fear that the sale of its stockholdings would increase the economic power of already powerful groups, since there is no mechanism to assure that the stocks would be widely bought or widely held. Nor has NAFIN cared to hand over going concerns to those who have not performed the entrepreneurial function."[146] NAFIN's problems in turning over enterprises are thus not atypical, but the caution NAFIN has displayed appears to be based, at least in part, on legitimate public policy grounds. To some, the virtues of NAFIN extend even further: ". . . its profits and profit-mindedness have been of great value to the country in helping the selection of the most suitable projects and in encouraging industrial efficiency. . . . But governments of all countries are likely to want to subsidize a number of projects on social or political grounds, and it has been to Mexico's advantage that the government has been able to do this through Nacional Financiera and its profits rather than resort to perpetual transfers through the tax system."[147]

Taiwan

Taiwan's successful economic development in the last generation is widely known, its use of mixed enterprise scarcely at all. "Public enterprise" or "joint venture" are familiar terms in Taiwan, but the government has given little publicity to unions of government and domestic capital, a fact which inhibits this discussion severely. Before describing the more recent past, however, it is appropriate to note that mixed enterprise was no stranger to the development of Taiwan when the mainland Chinese arrived in 1949.

Under Japanese rule (1895-1945), mixed enterprise was a prime instrument of industrial development. The government flirted with the concept in 1900 when it stimulated the creation of the Taiwan Sugar Company, formed in response to the government's promise to Japanese investors of a guaranteed dividend of 6 percent of their investment for the first six years. The major investors were the Japanese Imperial Household and the Mitsui and the Mori families.[148] Though the government had no shares in the sugar company, it was part-owner of the Taiwan Electric Power Company (TEPC), created in 1919. Other major investors included Mitsui and the Japan Life Insurance Company. When the government decided to industrialize the island in the mid-1930s, TEPC "expanded its operations and became the entrepreneur-investor for the government in heavy industry."[149] One of the company's major accomplishments was the creation of the Japan Aluminum Company, the most important metal producer in Taiwan. This company was also a mixed enterprise, as its backers were Mitsui and Mitsubishi, in addition to TEPC. Though TEPC was joined in its industrialization efforts in 1936 by a government-owned company, industrialization achieved only limited success prior to World War II.

Because of heavy American bombing and the repatriation of Japanese managers after World War II, big-scale industry in Taiwan was feeble when the mainland Chinese arrived. Anxious to strengthen their economic base, they placed all major industrial establishments in Taiwan in the hands of the government.[150] These enterprises, it has been said, "bore the burden of industrialization from the start. The subsequent process of industrialization took the form of private enterprises catching up with and surpassing public enterprises."[151] Industrialization, like other development in Taiwan after 1949, was immensely helped by large-scale American assistance. Weighed against total gross investment in the economy, American aid averaged about 34 percent over the period from 1951 to 1965.[152] In 1961, Taiwan's Economic Affairs Minister observed that the United States had supplied an average of 20 percent of the funds invested in private enterprise between 1952 and 1959.[153]

Although American aid eventually helped build a powerful private enterprise sector, which the Americans sought more avidly than the Taiwan government at the outset,[154] it was achieved only indirectly. Thus, for the 1951-65 period, American aid to industry was only a poor fourth after contributions to infrastructure, human resources, and agriculture.[155] The heavy investment in infrastructure was essential to the growth of large-scale industry, and the government's policy of refurbishing established private industries and beginning certain new ones also aided the private sector.

Mixed Enterprise

The statistics on aid suggest how strongly the government was relying on mixed enterprise in this early period. Two-thirds of all American aid went to public enterprises and agencies, about 27 percent to projects of mixed public and private ownership, or to agencies that served both kinds of enterprises, while only about 6 percent went to private enterprise.[156] This emphasis on mixed enterprise appears to have followed a policy announced by Chiang Kai-Shek on the mainland in 1945. In a National Day broadcast, he stated, "The government should give financial aid to or make investment in private enterprises which are short of capital."[157] The transfer of enterprises to the private sector went more slowly than the Americans wished. Though the Americans never questioned the government ownership of transportation, communication, and power firms, they pushed hard for the privatization of banking, fertilizer, sugar, aluminum, iron and steel, and other industries that were not natural monopolies.[158]

Although some Chinese officials were reluctant to transfer public enterprises to the private sector,[159] there appears also to have been a feeling that even the public enterprises were not well enough developed to avoid direct action by government. Thus, the Economic Affairs Minister maintained in 1961 that, although development banks or similar institutions had promoted the development of private enterprise in a number of countries, "on Taiwan, the Chinese government had to perform these functions until banking and similar institutions are established and ready to take over these tasks."[160] The same official made clear, nevertheless, that his government had given every encouragement to private enterprise. The government had sought to restrict the expansion of public enterprise and avoid competition with private enterprise; it had given direct assistance to private enterprise through taxes, tariffs, loans, and foreign exchange and international trade measures. In order to get a textile industry underway, textile goods had been placed on a restricted import list and the government supplied raw cotton, working capital, and marketing assistance. Government funds paid for exploration costs, later repaid, for the mining of coal and other minerals. An Industrial Development Commission formulated plans for various industries, interested private companies in them, and assisted them in obtaining funds.[161] The government's flexible promotional attitude was typified by two actions taken in 1953. It had an agent take over the only soda ash company, nurse it back to economic health, and return it to its owners a year later with no strings attached. The government also announced a policy of "transferring all public enterprises to private ownership except monopoly enterprises, industries vital to national defense and a few special industries."[162]

The same announcement gave specific recognition to mixed enterprise. "Government-owned enterprises" were defined as: (1) "Enterprises operated by the Government alone." (2) "Enterprises jointly operated by the various levels of government." and (3) "Enterprises jointly operated by the government and private persons in accordance with the Company Law and in which the government's stock exceeds 50%."[163]

Under this law and as part of a land reform program, four important enterprises with mixed capital were shifted to private ownership almost immediately. Because of the publicity given this move and the precedent it set for other nations, such as South Vietnam, it is worth reviewing in some detail. Between 1949 and 1953, with the aid of the Chinese-American Joint Commission on Rural Reconstruction, a series of land reform steps were undertaken. These had the object of improving the unfavorable conditions under which lands were leased to tenants. The first step consisted of reducing farm rent and protecting tenants' rights more adequately. Thereafter, the government began selling public lands used for farming to those who had tilled the land. In 1952, the third measure, known as the Land-to-the-Tiller program, went into action. Under it, the government purchased private holdings in excess of a stated area and resold them to the tenant farmers who had been tilling them. It was in compensating the landlords that the link to industry was achieved. As a matter of fact, a publication issued by the Joint Commission on Rural Reconstruction viewed the compensation program as achieving the double purpose of coordination with the enforcement of the Land-to-the-Tiller Act and with the policy statements of the government about enlarging the private enterprise area.[164]

Of the total compensation, landlords were paid 70 percent in commodity bonds and 30 percent in stocks of public enterprises. As the former, compensation for paddy fields was paid with rice bonds and for dry land, with sweet potato bonds. This novel transaction has been touted as preserving the value of the sales price against inflation, relieving the government of the necessity of turning to the printing press, and permitting the tenants to benefit from easy repayment.[165] Another hoped-for advantage was a boost to the private economy created by the requirement that landlords purchase stock in public enterprises.

Although most accounts of the landlord compensation transaction simply refer to the sale of shares in "public" enterprises, an examination of the ownership of the four corporations (plus a fifth, involved contingently) in which the landlords were to purchase stock indicates that all were actually "mixed" enterprises, though not always with central government participation. The ownership breakdown is shown in Table 6-2.

A complex procedure was involved in effecting the transfer of stock. Because of a currency change to New Taiwan dollars in 1949 and the requirements of the 1953 statute dealing with the transfer of enterprises, it was necessary to reassess the capital value of the five corporations, a task accomplished by a fifteen-member committee with a wide-ranging membership. During the first half of 1953, subcommittees inspected the books and physical plant of the corporations. On the basis of the new valuation, the corporations then issued new stock at a uniform face value of ten dollars per share. Formal approval for the sale of the two provincially-owned corporations was obtained from the provincial assembly and for the sale of the three nationally-owned corporations from the national legislature in June.[166] Priority of sale was also established by committees of the national legislature. The Fertilizer Corporation was not to be sold unless the proceeds from the other four corporations were adequate. Of the four corporations, the cement and paper and pulp corporations were deemed more attractive to investors because they were more profitable and more manageable.[167] Therefore, 70 percent of the stock compensation to landlords was allocated to these two corporations. "Each landlord had to take a bundle of all four stocks: 37 percent of stocks in the Taiwan Cement Corporation, 33 percent in the Taiwan Paper and Pulp Corporation, 13 percent in the Taiwan Agricultural and

Table 6-2
Ownership of Enterprises to be Sold to Taiwan Landlords

Enterprise	Ownership of Shares (Percent)			
	National Govt.	Provincial Govt.	Private Individuals	Private Corporations
Taiwan Agriculture and Forestry Corp.	–	95.91	3.45	0.64
Taiwan Industrial and Mining Corp.	–	73.64	14.06	12.30
Taiwan Fertilizer Co.	57.64	37.07	1.36	3.93
Taiwan Paper and Pulp Corp.	44.34	29.03	1.18	25.45
Taiwan Cement Corp.	52.01	33.78	0.90	13.31

Source: Sino-American Joint Commission on Rural Reconstruction, *Annual Report on Land Reform in the Republic of China* (October 1965), p. 72.

Forestry, and the remaining 17 percent in the Taiwan Forestry and Development Corporation."[168]

Once the sale of the four corporations was completed, government assistance helped them on their way. They were provided with the same facilities for short-term loans utilized by public enterprises; the allotment of foreign exchange was provided on a similar basis; and they were given various other kinds of help, including aid in the marketing of their products.[169] Although the subsequent history of three of the corporations was rather spotty, the Taiwan Cement Corporation doubled its production and the market value of its stocks over the next decade.[170]

Despite the government assistance to the corporations, which continued until 1957, the landlords were disinclined to keep their stock, though the Cement Corporation retained the allegiance of the landlord-stockholders better than did the other corporations. Even so, only a small fraction of the Cement Corporation stockholders kept their stock. The percentage of retention varied between 4.5 percent of those who sold less than 0.5 hectare of paddy land to 9.3 percent for those who sold land between two to three hectares in size.[171] It can be seen that the larger landlords were most inclined to keep the shares of the companies. Even their retention rate, however, scarcely appears to justify the lavish praise often given to the plan to repay landlords in shares of industrial enterprises. For example, the reported conclusion of "many speakers" at an international land reform conference held in Taiwan in 1968 was that the transaction had "redirected the landlords' energies and capital toward industry" and had thereby "reinforced the breaking up of the traditional, stagnant subsistence-farming society and heightened the wholesale restructuring of society."[172] In short, the land reform aim of the measure appears to have been more nearly achieved than the process of involving agrarian capital in industry. The sale of the four public enterprises did, nevertheless, signify the intention of the Taiwan government to act on its policy of transferring enterprises, and substantial ones at that, to the private sector. The president of the Taiwan Cement Corporation, writing in 1965, credited the transaction with bringing about "a new outlook of the people toward private enterprise and a basic knowledge of the industrial society."[173] The experiment also had some influence abroad. In South Vietnam, Taiwan's close associate, a rather similar program was attempted in 1957.[174]

Though statistics are largely lacking, the government apparently transferred various enterprises to the private domain after 1953, in line with its proclaimed policy. One scholar has reasoned that the substantial decline in the value of public enterprise production as compared with private enterprise output between 1952 and 1960 suggests "a gradual transfer to private enterprise."[175] The ratio of the former to the latter changed from 41-59 in 1952 to 60-40 in 1960. It must be noted, however, that there was a remarkable expansion of private industry in this period; between 1952 and 1964, its output multiplied seven times at an average annual rate of 18.8 percent, compared with 7.6 percent for enterprises in which the government had a total or partial interest.[176] How much these statistics were affected by transfers of firms is uncertain. Whatever the precise facts, the policy of transfer was later reinforced. In 1965, an amendment to the 1960 Statute for Encouragement of Investment provided for the transfer of state enterprises to private ownership through public sale of their shares.[177]

Private industry's advancement was thus accomplished with the full coopera-tion of the government, which took a number of additional steps to curb public entrepreneurial efforts and to encourage those of the private sector. In 1960, the government announced it would no longer invest "in those enterprises which private owners can operate except in utilities and in those enterprises that are pilot plants or in the nature of demonstrations."[178] The government also assisted the private sector by starting an elaborate loan program, substantially financed by American aid;[179] by establishing a center in the middle 1950s to give technical assistance, mainly to small and medium-sized industries;[180] by creating an industrial planning and coordination group within the Ministry of Economic Affairs in 1958;[181] and by setting up an Industrial Development and Investment Center, which "performs a wide range of preinvestment services and postinvestment trouble-shooting activities" and "serves as a bridge between the government and the private enterprise as well as a focal point for foreign investors."[182]

Consistent with the lack of precise statistics on investments in enterprises associated with the government is the gap in information on the composition of boards. In 1953, a writer asserted that private shareholders were permitted to elect one director to the board of each of eight corporations owned 60-40 by the central government and provincial government, with a "trace" of private ownership.[183] The assertion loses some of its force when it is realized that three of the eight corporations are the last three listed in Table 6-2 above. The private ownership appears to be much more than a trace in at least two of the three.

Planning and Mixed Enterprise

Enough has been said above to indicate the outlines of a strong government hand in development. In seeking economic growth, the government has, for example, often overruled revenue officials "in order to give additional incentives to entrepreneurs," to quote the words of Premier C.K. Yen.[184]

The quality of formal planning, nevertheless, has been of a rather primitive character and has been shaped by immediate, pragmatic factors. As United States aid became more significant after 1956, it enabled the Taiwan government to use planning for the purpose of preparing industries for competition in foreign markets.[185] American aid officials encouraged broad goal-setting efforts by the government, although they carefully avoided elaborate planning of the

Indian variety.[186] The main objective of the First Four-year Plan (1953-1956) was to allocate and coordinate United States economic aid.[187] Subsequent plans emphasized agro-based industries and those based upon mineral resources as well as export industries. The Fifth Plan (1969-1972) "aims at improving the infrastructure and changing the emphasis from the labour-intensive industries to more capital-extensive industries, such as petrochemicals, electronics, precision equipment and heavy electrical machinery."[188] At first, the economic affairs and communications ministries produced the plans,[189] but in 1963, this process was taken over by a cabinet group headed by the premier, the Council for International Economic Cooperation and Development.[190] Plan goals were consistently achieved and exceeded. From 1964 to 1968, "on an annual basis, a planned 7 percent growth turned out to be 10.5 percent in practice, second only to Japan in the entire world."[191] In one analyst's view, the success of Taiwanese planning can be attributed to the ease of administrative control in a compact island economy and to "a certain degree of political regulation of the distribution or incomes, the distribution of investments, and the flow of material goods and services."[192]

The emphasis on accelerating economic growth brought both private companies and public corporations into closer cooperation with the government.[193] The latter were involved in planning through their respective ministries. Publicly willing to cooperate but privately skeptical of the government's adroitness in planning, private companies, especially the larger ones, nevertheless, were increasingly drawn into a mutually-beneficial arrangement with the government.[194]

In cooperating, private industry was undoubtedly encouraged by the official policy of transferring public and mixed enterprises to the private realm. It is worth noting that the 1953 statute putting this policy into effect stated, "Funds realized from the transfer of government-owned enterprises to private ownership shall be used exclusively for the purpose of economic development."[195] In 1966, plans were made to transfer four by-product factories of the Taiwan Sugar Corporation, the largest public enterprise, to private ownership.[196] In the opinion of one American scholar, financial pressures on the government after American aid ceased in 1965 seemed likely to increase pressures to implement the policy of transfer.[197]

The outlook for mixed enterprise appeared to be favorable but geared closely to the goal of private-enterprise-flavored development. For example, the 1958 statute providing for the transfer of public enterprises to private hands was amended a decade later to establish a development fund with the proceeds from the sale of such enterprises. According to Premier C.K. Yen, these proceeds were to be used to invest in enterprises beyond the capability of private investors and "to finance joint investment projects, which are promoted by private investors but in which the private sector has insufficient capital."[198] Such mixed enterprises were to be temporary, with the proceeds from their sale accruing to the fund on a revolving principle. To give another example, a composite enterprise was chosen as the preferred vehicle for creating a steel-production complex, beginning in 1968. Recognizing the great cost of the first phase of the project, a steel mill, Minister of Economic Affairs K.T. Li pushed plans calling for three-fifths of the funds to come from private sources, foreign and domestic, and three-fifths to come from the government.[199] These examples suggest that despite the great strides made by private enterprise in Taiwan, the government uses mixed enterprise to hover protectively over the further development of the economy.[e] This is consistent with a surprising reliance—in view of the secular drive to strengthen the private sector—on public enterprise in Taiwan. A kind of resurgence has apparently occurred. In 1965, as a result of a deliberate policy of promoting private business, capital investment in the government sector had dropped to 30 percent of that for the private sector. By 1970, however, the ratio was 70 percent, the high economic growth rate was being paced by state enterprises, and a proposed government directive urged the public corporations to make a profit of 10 percent.[201]

Conclusion

An initial impression of high government paternalism in three diverse countries— Israel, Mexico, and Taiwan—is borne out upon closer examination. The perilous conditions under which Israel and Taiwan (under the Chinese Nationalists) came into existence and struggled to survive may go far to explain the orientation of their governments. The explanation for Mexico may also be tied to a dramatic event—the revolution—but a more important factor appears to have been the later determination of the government party to achieve a high rate of industrial growth.

For historical reasons, Israel has a most unusual trisector economy, with endless permutations that often make its enterprises "mixed" in a manner no other country can match. Though there are departmental enterprises and public corporations, government companies have been the chief vehicle for commercial efforts, and most companies have mixed ownership. The government appears to have had more success in joining with the workers' sector than the purely private sector. Though planning has been of a minimal nature, the government's hand appears to be everywhere, just as in the other two countries examined.

Like the Israelis, the Mexican government has not hesitated to invest directly in industry and finance where needed from the perspective of sustaining a drive for development. Though its economy lacks the intricacy of Israel's, public and private influence over the economy is so intertwined as to baffle observers.

---

[e]This represents a continuation of the view, expressed by a government spokesman in 1965, that "the Chinese government assigned from the very beginning the role of pioneering to government enterprises and this policy has paid off handsomely."[200]

Mixed enterprises are found among the country's largest enterprises as well as those of modest size, and through Nacional Financiera, a giant mixed-enterprise development bank, the mixed enterprise idea has been extended broadly through the economy. Partial ownership of important industry permits NAFIN to participate in the government's surveillance efforts over industry, some of which have regulatory overtones. Government planning is a rather haphazard, unpublicized process, but strong economic growth has continued.

The foreign influences over the island of Taiwan have been pervasive in the twentieth century, and mixed enterprise has been prominent in the story. The Japanese employed mixed enterprise as a major development tool. In the period soon after the Chinese Nationalists came to Taiwan, more than one-fourth of the lavish American aid went to public-private ventures. Yet, mixed enterprise has customarily not been differentiated from public enterprise, and the precise scope of the former is difficult to picture. The well-known transfer of public enterprises to private ownership in connection with land reform turns out to have been a transfer of mixed enterprises. Though there were subsequent transfers under a government policy encouraging them, the proportion of these that were mixed enterprises has not been publicized. Planning in Taiwan, as in the other countries surveyed in this chapter, has been rather primitive, a fact for which government activism has again compensated. Economic development has exceeded plan estimates. A measure of devotion to development is the policy of placing proceeds from the sale of public enterprises into economic development.

7 Perspectives on Mixed Enterprise and Development

Mixed enterprise, an old institution, is newly relevant in an era when there are many new nations seeking to modernize. Economic development means many things to many people, but in the twentieth century one of its chief components, rightly or wrongly, has been industrialization. If industry and finance, its supporting arm, have been the center of the modernization effort, they are also the major locus for mixed enterprise. Accordingly, these fields have been the principal foci of the country surveys contained in this volume. In examining mixed enterprise in conjunction with development aims, there is the possibility of glimpsing relations between the public and private sectors, as well as something of the development style chosen by the respective countries.

To approach mixed enterprise from a developmental perspective does not mean that mixed enterprise cannot be viewed persuasively in other terms. A statement made in Chapter 2 about public enterprise can be applied to mixed enterprise almost as aptly: "Public enterprises were a common phenomenon long before economic growth became a popular aim, some governments are still not growth-oriented, and various public enterprises have been created for such purposes as bringing in revenue to the state, providing a favorable display, or as locales for patronage appointments." Furthermore, finding reliable criteria to relate mixed enterprise to development probably is no easier than for public enterprise and development, a topic dealt with at some length in Chapter 2. The criterion that has been mainly employed in this study has been national economic planning, and its suitability will be commented on below.

In pursuing the development theme for mixed enterprise, this study has not emphasized a watertight separation of development from other purposes. Stated development goals often become intertwined with other ends. Also, a nation's judgment on what constitutes economic development may be in a state of flux, as when a country shifts from economic growth to social improvement. Individual events involving mixed enterprises can lend themselves to differing interpretations. For example, if a nation continues an undertaking on a mixed basis after the private sector has defaulted, accident or inertia may be offered as an explanation, or it might be emphasized that continuation suggests the importance of the undertaking for the country's continued economic growth or stability. To give another illustration, if a government in effect subsidizes mixed enterprise by charging low interest rates or not taking profits, the process can be viewed as emphasizing the weakness of the mixed enterprise or it can be seen as a necessary price paid by the government for maintaining an effort regarded as essential for development. The major reason for approaching the development theme so generally remains to be stated. This volume is an introduction to a large topic, and it will take field studies to answer the question of whether specific mixed enterprises are actually contributing to a nation's development in the terms it has set for itself. That development goals have relevance for mixed enterprise has, however, been assumed.

Although the country experiences reported in the preceding chapter are necessarily brief and somewhat episodic, they provide rough impressions of the use of mixed enterprise in a developmental context. These experiences need, however, to be placed in the perspective of the rather sparse mixed enterprise literature. In addition, the first chapter speculated about the topic, and further comment is now in order. The discussion is organized under the headings of development and mixed enterprise characteristics, transience and permanence, and concepts of behavioral patterns. In the first two sections, the literature is reviewed initially, followed by commentary on the country experiences and on the first-chapter hypothesizing. The final section reviews and evaluates some patterns of mixed enterprise and development that have been postulated in the literature.

Development and Mixed Enterprise Characteristics

Perhaps because mixed enterprise is a continental European feature, there appears to be little mention of it—and less of its ties to development—in works in the English language prior to World War II. In 1941, Marshall Dimock proposed "Les Entreprises Mixtes" as a replacement for the unsatisfactory process of regulating public utilities.[1] Six years later, John Thurston, another American writer on public enterprises, suggested that mixed enterprise might operate successfully "where the government is conservative and essentially at one with the propertied classes. . . ."[2] In the atmosphere of the depression, however, he felt there was too much hostility between them to warrant the experiment. In England, Sir William Hart saw advantages in "mixed undertakings" at the local government level under certain conditions.[3]

Though there has been an extensive development literature of the last generation, the question of the usefulness of mixed enterprise has been discussed in it only occasionally. In the late 1950s, Daniel L. Spencer articulated its appeal in the Indian setting.[4] Small investors were usually reassured by the presence of the state as to the security of principal and return. The hope of obtaining preferential treatment, especially of becoming the principal supplier to the mixed enterprise, held an allure for entrepreneurial investors. For the government, the advantage of combining with private capital (especially foreign) was thought to be from the infusion of business efficiency in the mixed undertaking. Though often unrealized in practice, the income from participation in enterprises could be used as a source of revenue and as an instrument of fiscal control. Spencer's observations have a familiar ring. An interesting government motive for establishing mixed enterprise has been suggested by David Apter. Although governments in excolonial areas tend to be wary of private industry, it is one of the groups to which they are accountable and one which they often need for development. Especially where there is a fear of private investors, perhaps because of a hangover from Marxist conceptions of exploitation, the mixed enterprise will be useful. "Run on a purely commercial basis," Apter argues, "government has a policy stake, yet is less accountable to private investors."[5] One might add that from the standpoint of the private participants, sharing in an enterprise financially supported by the government often makes for smoother sailing through the rough seas of government regulation than if the private parties set out on their own. Most of the briefer arguments for mixed enterprise in the literature resemble this statement from Jan Tinbergen's *Design for Development*: "Mixed ownership may sometimes afford a means of combining private efficiency with the desirable direct public control."[6] Mixed undertakings undoubtedly reflect the good and bad features of both government and private enterprise. This is the view of S.K. Allen, whose summary of mixed enterprise's strengths and weaknesses is worth quoting in its entirety to end the summary of writings on the present topic:

The sources of strength in the government-private joint venture are impressive. First, the amount of potential capital is augmented to the fullest extent by the joint arrangement. Second, the ability of the government to absorb losses or to wait long periods while an enterprise develops, exceeds that of private investors. Third, commitment of government funds to a venture tends to generate a feeling of confidence on the part of the private participants, including creditors, that the undertaking is sound, that it will receive favorable treatment from the government, that injustices of management to absentee or minority investors will be minimized, and that the project will be carried through to ultimate success. Fourth, the leadership of the government, because of close and continuous contact with the private participants, can be used effectively to develop managerial skills and to nurture new entrepreneurs.

The weaknesses which tend to reduce the effectiveness of government-private joint ventures are mainly qualifications of the advantages just mentioned. First, while potentially all sources of capital in a country can be tapped by the joint arrangement, the presence of government in the enterprise will deter some investors who dislike or mistrust the influence of government or who would rather be free to manage the business and reap the entire rewards, without interference, particularly since managing the joint enterprise is likely to be a cumbersome job. Secondly, changing regimes or shifting political attitudes may affect the patience and perseverance of the government. In the third place, enterprises which do not have government participation may be placed at a competitive disadvantage. Finally, the leadership of the government in developing entrepreneurs may not be inspiring because of the weak personal incentives and lack of successful business experience which often characterize government employees.[7]

The survey of country experiences reported in earlier chapters prompts a number of observations, some of which relate to the speculation in Chapter 1. As expected, government origination and domination of mixed enterprises is extensive, but the picture is more complicated than anticipated at the outset of this study. In the developed countries, especially France and Italy, mixed enterprises have often originated, not out of government initiative, but private bankruptcy. Government domination is least evident in the United States, where powerful interest groups have been able to create rather advantageous circumstances for themselves in joint arrangements with the government. The absence of fixed capital investments by the federal government probably limits assertions of its own authority in such mixtures. Elsewhere, government dominance has in practice sometimes turned out to be stronger than intended by the government itself. Thus, the Mexican government has been forced to take up some shares intended for private parties; Pakistan has found it difficult to dispose of its holdings in industrial enterprises; Israel has found it much easier to combine with the workers' sector than the private sector in enterprises; and Japan in the 1880s ended up with public enterprises whereas it had planned to have mixed enterprises.

The tendency toward government dominance of mixed enterprise is lessened to the degree that government is satisfied with a minority interest or minority representation on the board. France, Italy, Mexico, and Israel have numerous enterprises in which the government has less than half the shares. It is true, however, that these same nations have various means that can be used to increase the government's sway over these enterprises. In France, it is aggressive planning and a close relationship with the private sector; in Italy, it is the wide dispersion of shares, which permits IRI and ENI (not the government, in this case) to control with only a minority of shares; in Mexico, it is the practice of including such institutions as the Bank of Mexico among the representatives of the "general public"; in Israel, it is the fact that the government can call on representatives of the "national institutions" for support on the boards of the enterprises. Though Pakistan and India have proportionately fewer enterprises in which the government has a minority interest, they have also taken measures to diminish private influence over the enterprises. In Pakistan, there is a tendency to give the government a majority of the directors, even when it does not have a majority of the capital. In India, the nationalization of insurance and banks plus reorganization of financial agencies appear to have given the government majority control of some financial institutions in which it was once in a minority.

Classifying countries according to development levels (see Table 7-1) leads to several questions which were briefly mentioned in Chapter 1: (1) Has there been

Table 7-1

Estimates of Total and Per Capita Gross National Product of Developed and Less Developed Countries (Expressed in United States Dollars)

	Year	G.N.P. at Market Prices Millions of Dollars	Per Capita G.N.P. at Market Prices Millions of Dollars
Developed			
United States	1968	880,774	4,379
France	1968	126,623	2,537
Japan	1968	141,882	1,404
Italy	1968	74,786	1,418
Less-Developed			
Israel	1968	4,007	1,460
Mexico	1968	26,744	566
Taiwan	1968	4,199	312
Pakistan	1968	15,287	140
India	1967	41,114	80

Source: Adapted from United Nations Department of Economic and Social Affairs. *Year-Book of National Accounts Statistics 1969.* United Nations/New York (1970), pp. 15-21.

a conscious transfer of mixed-enterprise experience from the developed countries to the less-developed (LDCs)? (2) Is there greater use of mixed enterprise, particularly to advance development, in the poorer countries as compared with the richer? (3) Is mixed enterprise more likely to be present when economic planning is elaborate?

(1) The temporal priority of mixed-enterprise experience in certain developed countries has furnished an opportunity for the LDCs to capitalize on it. The extent to which a conscious effort at transfer was made needs closer study than this survey can provide. Pakistan, it has been suggested, modeled its attempt to transfer enterprises to the private area upon the experience of Japan. India and Pakistan had the example of the princely states' use of mixed enterprise under British rule. Japan's use of mixed enterprise in Taiwan when it dominated the island can be documented, but there is no evidence that this is the reason that the Chinese nationalists, when they came to Taiwan, employed mixed enterprise. There are occasional references to experience in the developed countries. For example, in India the Italian experience with sector corporations or holding companies was used as the basis of a recommendation for a similar system in India.

(2) The customary weakness of the private sector in the LDCs suggests that they might welcome mixed enterprise as a device for speeding economic development. With one exception, this seems to be an accurate expectation. The exception, India, has by far the lowest per capita gross domestic product, but its

failure to employ mixed enterprise widely outside of the financial area may have other explanations, as is suggested below. As to developed countries, their use of mixed enterprise is greater than might be expected, given the vigorous state of their private economies. The use of mixed enterprise among developed countries is often numerically as great as among the LDCs, but the greater size and vigor of the private sector tends to make mixed enterprise less prominent in the economy. There is again one exception. Italy, which has the weakest economy among the developed nations included in the survey, not only gives mixed enterprise a leading role in the economy but attempts, not always successfully, to employ it for development. The greater-than-expected numbers of mixed enterprises in developed countries can be traced partly to defaulting private enterprise, especially in France and Italy.

(3) "If government actively manipulates the economy in order to obtain compliance with a national plan," it was said in the first chapter, "then it can probably be assumed that mixed enterprise will be regarded as one of the instruments to manipulate." Judging from the survey, this statement needs some qualification. The elaborateness of planning employed by a country does not appear to be an especially accurate guide to the use of mixed enterprise to accomplish development goals. France, India, and Pakistan probably have established more elaborate plans and planning machinery than the other countries. All three appear to include mixed enterprises in the public enterprise sections of their plans, but with no special attention to features that distinguish mixed enterprise from public enterprise. India, which has made planning a minor religion, probably makes less use of mixed enterprise than any of the countries surveyed except the United States. Italy, Japan, Israel, Mexico, and Taiwan, in which planning appears to be fairly rudimentary, have at the same time employed mixed enterprise for development with considerable force and skill. They, too, have not differentiated mixed enterprise from public enterprise as to treatment, but they have used it just as resolutely as the other group of countries, and in some cases, considerably more so. The United States is again a special case, but it can probably be lumped more naturally with the latter group of countries than the former.

Two remarks about the use of mixed enterprise in a developmental context are appropriate in closing this section on the topic of development and mixed enterprise characteristics. The first confirms the notion of the intertwining of developmental with other purposes that was mentioned at the beginning of the chapter. In Japan, for example, bureaucrats are said to cultivate relations with certain public enterprises in order to enhance their chances of appointments to their governing boards. There is no reason to think that the mixed enterprises among the government corporations listed by the Japanese government as being associated with economic development are excluded. Not only are there apparently similar bureaucratic drives in Italy, but, in addition, a continual struggle by the government to assert itself against rival power centers, represented partly by the huge mixed-enterprise aggregations.

The second remark has to do with ideology. As expected, it appears to have no major role in the developmental use of mixed enterprise. There have been some marginal influences. In France, at the time of the Popular Front and until about 1946, mixed enterprise suffered from an association with a business-dominated past, but it survived this period virtually intact. In Italy, the near-autonomy achieved by IRI and especially ENI induced the left-of-center parties to be cautious about setting up other power centers in the public sphere, but the mixed enterprises within the two organizations were not the bone of contention. In India, the government has appeared to be reluctant to give the small investor a chance to invest in mixed enterprises, and it is conceivable, as a writer suggests in the section that follows, an ideological motive may help explain the reluctance.

Transience and Permanence

The common condition of a lack of sufficient capital often forces development-minded governments to begin enterprises by themselves or in conjunction with private capital. Subsequently, as capital continues to remain scarce, the question may arise as to whether the government capital invested in a particular enterprise can be used to greater advantage elsewhere. Alternatively, more private capital may become available, and it may be thought that a market can be found for an enterprise begun wholly or partly with government money.

These situations have drawn some attention in the literature. One view is that mixed enterprise is most useful when units are sold as soon as they are financially attractive to private buyers. This practice, wrote the late A.H. Hanson, "limits the Government's own managerial responsibilities and it makes available a 'revolving fund' which can be used for a succession of pioneering industrial ventures."[8] Despite the advantages he saw for transient mixed enterprise, Hanson believed "this method of creating a capitalist sector of the economy is a confession of the inadequacy of the whole 'private enterprise' perspective."[9] Another view of whether mixed enterprise should be sold or retained would have the decision depend on the satisfaction of certain conditions. This stand was articulated in 1967 by Yaacov Arnon, director-general of the influential Ministry of Finance in Israel. Assuming that private investors are ready to buy an existing government company but not to undertake a new venture, that government investment in other parts of the economy is still necessary, and that public ownership is not a matter of principle, Arnon endorsed the revolving fund concept.[10] He rejected a suggestion made by Simon Kuznets to have an independent body, such as a supreme economic court, make the decision about selling, which Kuznets thought a government might be reluctant to make.[11] In the unlikely possibility that government investment is not needed for further development, Arnon would favor retaining the enterprises so that the government does not merely have idle funds on its hands.[12] More than one writer would eliminate from the sale category those enterprises which may be counted as infrastructure. Transience or permanence is, however, a difficult decision. In commenting on the policies of retaining infrastructure and selling enterprises created because of earlier barriers to private initiative, one writer has suggested that "it remains to be seen whether growth is in fact encouraged by such policies and, if it is, whether it will be politically possible to shift the successful 'commercial' enterprises from the public sector to the private sector."[13]

In a framework devised by Ignacy Sachs, a Marxist writer, the question of selling or retaining enterprises is visualized in somewhat ideological terms. Mixed enterprises (in Sachs' terminology, including almost any mixture but especially government combinations with foreign private capital as well as domestic private capital), he believes, can serve either of two patterns.[14] Under the "Indian Pattern," the government utilizes the mixed enterprises "as a means of supplementing its financial resources," but it retains the initiative and exercises supervision. In practice, few such enterprises are created because governments using the Indian pattern "rather prefer to set definite limits between the spheres of activity of the public and private sector. . . ." Under the other approach, the "Japanese Pattern," mixed enterprises serve as a handy way of transferring public resources to the private sector, with the aim of preparing it for self-sustained growth. The "overall social interest" suffers, according to Sachs, because "mixed enterprises appear in fields of production particularly interesting for private capitalists and their activity is guided primarily by considerations of profit for the private shareholders."

In the nine-country survey, it is apparent that selling mixed enterprises has not been a dominant theme, though the so-called Japanese Pattern has made an impression. As noted, its fame rests upon Japan's sale, in the 1880s, of enterprises intended to be mixed but actually public because of default of the private sector. Through its Industrial Development Commission and the provincial commissions which succeeded it, Pakistan far less successfully attempted to sell its industrial mixed enterprises.

Two other countries tried, at fairly early stages in their mixed-enterprise history, to get the private sector to buy undertakings. Soon after Mussolini established IRI to take over bankrupt private operations, an attempt was made to sell them back to private buyers. The attempt, never successful, was aborted, when Mussolini launched Italy on the path of self-sufficiency and preparation for war, using IRI as an instrument in this effort. Mexico made an even less convincing attempt. In 1955, Nacional Financiera announced an intention to sell its enterprises to the private sector, but, for various reasons, the transactions fell through.

Two additional countries have exhibited great flexibility about retaining or selling public and mixed enterprises. Taiwan has announced a policy of selling at several times in its brief history under Chinese Nationalist rule, but the precise extent of its success has been difficult to trace apart from the well-known sale of four mixed enterprises in 1953 in connection with the agrarian reform program. Israeli spokesmen have periodically proclaimed their lack of dogmatism about the retention of enterprises, and their wish to put development by whatever means ahead of any wish to retain enterprises. At the same time, great success in actually transferring enterprises has not been apparent.

As for the three remaining countries, France, the United States, and India, little or no emphasis has been placed on the transfer of enterprises. In France, the pattern stabilized long ago. In the United States, the present lack of a government contribution to capital means that the relatively few existing mixed enterprises, based on mixed boards, represent political compromises in special areas. Indian mixed enterprise has been too basic in the financial area to be transferred and too marginal in industry to arouse interest in transfer.

In all this, there does not seem to be a separate pattern for the developed countries as compared with the less-developed. If there has been any dominant guide to action, it centers on pragmatism. Announced intentions to sell have been thoroughly dependent upon the willingness of the private sector to buy, not on the announcements. Considering only intentions, however, the less-developed countries, apart from India, have been, in varying degrees, associated with the so-called Japanese Pattern of employing mixed enterprise. The proto-type of the Indian Pattern fits into Sachs' description of behavior under this approach: no attempt to sell its mixed enterprises has been made and their small number suggests a lack of emphasis on the mixed-enterprise concept. In sum, the less-developed countries mainly follow the idea that mixed enterprises are a halfway house to private enterprise, while the developed countries, who largely inherited rather than created mixed enterprises, keep them, not, apparently, out of love for the Indian pattern, but because there is no alternative. In the first chapter, it was hypothesized that, as economic growth occurs in a less-developed country, mixed enterprise would decline because private enterprise had less need of government participation. The persistence of mixed enterprise in developed countries does not directly contradict this notion, but it does suggest that the fallout from unsuccessful but essential private enterprise may minimize a decline in the number of mixed enterprises. As the private sector grows, of course, the relative importance of mixed enterprise is likely to decline.

Concepts of Behavioral Patterns

The preceding sections have reviewed a variety of features of mixed enterprise, seen from a developmental perspective. Greater precision awaits field studies, as has been suggested. They can shed light on such complicated matters as the degree of adherence to planned development, effects of pricing and profitability policies on the accomplishment of development goals, or the relevance of internal management practices for the integration of mixed enterprises into a development plan. On a more cosmic level, field studies can relate mixed enterprises to the political system and the society. In closing this introductory study, however, it is appropriate to call the attention of possible field investigators to several policy issues and approaches to mixed enterprise in action.

A break-even pricing policy is not feasible for a mixed enterprise as profits are needed to attract private investors.[15] The desirability of making some profits is widely conceded even for wholly-owned government enterprises.[16] Thus, the question of the disposition of profits is raised. A view which has evolved ever more strongly in these days of increased planning is that "there is a very strong case indeed against allowing the individual public corporation the free disposal of its own profits. These ought to be regarded as resources generally available for economic development in accordance with the Government's plan and should not in every case be ploughed back into the enterprise which has made them."[17] Spencer is in agreement and would apply this reasoning to the state's share of profits in mixed enterprises. Whether the general welfare would benefit depends, in his view, on circumstances surrounding each of three likely uses for the proceeds. If they are used as tax offsets, and the product is a luxury, higher prices and profits will penalize upper economic groups; if the product is a necessity, higher prices and profits may burden the masses. Successful use of the proceeds as a development fund assumes that private savings will take place and will be channeled into productive investment. Mixed enterprise fulfills the function partially, leaving room for capital formation in the private sector and, Spencer argues, encouraging it. Finally, the proceeds might be used as a tool of fiscal policy. For example, when deflation threatens, lower prices might be instituted to stimulate demand, where it is elastic, for larger purchases of the product; but this would be significant only where mixed enterprises were sufficiently important as a total part of economic activity.[18]

The need for equality of operating conditions between public and private enterprise and the need to regard mixed enterprise as belonging to one or the other category but not to both have been asserted by Pasquale Saraceno, formerly chief economist at IRI.[a] Furthermore, "any additional cost imposed upon public firms by public-interest purposes assigned to them should be covered by special government subsidies."[20] Developing countries that desire to transfer firms to private hands particularly need equality of conditions between public and private enterprise, Saraceno argues, because neither artificial privileges nor burdens can be transferred.[21] In claiming that there need be no third world of mixed enterprise, Saraceno emphasizes, "There is in practice always some mechanism by which one partner prevails when opinions differ."[22] A

---

[a]He is aware of the fact that the "cost-reducing market discipline" may not exist for public enterprise (nor for private monopolists) and that "public firms therefore have to solve the problem of cost reduction internally."[19]

mixed enterprise is to be preferred to a nationalized undertaking because, as Andrew Shonfield has summarized Saraceno's views, "It has the advantage of being constantly subject to the tension between the objectives of public policy on the one hand, and the need to satisfy shareholders that their capital is being used on projects which will show a good return on the other."[23]

Taking the duality of aims in mixed enterprise as a given, Spencer attempts to predict behavior under various market conditions. If the aims of shareholders and managers in ordinary large firms tend to diverge, alternative motivations are even more marked in a mixed enterprise, as he sees it.[24] In his model, he assigns profit maximization to the representatives of the private sector and social aims to government or public representatives. Even when one side dominates, the behavior of a mixed enterprise is likely to be different than when ownership is not split at all.[25] Behavior is posited as different under conditions of competition, monopoly, and oligopoly. Under the first, Spencer predicts that the firm would be "forced to move in accordance with the forces of the market"; under the second, "though the private interest would be tractable, they would undoubtedly insist on some degree of super-normal profits" and fiscal considerations would affect the government representatives' votes; and, if the mixed firm was a leader of an oligopoly group, "the oligopoly would behave like monopoly because the government participation would tend to unify the group and preserve the status quo."[26]

The contrast between this economist's view of mixed enterprise and the emphasis upon political-administrative factors in the writings of two political scientists, Fred W. Riggs and Frank P. Sherwood, is striking. Though Riggs' imaginative and perceptive works on modernization deal only fleetingly with public enterprise and not at all with mixed enterprise, Sherwood has called attention to the manner in which Riggs' approach enriches the literature of public enterprise, viewed developmentally, and, in the same spirit, he has added observations of his own on mixed enterprise.

In Riggs' complicated model of a "prismatic" society—which cannot be fairly described here but which envisons a political community somewhere between traditional (fused) society and one fully modernized (diffracted), public enterprises "cannot be operated profitably."[27] "Arena factors" such as considerations which determine balance-of-power, prestige, and solidarity vie with market factors and tend to overwhelm them.[28] Theoretically, public enterprise can be used as an effective means of economic development, but only if there are "political institutions capable of controlling bureaucracy, and officials who have to administer public capital efficiently."[29] As these factors are lacking, public enterprise should not be touted as a panacea for the inability of private enterprise to achieve economic growth. "This chimera," says Riggs, "augmented by a passion for planning, reinforces bureaucratic expansionism."[30] Officials see public enterprises as providing employment for job-seekers, expanding the number of agencies under their control, and increasing sales income. Private enterprise finds only slightly more hope in this society. Ambitious entrepreneurs belonging to outgroups ("pariah entrepreneurs") offer a chance of progress, but they "would be permitted by influential officials to carry on their activities, provided they contributed financially to the private incomes of their protectors and patrons in government."[31] The dependence of pariah entrepreneurs upon the favor of government officials prevents real competition between public and private enterprise. If the bureaucratic elite permits the private entrepreneurs to operate, "it is not because they lack the power but because they find it more profitable to retain them as a source of tributary taxes than to undertake the more arduous and possibly less profitable task of running state enterprises."[32]

Sherwood's concern that the public responsibility of public enterprise be emphasized leads him to the conclusion that mixed enterprise may pose even more of a problem. "A bastardized organ which can neither optimize self-interest nor fully serve the public interest may turn out to represent the worst of all worlds."[33] Applying Riggs' thesis, Sherwood argues that mixed enterprise can no more create a market than public enterprise can.[34] Intentions to sell mixed enterprises to private investors are rarely carried out, and little private capital is attracted to those not sold. The governments of the less-developed countries, nevertheless, adore the fiction of the market and sometimes pay dividends to private investors in mixed enterprises even while subsidizing them.

Because models abstract from reality rather than describe it, they enhance our ability to grasp a situation. Taken together, the models reviewed above sharpen awareness about contrasting ways of perceiving the same phenomena. The Riggs-Sherwood approach is particularly useful because it places the difficulties faced by mixed enterprise in a societywide context frequently found in the poor nations. As a representation of their likely dilemmas, the Riggs-Sherwood picture is more persuasive than Spencer's. As an early student of mixed enterprise in India, Spencer might well agree. His assumptions about the contrasting motivations of the public and private representatives on the boards of mixed enterprises were made for purposes of "systematic analysis," and he recognized that the public representatives "too may have personal considerations of bureaucratic empire building, managerial prestige and even personal gain."[35]

The present volume has been intended as a bridge between such models and the more refined models that might be drawn from comparative field studies. For all its shrewdness about the difficulties and dilemmas of the less-developed nations, the Riggs-Sherwood model appears to assume a uniformity of motivation and behavior that may not be warranted, even granted that models deliberately abstract from reality and simplify it. Although the nine countries here surveyed can fairly logically be grouped into categories labeled developed and less-developed, and differences between them perceived, the variety among nations within each category is more impressive.

Notes

Notes

Chapter 1
Mixed Enterprise: Contour and Context

1. The respective sources for the information are: Department of External Affairs, *Canadian Weekly Bulletin*, Ottawa, Canada, August 21, 1968, p. 1; *Time*, December 29, 1967, p. 58; T.C. Daintith, "The Mixed Enterprise in the United Kingdom," in W. Friedmann and J.F. Garner, eds., *Government Enterprise: A Comparative Study* (New York: Columbia University Press, 1970), p. 53; Mordechai E. Kreinin, "Joint Commercial Enterprises as a Vehicle for Extending Technical Aid," *Social and Economic Studies*, XII (December 1963), pp. 459-470; Amba Prasad, "The Theory and Practice of the Public Corporation in a Democracy," *Indian Journal of Public Administration*, VI (January-March, 1960), 33; *New York Times*, 27 June 1969 and 22 December 1970; Nai-Ruenn Chen and Walter Galenson, *The Chinese Economy under Communism* (Chicago: Aldine Publishing Co., 1969), pp. 145-146; *New York Times*, 19 August 1968; ibid., 15 September 1968; and *Time*, November 16, 1970, p. 90.

2. P.J.D. Wiles, *The Political Economy of Communism* (Cambridge, Mass.: Harvard University Press, 1962), pp. 2-12.

3. Richard L. Meier, *Developmental Planning* (New York: McGraw-Hill Book Co., 1965), pp. 153-54.

4. Eugene Staley, "The Role of the State in Economic Development," in Myron Weiner, ed., *Modernization: The Dynamics of Growth* (New York: Basic Books, Inc., 1966), p. 303.

5. Richard D. Robinson, *International Business Policy* (New York: Holt, Rinehart and Winston, Inc., 1964), p. 147, n. 3; see also, Wolfgang G. Friedmann and George Kalmanoff, eds., *Joint International Business Ventures* (New York: Columbia University Press, 1961), pp. 5-6.

6. Daniel L. Spencer, *India, Mixed Enterprise and Western Business: Experiments in Controlled Change for Growth and Profit* (The Hague: M. Nijhoff 1959), pp. 82-90.

7. It should be pointed out, as a mark of terminological confusion, that any of these combinations are called "mixed enterprises" in United Nations, Technical Assistance Administration, *Some Problems in the Organization and Administration of Public Enterprises in the Industrial Field* (New York: United Nations, 1954), p. 12.

8. In addition to the sources cited in note 5, above, see, e.g., Raymond Vernon, *Sovereignty at Bay: The Multinational Spread of U.S. Enterprises* (New York: Basic Books, Inc., 1971); Robert J. Ballon, ed., *Joint Ventures and Japan* (Tokyo: Sophia University, 1967); and Homer G. Angelo, Multinational Corporate Enterprises: Some Legal and Policy Aspects of a Modern Social-Economic

Phenomenon," in *Recueil des Cours: Collected Courses of The Hague Academy of International Law, III, 1968* (Leyden: A.S. Sijthoff, 1970), pp. 443-607.

9. "Multinational Enterprise & National Sovereignty," *Harvard Business Review*, XLV (March-April 1967), pp. 156-158 ff. The amount was estimated at 65 billion dollars in 1970 by A.T. Knoppers, "The Multinational Corporation in the Third World," *Columbia Journal of Business*, V (July-August 1970), pp. 33-39.

10. Jean Jacques Servan-Schreiber, *The American Challenge* (New York: Antheneum Publishers, 1968).

11. See Eli F. Heckscher, *Mercantilism* (2 vols.), authorized translation by Mendel Shapiro (London: Allen & Unwin, 1934), I, pp. 392-415.

12. For a broad survey, now somewhat dated, see Wolfgang Friedmann, ed., *The Public Corporation: A Comparative Symposium* (Toronto: Carswell Co., 1954).

13. United Nations, Department of Economic and Social Affairs, *A Handbook of Public Administration: Current Concepts and Practices with Special Reference to Developing Countries* (New York: United Nations, 1961), p. 73.

14. For documentation, see Spencer, *India, Mixed Enterprise and Western Business*, pp. 73-76.

15. Ibid., and A.H. Hanson, *Public Enterprise and Economic Development* (London: Routledge & Kegan Paul Ltd., 1959), are notable exceptions, but both were published some time ago.

16. For a clear discussion of the concept and consequences of formalism, see Fred W. Riggs, *Administration in Developing Countries: The Theory of Prismatic Society* (Boston: Houghton Mifflin, 1964), pp. 15-19, 182-184.

Chapter 2
Public Enterprise and Development Planning

1. Joan Mitchell, *Groundwork to Economic Planning* (London: Martin Seeker & Warburg, Ltd., 1966), p. 15.

2. Richard L. Meier, *Developmental Planning* (New York: McGraw-Hill Book Co., 1965), p. 33.

3. Neil W. Chamberlain, *Private and Public Planning* (New York: McGraw-Hill Book Co., 1965), p. 2.

4. J. Tinbergen, "Economic Planning: Western Europe," in *International Encyclopedia of the Social Sciences*, XII (New York: Macmillan Co., 1968), 102.

5. Robert Shone, "The Machinery for Economic Planning: II. The National Economic Development Council," *Public Administration* XLIV (Spring 1966), 14-15. See also, P.J. Verdorn, "Government-Industry Planning Interrelationship," *California Management Review*, VIII (Winter 1965), 51-58. But for a

deflation of the trend, especially in England, see Norman Macrae, "Whatever Happened to British Planning?" *Public Interest* (Fall 1970), pp. 140-158.

6. Gunnar Myrdal, *Asian Drama: An Inquiry into the Poverty of Nations* (3 vols., New York, 1968), II, Part Four. The quotation is from p. 711.

7. Gerhard Colm and Theodore Geiger, "Public Planning and Private Decision-Making in Economic and Social Development," in United States Papers prepared for the United Nations Conference on the Application of Science and Technology for the Benefit of the Less Developed Areas, VIII: *Organization, Planning, and Programming for Economic Development* (Washington, D.C., 1962), pp. 16-17.

8. Alexander Eckstein, "Individualism and the Role of the State in Economic Growth," *Economic Development and Cultural Change*, VI (January 1958), 82-83.

9. Friedrich A. Hayek, *Road to Serfdom* (Chicago: University of Chicago Press, 1944). For a sharp critique of British planning, see John Jewkes, *Public and Private Enterprise* (London: Routledge & Kegan Paul Ltd., 1965). A brief summary of the controversy over central planning may be found in James G. March and Herbert Simon, *Organizations* (New York: John Wiley & Sons, Inc., 1958), pp. 200-210.

10. A.H. Hanson, *The Process of Planning: A Study of India's Five-Year Plans, 1950-1964* (London: Oxford University Press, 1966), p. 3.

11. See, e.g., Charles T. Goodsell, "The Development Planning Mythos and the Real World," *Public Administration Review*, XXX (July-August 1970), 454-458; and Aaron Wildavsky, "Does Planning Work?," *Public Interest*, XXIV (Summer 1971), 95-104.

12. Chamberlain, *Public and Private Planning*, p. 2.

13. Ibid., p. 3.

14. For a concise discussion, see A. Faludi, "The Planning Environment and the Meaning of 'Planning'," *Journal of the Regional Studies Association*, IV (May 1970), 1-9.

15. Meier, *Developmental Planning*, pp. x-xi.

16. Mitchell, *Groundwork to Economic Planning*, p. 14.

17. Jacob Viner, "The Influence of National Economic Planning on Commercial Policy," in Wayne E. Leeman, ed., *Capitalism, Market Socialism, and Central Planning* (Boston: Houghton Mifflin Co., 1963), p. 278.

18. Ibid., p. 279.

19. Hanson, *The Process of Planning*, p. 7.

20. Jesse Burkhead, "Fiscal Planning—Conservative Keynesianism," *Public Administration Review*, XXXI (May-June 1971), 335.

21. United Nations, Department of Economic and Social Affairs, *World Economic Survey, 1967: Part One, The Problems and Policies of Economic Development: An Appraisal of Recent Experience*, paperbound edition (New York: United Nations, 1968), p. 98.

22. Andrew Shonfield, *Modern Capitalism: The Changing Balance of Public and Private Power* (London: Oxford University Press, 1965), p. 231.

23. W. Arthur Lewis, "Economic Planning: Development Planning," in *International Encyclopedia of the Social Sciences* (New York: Macmillan Co., 1968), XII, 118.

24. See Douglas Ashford, *Morocco-Tunisia; Politics and Planning* (Syracuse, N.Y.: Syracuse University Press, 1965) and Bertram M. Gross' prefatory comment.

25. Albert Waterston, *Development Planning* (Baltimore: Johns Hopkins Press, 1965), pp. 332-333. See also, Gerhard Colm and Theodore Geiger, "Country Programming as a Guide to Development," in the Brookings Institution Publication, *Development of the Emerging Countries: An Agenda for Research* (Washington, D.C.: Brookings Institution, 1962), pp. 51-52.

26. Two good sources on plan implementation are: Bertram M. Gross, "The Administration of Economic Development Planning: Principles and Fallacies," in *Studies in Comparative International Development*, Washington University, St. Louis, Missouri, v. III no. 5 (1967-1968), 89-110; and Max F. Milliken, "Comments on Methods for Reporting and Evaluating Progress under Plan Implementation," in *Planning and Implementation*, Papers Submitted to the Committee for Development Planning, United Nations, Department of Economic and Social Affairs (New York: United Nations, 1967), pp. 177-184.

27. Chamberlain, *Public and Private Planning*, p. 156.

28. Eckstein, "Individualism and the Role of the State in Economic Growth," pp. 82-83.

29. Edward S. Mason, "Some Aspects of the Strategy of Development Planning: Centralization vs. Decentralization," in United States Papers Prepared for the United Nations Conference on the Application of Science and Technology for the Benefit of the Less Developed Areas, VIII: *Organization, Planning, and Programming for Economic Development*, p. 4. See also, Myrdal, *Asian Drama*, II, 845-847.

30. United Nations, Department of Economic and Social Affairs, *Planning for Economic Development: Report of the Secretary-General Transmitting the Study of a Group of Experts* (New York: United Nations, 1963), p. 54.

31. R.L. Watts, "Recent Trends in Federal Economic Policy and Finance in the Commonwealth" in John D. Montgomery and Arthur Smithies, eds., *Public Policy*, XIV (Cambridge, Mass.: Harvard University, Graduate School of Public Administration, 1965), 385.

32. United Nations, *Planning for Economic Development*, p. 54.

33. Mason, "Some Aspects of the Strategy of Development Planning," p. 8.

34. "Organizational Aspects of Planning" in *Industrialization and Productivity*, Bulletin 9, Department of Economic and Social Affairs, United Nations (New York: United Nations, 1965), p. 8.

35. A.H. Hanson, "Report of Preliminary Study" in United Nations, Depart-

ment of Economic and Social Affairs, *Organization and Administration of Public Enterprises: Selected Papers* (New York: United Nations, 1968), p. 14. See also, W. Arthur Lewis, *Development Planning* (London: Allen & Unwin, 1966), p. 272.

36. Richard T. Gill, *Economic Development: Past and Present* (Englewood Cliffs, N.J.: Prentice-Hall, Inc., 1963), p. 103.

37. David Krivine, "Private Enterprise in an Underdeveloped Country," *Political Quarterly*, XXX (October-December 1959), 384.

38. United Nations, "Organizational Aspects of Planning," p. 8.

39. See, e.g., Murray D. Bryce, *Industrial Development: A Guide for Accelerating Economic Growth* (New York: McGraw-Hill Book Co., 1960), Ch. 3; and Hanson, ed., *Public Enterprise: A Study of its Organisation and Management in Various Countries* (Brussels: International Institute of Administrative Sciences, 1954), p. 401.

40. United Nations, *Planning for Economic Development*, p. 44.

41. Ibid., p. 30.

42. United Nations, "Organizational Aspects of Planning," p. 8.

43. Lewis, *Development Planning*, p. 265.

44. Mason, "Some Aspects of the Strategy of Development Planning," p. 9.

45. Frank H. Golay, *The Philippines: Public Policy and National Economic Development* (New York: Ithaca, N.Y.: Cornell University Press, 1961), p. 373.

46. John Kenneth Galbraith, *Economic Development*, Sentry Edition (Boston: Houghton Mifflin Co., 1964), Ch. VIII.

47. Raymond Aron, *The Industrial Society: Three Essays on Ideology and Development* (New York: Frederick A. Praeger, Inc., 1967), p. 114.

48. C.A.R. Crosland, "The Future of Public Ownership," *Encounter*, XVI (May 1961), 60.

49. Ben W. Lewis, "Comparative Economic Systems: Nationalized Industry; British Nationalization and American Private Enterprise: Some Parallels and Contrasts," *American Economic Review*, LV (May 1965), 50-64.

50. The literature is too vast to list here. A small sampling of American works might include: Marshall E. Dimock, "Government Corporations," *American Political Science Review*, XLIII (October-December, 1949), 899-921, 1154-64; C. Herman Pritchett, "The Paradox of the Government Corporation," *Public Administration Review*, I (Summer 1941), 381-389; Harold Seidman, "The Theory of the Autonomous Government Corporation: A Critical Appraisal," *Public Administration Review*, XII (Spring 1952), 89-96; and Lloyd D. Musolf, *Public Ownership and Accountability: The Canadian Experience* (Cambridge, Mass.: Harvard University Press, 1959).

51. Galbraith, *Economic Development*, p. 98.

52. A.H. Hanson, *Managerial Problems in Public Enterprise* (New York: Asia Publishing House, 1962), p. 133.

53. Lewis, "Comparative Economic Systems," p. 56.

54. William I. Abraham, *Annual Budgeting and Development Planning*, National Planning Association Methods Series No. 1 (Washington, D.C.: National Planning Association, December 1965), p. 15.

55. United Nations, *World Economic Survey, 1967: Part One*, p. 101.

56. Ibid.

57. Ibid.

58. Ibid., p. 67.

59. Ibid., p. 105.

60. Colm and Geiger, "Public Planning and Private Decision-Making," p. 24.

61. Jack Wiseman, "Guidelines for Public Enterprise: A British Experiment," *Southern Economic Journal*, XXX (July 1963), 44.

Chapter 3
Pioneers in Mixed Enterprise and Development:
France, Italy, and Japan

1. Paul Webbink, "Government Owned Corporations," in *Encyclopedia of the Social Sciences*, VII (New York: Macmillan Co., 1932), 107-108.

2. Ibid., and Daniel L. Spencer, *India, Mixed Enterprise and Western Business: Experiments in Controlled Change for Growth and Profit* (The Hague: M. Nijhoff, 1959), pp. 76-78. For recent English developments, see T.C. Daintith, "The Mixed Enterprise in the United Kingdom," in W. Friedmann and J.F. Gainer, eds., *Government Enterprise: A Comparative Study* (London: Stevens & Sons Limited, 1970), pp. 53-78.

3. The information on mixed enterprise that follows is drawn mainly from Warren C. Baum, *The French Economy and the State* (Princeton: Princeton University Press, 1958); Maurice Byé, "Le Conflit des tendances dans l'organisation du 'Secteur Public'," in Leon J. Morandiere and Maurice Byé, eds., *Les Nationalisations en France et à l'étranger* (Paris: Presses Universitaire, 1948), vol. I, *Les Nationalisations en France*, pp. 5-59; Byé "Nationalization in France," in Mario Einaudi, Maurice Byé, and Ernesto Rossi, *Nationalization in France and Italy* (Ithaca: Cornell University Press, 1955), pp. 65-188; Republique Française Ministère des Finances, *Inventaire de la situation financière* (Paris: Imprimerie Nationale, 1946), pp. 512-513; and William A. Robson, "Nationalized Industries in Britain and France," *American Political Science Review*, XLIV (June 1950), 299-322. Descriptions of the legal forms used for mixed enterprise and public enterprise in general can be found in Winfield Dallmayr, "Public and Semi-Public Corporations in France," *Law and Contemporary Problems*, XXVI (Autumn 1961), 755-793, and in R. Drago, "Public Enterprises in France," in Friedmann and Gainer, eds., *Government Enterprise*, pp. 107-122.

4. Andrew Shonfield, *Modern Capitalism: the Changing Balance of Public and Private Power* (New York: Oxford University Press, 1965), p. 82.

5. Information on French planning and mixed enterprise comes principally from Pierre Massé, "The Guiding Ideas Behind French Planning," in Wayne A. Leeman, ed., *Capitalism, Market Socialism, and Central Planning* (Boston: Houghton Mifflin Co., 1963), pp. 363-372; Hans Schollhammer, "National Economic Planning and Business Decision-making: The French Experience," *California Management Review*, XII (Winter 1969), 74-88; Jean Ripert, "The Implementation of the French Plans," in *Planning and Plan Implementation*, Papers Submitted to the United Nations Committee for Development Planning (New York: United Nations, 1967), pp. 68-83; Vera Lutz, *French Planning* (Washington, D.C.: American Enterprise Institute, 1965); John Hackett and Anne-Marie Hackett, *Economic Planning in France* (Cambridge, Mass.: Harvard University Press, 1963); Stephen Cohen, *Modern Capitalist Planning: the French Model* (Cambridge, Mass.: Harvard University Press, 1969); Pierre Bauchet, *La Planification française; quinze ans d'experience* (2d. ed., Paris: Editions du seuil, 1962); Charles P. Kindleberger, "French Planning," in Max F. Millikan, ed., *National Economic Planning: A Conference of the Universities–National Bureau Committee for Economic Research* (New York: Columbia University Press, 1967), pp. 296-297; J.R. Boudeville, *Problems of Regional Economic Planning* (Edinburgh: Edinburgh University Press, 1966); Baum, *The French Economy and the State*; Shonfield, *Modern Capitalism*; Group d'Etudes sur les Enterprises Publiques, "Rapport de la section française," Treizième Congres International des Science Administratives (Paris, 1965), mimeo; and John Sheahan, *Promotion and Control of Industry in Postwar France* (Cambridge, Mass.: Harvard University Press, 1963).

6. Massé, "Guiding Ideas Behind French Planning," p. 364.

7. Bauchet, *La Planification française*, p. 127.

8. Schollhammer, "National Economic Planning," p. 80.

9. See e.g., Kindleberger, "French Planning," pp. 284-285; and Hackett and Hackett, *Economic Planning in France*, p. 242.

10. Ripert, "The Implementation of the French Plans," pp. 69, 71.

11. Cohen, *Modern Capitalist Planning*, pp. 133-134, 166, and 237.

12. Richard B. Du Boff, "The Decline of Economic Planning in France," *Western Political Quarterly*, XXI (March 1968), 99.

13. Jean Marchal, "Investment Decisions in French Undertakings," *Annals of Public and Co-operative Economy*, XXXIV (October-December 1964), 265.

14. Hackett and Hackett, *Economic Planning in France*, p. 69.

15. Baum, *The French Economy and the State*, p. 170, n.

16. Shonfield, *Modern Capitalism*, p. 86, n. 33.

17. Hackett and Hackett, *Economic Planning in France*, p. 69.

18. Shonfield, *Modern Capitalism*, pp. 83-84.

19. The chief sources of information on Italian mixed enterprise are Joseph LaPalombara, *Italy: The Politics of Planning* (Syracuse: Syracuse University Press, 1966); M.V. Posner and S.J. Woolf, *Italian Public Enterprise* (Cambridge, Mass.: Harvard University Press, 1967); Shonfield, *Modern Capitalism*; Rossi,

"Nationalization in Italy," in Einaudi, Byé, and Rossi, *Nationalization in France and Italy*, pp. 189-246; annual reports of IRI; P.H. Frankel, *Mattei: Oil and Power Politics* (New York: Frederick A. Praeger, Inc., 1966); and Dow Votaw, *The Six-Legged Dog: Mattei and ENI—A Study in Power* (Berkeley: University of California Press, 1964).

20. Shonfield, *Modern Capitalism*, p. 179.

21. For details, see Vicenzo Apicella, "The Development of the Public Sector," *Annals of Public and Corporate Economy*, XXXV (January-March 1964), 22, 30, and Appendix A.

22. Rossi, "Nationalization in Italy," p. 205.

23. "The Instituto per la Ricostruzione Industriale, Rome," *Annals of Collective Economy*, XXVIII (January-March 1957), 23.

24. Posner and Woolf, *Italian Public Enterprise*, p. 72. See also Rossi, "Nationalization in Italy," p. 205.

25. Information on planning and mixed enterprise is drawn mainly from Rossi, "Nationalization in Italy"; LaPalombara, *Italy: The Politics of Planning*; Lutz, *Italy: A Study in Economic Development* (London: Oxford University Press, 1962); Posner and Woolf, *Italian Public Enterprise*; George C. Maniatis, "Executive Control Over State Holding Companies and Their Subsidiaries in Italy," *Indian Journal of Public Administration*, XII (October-December 1966), 743-756; Giorgo Stefani, "Public Undertakings in Italy and the Prospects for Economic Programming," *Annals of Public and Corporate Economy*, XXXVII (January-March 1966), 43-63; Apicella, "Development of the Public Sector"; S. Moos, "An Experiment in Mixed Enterprise," *Oxford University Institute of Economics and Statistics Bulletin*, XXVI (May 1964), 195-204; Nigel Despicht, "Long Range Planning and Regional Policy: 2. France and Italy—Latecomers to the Industrial Urban Scene," *Long Range Planning*, III (September 1970), 75-85; and Glauco Della Porta, "Planning and Growth Under a Mixed Economy, the Italian Experience," *Review of the Economic Conditions in Italy*, XIX (November 1965), 443-458.

26. Despicht, "Long Range Planning and Regional Policy," p. 83.

27. LaPalombara, *Italy: The Politics of Planning*, pp. 89-90.

28. For an informative account of its aims and activities, see LaPalombara, *Italy: The Politics of Planning*, pp. 35-50. Despicht, "Long-Range Planning and Regional Policy" has recent information.

29. Rossi, "Nationalization in Italy," p. 232.

30. Maniatis, "Executive Control Over State Holding Companies," p. 747.

31. See, e.g., Votaw, *The Six-Legged Dog*, pp. 120-121; LaPalombara, *Italy: The Politics of Planning*, p. 56; and Posner and Woolf, *Italian Public Enterprise*, p. 39.

32. Maniatis, "Executive Control Over State Holding Companies," p. 753.

33. Lutz, *Italy: A Study in Economic Development*, p. 283.

34. Istituto per la Ricostruzione Industriale, *1968 Annual Report* (abridged English version, Rome: Istituto per la Ricostruzione Industriale, 1969), p. 84.

35. Ibid., p. 85.
36. Istituto per la Ricostruzione Industriale, *1969 Annual Report* (abridged English version, Rome: Istituto per la Ricostruzione Industriale, 1970), p. 17.
37. Joe S. Bain, *International Differences in Industrial Structure* (New Haven: Yale University Press, 1966), pp. 96-97.
38. Ibid., p. 101.
39. LaPalombara, *Italy: The Politics of Planning*, p. 106.
40. Brian Chapman, *The Profession of Government: The Public Service in Europe* (London: Macmillan Co., 1959), p. 59.
41. Shonfield, *Modern Capitalism*, p. 188.
42. Ibid., p. 189.
43. Information on mixed enterprise and development through World War II is mainly derived from E.S. Crawcour, "The Tokugawa Heritage," in William W. Lockwood, ed., *The State and Economic Enterprise in Japan: Essays in the Political Economy of Growth* (Princeton: Princeton University Press, 1965), pp. 17-44; Lockwood, *The Economic Development of Japan* (Princeton, 1954); George C. Allen, *A Short Economic History of Modern Japan, 1867-1937* (London: Macmillan & Co., 1947), and *Japan's Economic Expansion* (London: Oxford University Press, 1965); Thomas Smith, *Political Change and Industrial Development in Japan: Government Enterprise, 1868-1880* (Stanford: Stanford University Press, 1955); Angus Maddison, *Economic Growth in Japan and the U.S.S.R.* (New York: W.W. Norton & Co., 1969); Henry Rosovsky, *Capital Formation in Japan, 1868-1940* (New York: Free Press, 1961); Robert T. Holt and John E. Turner, *The Political Basis of Economic Development: An Exploration in Comparative Political Analysis* (Princeton: D. Van Nostrand Co., 1966); Martin Bronfenbrenner, "The Japanese 'Howdunit'," *Trans-Action*, VI (January 1969), 32-36; and Gustav Ranis, "The Financing of Japanese Economic Development," *Economic History Review*, XI (April 1959), 440-454.
44. Ranis, "The Financing of Japanese Economic Development," p. 450.
45. Allen, *A Short Economic History of Japan*, p. 30.
46. Rosovsky, *Capital Formation in Japan*, p. 25-26.
47. Smith, *Political Change and Industrial Development in Japan*, pp. 36-40.
48. Ibid., p. 43.
49. Ignacy Sachs, *Patterns of Public Sector in Underdeveloped Economies* (Bombay: Asia Publishing House, 1964), p. 87.
50. Smith, *Political Change and Industrial Development in Japan*, p. 100.
51. Allen, *Japan's Economic Expansion*, p. 58.
52. Lockwood, *The Economic Development of Japan*, p. 509.
53. Information on this period is drawn principally from Toshiyuki Masujima, "Government Corporations in Japan," Administrative Management Agency, Office of the Prime Minister, Tokyo, 1969 (mimeo); "Government-Affiliated Agencies," [1 and 2], *Oriental Economist*, XXXIV (November and December, 1966), 662-666 and 715-720; and Allen, *Japan's Economic Expansion*.
54. Allen, *Japan's Economic Expansion*; p. 158. *Time*, April 13, 1970, p. 92.
55. The information in this sentence and the succeeding one is based on a

letter from Mr. Toshiyuki Masujima of the Administrative Management Agency, Office of the Prime Minister, Tokyo, Japan, dated October 6, 1970.

56. The principal sources of information on planning and on its relation to mixed enterprise are Maddison, *Economic Growth in Japan and the U.S.S.R.*; B.G. Hickman, "Introduction," in B.G. Hickman, ed., *Quantitative Planning of Economic Policy*, (Washington, D.C.: Brookings Institution, 1965), 1-13; Shuntaro Shishido, "Japanese Experience with Long-Term Economic Planning," in Hickman, ed., *Quantitative Planning of Economic Policy*, pp. 212-232; Saburo Okita, "The Role of Economic Plans and Budget Compilation in Japan," in United Nations, *Planning and Plan Implementation*, pp. 156-168; Tsunehiko Watanabe, "National Planning and Economic Growth in Japan," in Hickman, ed., *Quantitative Planning of Economic Policy*, pp. 233-251; Economic Planning Agency, Government of Japan, *New Long-Range Economic Plan of Japan, 1961-1970: Doubling National Income Plan* (Tokyo: The Japan Times, Ltd., 1961); Economic Planning Agency, Government of Japan, *Economic and Social Development Plan, 1967-1971* (Tokyo: The Japan Times, Ltd., 1967); Isdmu Miyazaki, "Economic Planning in Postwar Japan," *The Developing Economies,* VIII (December 1970), 369-385; Shigeto Tsuru, "Formal Planning Divorced From Action: Japan," in E.E. Hagen, ed., *Planning Economic Development* (Homewood, Ill.: Richard D. Irwin, Inc., 1963), pp. 119-149; Chitoshi Yanaga, *Big Business in Japanese Politics* (New Haven, 1968); and M.E. Dimock, *The Japanese Technocracy* (New York: Walker and Co., 1968).

57. Shishido, "Japanese Experience with Long-Term Economic Planning," p. 232.

58. Tsuru, "Formal Planning Divorced From Action," p. 148.

59. Watanabe, "National Planning and Economic Growth in Japan," p. 249.

60. Economic Planning Agency (Japan), *New Long-Range Economic Plan*, p. 19.

61. See Yanaga, *Big Business in Japanese Politics*; and Masujima, "Government Operations in Japan."

62. Bain, *International Differences in Industrial Structure*, p. 102. On Japan, see also Holt and Turner, *The Political Basis of Economic Development*, p. 248.

63. Maniatis, "Private Minority Shareholding Interest in Italian Mixed Companies," *Land Economics*, XLIII (February 1967), 119.

Chapter 4
The United States: Private Power and Partial Planning

1. For a quick, penetrating review of the research of economic historians, see Robert A. Lively, "The American System," *Business History Review*, XXIX (March 1955), 81-96.

2. For a summary of views and citations to original sources, see Murray

Weidenbaum, *The Modern Public Sector: New Ways of Doing the Government's Business* (New York: Basic Books, Inc., 1969), pp. 32-35.

3. Eli Ginzberg, Dale L. Hiestand, and Beatrice G. Reubens, *The Pluralistic Economy* (New York: McGraw-Hill Book Co., 1965), p. 15.

4. Weidenbaum, *The Modern Public Sector*, p. vii.

5. This summary is from *P.S.*, I (Spring 1968), 47.

6. Bruce L.R. Smith, "The Future of the Not-for-Profit Corporations," *The Public Interest* (Summer 1967), pp. 75-87.

7. See, e.g., Barbara Carter, "Sargeant Shriver and the Role of the Poor," *The Reporter*, XXXIV (May 5, 1966), 17-20.

8. See Cyril B. Upham and Edwin Lamke, *Closed and Distressed Banks: A Study in Public Administration* (Brookings Institution, Washington, D.C., 1934); Bascom N. Timmons, *Jesse H. Jones: The Man and the Statesman* (New York: Henry Holt & Co., 1956); and Jesse H. Jones, *Fifty Billion Dollars: My Thirteen Years with the RFC* (New York: Macmillan Co., 1951).

9. H.R. 19333, reprinted in *Congressional Record* (daily edition), December 1, 1970, pp. H 10927 - H 10934.

10. U.S. Congress. Senate, *Financial Control of Government Corporations*, S. Rept. No. 694, 79th Cong., 1st sess., p. 4.

11. *Special Analyses, Budget of the United States, Fiscal Year 1971* (Washington, D.C., 1970), p. 77 (italics added). The same section of the 1972 Budget (p. 81) adds a seventh, the Federal Home Loan Mortgage Corporation, whose board of directors is composed of the members of the Federal Home Loan Bank Board.

12. Harold Seidman, *Politics, Position, and Power: The Dynamics of Federal Organization* (New York: Oxford University Press, 1970), pp. 252-255.

13. *Public Law* No. 518, 91st Cong., 2d sess. (October 30, 1970), "Rail Passenger Service Act of 1970."

14. Report of Secretary of the Treasury Alexander Hamilton of a plan for the institution of a National Bank, December 13, 1970, reprinted in *Legislative and Documentary History of the Bank of the United States, Including the Original Bank of North America*, compiled by M. St. Clair Clarke and D.A. Hall (Washington, D.C.: Gales and Seaton, 1832), p. 28 (hereafter cited as *History*).

15. Ibid., p. 29.

16. Ibid., p. 30.

17. Ibid., p. 35.

18. Information in this paragraph and the one that follows is from Paul Studenski and Herman E. Krooss, *Financial History of the United States*, 2nd ed. (New York: McGraw Hill Book Co., 1963), pp. 55-72.

19. St. Clair and Hall, *History*, p. 661. The information in this paragraph is from pp. 654-694.

20. The portion of the speech dealing with the Bank of the United States is reprinted in James W. Gilbart, *The History of Banking in America*, reprint edition (New York: Augustus M. Kelley, 1967), pp. 28-31.

21. Bray Hammond, *Banks and Politics in America: from the Revolution to the Civil War* (Princeton: Princeton University Press, 1957), p. 412.

22. Gilbart, *The History of Banking*, p. 37.

23. Robert W. Fogel, *The Union Pacific Railroad: A Case in Premature Enterprise* (Baltimore: Johns Hopkins Press, 1960), p. 27.

24. Ibid., p. 40.

25. Ibid., p. 47.

26. This information and that in the remainder of the paragraph is from Herman Schwartz, "Governmentally Appointed Directors in a Private Corporation—the Communications Satellite Act of 1962," *Harvard Law Review*, LXXIX (December 1965), 359-361; and Nelson Trottman, *History of the Union Pacific: A Financial and Economic Survey*, reprint edition (New York: Augustus M. Kelley, 1966), pp. 102-104, 204-206, and 252-257.

27. See Lloyd D. Musolf, ed., *Communications Satellites in Political Orbit* (San Francisco: Chandler Publishing Co., 1968).

28. Letter to President John F. Kennedy, October 25, 1962, *Congressional Record—Senate*, April 24, 1963, p. 6992.

29. Ibid.

30. Schwartz, "Governmentally-Appointed Directors," p. 361.

31. Ibid., p. 362.

32. U.S. Congress. House. Hearings before a Subcommittee of the Committee on Government Operations on H.R. 12092, *Making the Federal Deposit Insurance Corporation Subject to Annual Budget Review*, 86th Cong., 2d sess., June 21, 1960 (Washington, D.C., 1960), p. 25.

33. Ibid., p. 21.

34. Ibid., pp. 21-28.

35. Ibid., p. 46.

36. General Accounting Office, *Report on the Audit of Corporations of the Farm Credit Administration, for the Fiscal Year Ended June 30, 1945* (Washington, D.C.: U.S. Government Printing Office, 1946), p. 4.

37. General Accounting Office, *Report on the Audit of Corporations of the Farm Credit Administration, for the Fiscal Year Ended June 30, 1947* (Washington, D.C.: U.S. Government Printing Office, 1948), p. 26.

38. Commission on the Organization of the Executive Branch of the Government, *Lending, Guaranteeing, and Insurance Activities, A Report to the Congress, March 1955* (Washington, D.C., 1955), p. 52.

39. Representative Sidney R. Yates, *Congressional Record—House*, May 31, 1956 (daily edition), p. 8435.

40. See, e.g., John A. Prestro, "The Ever-Growing Farm Credit System," *Wall Street Journal*, 3 November 1970; and Vincent Massaro, "The Expanding Role of Federally Sponsored Agencies," *The Conference Board Record* (April 1971), pp. 14-20.

41. *The Budget of the United States Government, Fiscal Year 1958* (Washington, D.C.: U.S. Government Printing Office, 1957), p. M 22.

42. U.S. Congress. House. Hearings before a Subcommittee of the Committee on Government Operations on H.R. 8332, *Amending the Government Corporation Control Act*, 85th Cong., 2d sess., February 18, 20, and 24, 1958 (Washington, D.C., 1958), p. 183 (hereafter cited as *1958 Hearings*).

43. Comptroller General of the United States Elmer B. Staats, "Coverage of the Budget—Government-Sponsored Enterprises," in President's Commission on Budget Concepts, *Staff Papers* (Washington, D.C.: U.S. Government Printing Office, 1967), p. 192.

44. See *1958 Hearings*, pp. 6-10, and *1960 Hearings*, pp. 21-26 (see notes 44 and 33, respectively, supra).

45. *Special Analyses, Budget of the United States, Fiscal Year 1972*, (Washington, D.C.: U.S. Government Printing Office, 1971), p. 37.

46. See *1958 Hearings*, pp. 40-41.

47. *Special Analyses, Budget of the United States, Fiscal Year 1972* p. 83.

48. President's Commission on Budget Concepts, *Report* (Washington, D.C.: U.S. Printing Office, 1967), pp. 29-30.

49. *The Budget of the United States Government, Fiscal Year 1972* (Washington, D.C.: U.S. Government Printing Office, 1971), p. 18.

50. See, e.g., the publications cited in note 44, supra.

51. *The Budget of the United States Government, Fiscal Year 1972*, p. 18.

52. The proposal is described in a speech by Paul A. Volcker, undersecretary of the Treasury for monetary affairs, given in New York, June 10, 1971, and reproduced in a Treasury news release.

53. See, e.g., Massaro, "The Expanding Role of Federally Sponsored Agencies."

54. Reported in the Volcker speech (see note 52).

55. United Nations, Department of Economic and Social Affairs, *Planning for Economic Development, Volume II. Studies of National Planning Experience, Part 1. Private Enterprise and Mixed Economies.* The paper submitted by the United States government is on pp. 220-237, and the quotation is from p. 237.

56. Jesse Burkhead, "Fiscal Planning—Conservative Keynesianism," *Public Administration Review*, XXXI (May-June 1971), 335.

57. Dean S. Ammer, "The Side Effects of Planning," *Harvard Business Review*, XLVIII (May-June 1970), 32.

58. See U.S. Congress. Joint Economic Committee, *Twentieth Anniversary of the Employment Act of 1946: An Economic Symposium*, 89th Cong., 2d sess., February 23, 1966 (Washington, D.C.: U.S. Government Printing Office, 1966), pp. 8 and 16.

59. For background, see Walter F. Mondale, "Reporting on the Social State of the Union," *Trans-Action* V (June 1968), 34-38. Other informative sources, some critical, are: Peter J. Henriot, "Political Questions about Social Indicators," *Western Political Quarterly*, XXIII (June 1970), 235-255; Michael Springer, "Social Indicators, Reports, and Accounts: Toward the Management of

Society," *Annals of the American Academy of Political and Social Science*, CCCLXXXVIII (March 1970), 1-13; Mancur Olson, "An Analytic Framework for Social Reporting and Social Analysis," ibid., pp. 112-126; and Eleanor Bernert Sheldon and Howard E. Freeman, "Notes on Social Indicators: Promises and Potential," *Policy Sciences*, I (Spring 1970), 97-111.

60. Stewart L. Udall, *1976: Agenda for Tomorrow* (New York: Harcourt, Brace & World, Inc., 1968), pp. 17-18.

61. See, e.g., Melvin R. Levin, "The Economic Development Districts: New Planning Regions," *Urban Affairs Quarterly*, III (March 1968), 81-102; and Richard H. Slavin, "A New Dimension of State Planning—Policy Development and Issue Analysis," *Annals of Regional Science*, IV (June 1970), 61-68.

62. Neil Chamberlain, *Private and Public Planning* (New York: McGraw-Hill Book Co., 1965), p. 94.

63. Gerhard Colm, *Integration of National Planning and Budgeting*, National Planning Association Planning Methods Series No. 5, (Washington, D.C.: National Planning Association, 1968), p. 18.

64. For a wide-ranging review, see "Symposium: Planning-Programming-Budgeting System Reexamined: Development, Analysis, and Criticism," *Public Administration Review*, XXIX (March-April 1969), 111-202.

65. Gerhard Colm, "The Government Sector: A Re-examination of Controversial Issues," in Conference on Research in Income and Wealth of the National Bureau of Economic Research, *Problems in the International Comparison of Economic Accounts* (Princeton: Princeton University Press, 1957) v. 20, p. 113.

66. Ibid., p. 122.

67. Ginzberg, Hiestand, and Reubens, *The Pluralistic Economy*, p. 20.

68. President's Commission on Budget Concepts, *Report*, pp. 29-30.

69. Elmer B. Staats, "Coverage of the Budget—Government-Sponsored Enterprises," p. 189.

70. *Special Analyses: Budget of the United States, Fiscal Year 1972*, p. 37.

71. For a discussion, see George F. Break, "The Treatment of Lending and Borrowing in the Federal Budget," in Wilfred Lewis, Jr., ed., *Budget Concepts for Economic Analysis* (Washington, D.C.: Brookings Institution, 1968), pp. 66-69.

72. U.S. Congress. House. Committee on Banking and Currency, *Sale of Participations in Government Agency Loan Pools*, House Report No. 1448, 89th Cong., 2d sess., April 25, 1966 (Washington, D.C.: U.S. Government Printing Office, 1966), p. 3.

73. Commission on Agricultural Credit, *The Farm Credit System in the 70's: Report* (Washington, D.C.: Farm Credit Administration, 1970), p. 25.

74. Paul Meek, "Financing Farm Credit in the 1970's," in *The Farm Credit System in the 70's: Appendix* (Washington, D.C.: Farm Credit Administration, 1970), p. 78.

75. Quoted in Harold T. Mason, "Farm Credit Bank Securities: History and

Effectiveness of This Means of Financing, and Other Means That Might Be Considered," in *The Farm Credit System in the 70's: Appendix*, p. 59.

76. Robert C. Turner, "Federal Loan Programs, Budgetary Myths, and a Move Toward Reality," *Challenge* XV (March-April 1967), 9.

77. See *Congressional Record, House*, (daily edition), April 5, 1967, p. H 3570, and ibid., Appendix (daily edition), May 18, 1967, p. A 2460.

78. Thomas B. Marvell, *The Federal Home Loan Bank Board* (New York: Frederick A. Praeger, Inc., 1969), pp. 34-35.

79. U.S. Congress. Joint Economic Committee, *Joint Economic Report, 1968*, Senate Report No. 1016, 90th Cong., 2d sess., March 19, 1968 (Washington, D.C.: U.S. Government Printing Office, 1968), p. 15.

80. Commission on Mortgage Interest Rates, *Report to the President of the United States and to the Congress, August, 1969* (Washington, D.C.: U.S. Government Printing Office, 1969).

81. See, e.g., *New York Times*, 29 September 1969, and 25 June 1970.

82. Marvell, *The Federal Home Loan Bank Board*, p. 81.

83. R. Bruce Ricks, "The Role of Federal Credit Agencies in the Capital Markets," *Federal Home Loan Bank Board Journal* (September 1971), pp. 7-12, 16.

84. "Government-Sponsored Credit Agencies," *Federal Reserve Bank of New York Monthly Review*, LII (April 1970), 87-91.

85. George F. Break, *Federal Lending and Economic Stability* (Washington, D.C.: Brookings Institution, 1965), p. 103.

86. Murray L. Weidenbaum, formerly assistant secretary of the Treasury for economic policy, "Financing and Controlling Federal Credit Programs," *Federal Home Loan Bank Board Journal* (September 1971), pp. 13-16.

Chapter 5
Contrasts and Convergences: India and Pakistan

1. Gunnar Myrdal, *Asian Drama: An Inquiry Into the Poverty of Nations* (New York: Pantheon Books, 1968), III, pp. 731-732, 756-757.

2. R.L. Varshney, "Government-Business Relations in India," *Business History Review*, XXXVIII (Spring 1964), 24.

3. Daniel L. Spencer, *India, Mixed Enterprise and Western Business: Experiments in Controlled Change for Growth and Profit* (The Hague: M. Nijhoff, 1959), p. 40.

4. Ibid., p. 41.

5. Paramanad Prasad, *Some Economic Problems of Public Enterprises in India* (Leiden, Stenfert Kroese, 1957), pp. 97-101.

6. Varshney, "Government-Business Relations in India," p. 27.

7. This paragraph and the one that follows rely on Spencer, *India, Mixed Enterprise and Western Business*, pp. 42-45, 104-115.

8. Quoted in Varshney, "Government-Business Relations in India," p. 36.

9. Quoted in Iqbal Narain, "The Management of Public Enterprises—A Study of Some Aspects in the Context of the 'Socialistic Pattern'," *Indian Journal of Public Administration* IV (July-September 1958), 302.

10. Quoted in ibid., p. 303.

11. A.H. Hanson, *The Process of Planning: A Study of India's Five-Year Plans 1950-1964* (New York: Oxford University Press, 1966), p. 461.

12. Ibid., p. 462.

13. Ibid., pp. 459-465.

14. John P. Lewis, *Quiet Crisis in India: Economic Development and American Policy* (Garden City, N.Y.: Doubleday & Co., Inc., 1964), p. 226.

15. Douglas S. Paauw, *Development Planning in Asia*, National Planning Association Planning Experience Series No. 1 (Washington, D.C.: National Planning Association, 1965), p. 19.

16. George B. Baldwin, "Public Enterprise in Indian Industry," *Pacific Affairs*, XXX (March 1957), 21.

17. Prasad, *Some Economic Problems of Public Enterprises*, p. 171; Om Prakash, *The Theory and Working of State Corporations* (New York: Frederick A. Praeger, Inc., 1963), p. 83.

18. H.K. Paranjape, "Evolving Pattern in the Organization and Administration of Public Enterprises," *Indian Journal of Public Administration* IX (July-September 1963), 398.

19. H.C. Dasappa, "Parliamentary Control and Accountability of Public Undertakings," *Indian Journal of Public Administration* VII (April-June 1961), 143.

20. Government of India, Ministry of Finance, Bureau of Public Enterprises, *Annual Report on the Working of Industrial and Commercial Undertakings of the Central Government, 1967-68* (New Delhi: Manager of Publications, 1969), p. 1.

21. M.M. Khullar, "Anatomy of Profits and Public Sector." Paper read at 53rd annual conference of Indian Economic Association, Gauhati, December 28-30, 1970, p. 27.

22. See Prakash, *The Theory and Working of State Corporations*, pp. 37-39, 77-80.

23. Government of India, *Industrial and Commercial Undertakings*, p. 127.

24. Ibid., p. 3.

25. Ibid.

26. See ibid., p. 119-126.

27. Quoted in K. Krishna Moorthy, "The 'Public or Private' Debate—People's Shares?," *Far Eastern Economic Review* 30 (December 15, 1960), p. 588.

28. Nabagopol Das, *The Public Sector in India*, 3rd ed. (New Delhi, 1966), p. 86.

29. Ibid., p. 87.

153

30. Prasad, *Some Economic Problems of Public Enterprises*, pp. 112-113.

31. Ibid., p. 111.

32. Moorthy, "The 'Public or Private' Debate," p. 588.

33. Government of India, Administrative Reforms Commission, *Report on Public Sector Undertakings* (New Delhi: Manager of Publications, 1967), p. 13.

34. Paranjape, "Evolving Pattern in the Organization," p. 400.

35. M.C. Shukla, *Administrative Problems of Public Enterprise in India* (New Delhi: S. Chand, 1959), p. 38.

36. Prakash, *The Theory and Working of State Corporations*, p. 82.

37. H. Venkatasubbiah, *Indian Economy Since Independence* (Bombay: Asia Publishing House, 1961), p. 175.

38. Paranjape, "Evolving Pattern in the Organization," p. 400.

39. Varshney, "Government-Business Relations in India," p. 39.

40. Hanson, *The Process of Planning*, p. 481. See also, L.C. Gupta, *The Changing Structure of Industrial Finance in India: The Impact of Institutional Finance* (Oxford: Clarendon Press, 1969), p. 89.

41. Venkatasubbiah, *Indian Economy Since Independence*, p. 177.

42. See Indian Chamber of Commerce, *Central Financing Institutions for Industry in India* (New Delhi: Manager of Publications, 1963), p. 5.

43. Ibid., p. 41.

44. Ibid., p. 53.

45. Information in this paragraph is largely from Gupta, *The Changing Structure of Industrial Finance*, pp. 89-92.

46. J.J. Anjaria, "New Dimensions in Central Banking," *Reserve Bank of India Bulletin* (September 1968), pp. 1166-1167.

47. Prakash, *The Theory and Working of State Corporations*, p. 54.

48. Ibid.

49. Spencer, *India, Mixed Enterprise*, p. 165.

50. V.T. Krishnamachari, *Fundamentals of Planning in India* (New York: Frederick A. Praeger, Inc., 1962), p. 178-179.

51. Prakash, *The Theory and Working of State Corporations*, pp. 54-55.

52. Spencer, *India, Mixed Enterprise*, p. 120.

53. Hanson, *The Process of Planning*, p. 478.

54. Ibid.

55. Spencer, *India, Mixed Enterprise*, p. 134.

56. Hanson, *The Process of Planning*, p. 481.

57. Ibid., p. 482.

58. Dr. Ramaswami Mudaliar, whose explanation to Parliament is quoted in Venkatasubbiah, *Indian Economy Since Independence*, pp. 177-178.

59. Ibid., p. 178.

60. Ibid., p. 181.

61. Ibid., p. 182.

62. Krishnamachari, *Fundamentals of Planning*, pp. 80-88.

63. Ibid., p. 83.

64. Wilfred Malenbaum, "Industrial Progress in India Under Planning," *Current History* LIV (April 1968), 206.

65. Ibid., p. 208; and Paul Streeten and Michael Lipton, eds., *The Crisis of Indian Planning* (London: Oxford University Press, 1968), pp. 6-7.

66. See *New York Times*, 7 June 1971. For criticism of the revised plan, see Indian Institute of Public Opinion, "The Untenable Plan: A Critique of the Fourth Five-Year Plan," *Monthly Commentary on Indian Economic Conditions* (Blue Supplement), XI (May-June 1970), pp. I-XV.

67. *Economic and Political Weekly*, May 8, 1971.

68. See Arvind K. Sharma, "The Reorganization of the Planning Commission in India," *International Review of Administrative Sciences*, XXIV (1968), p. 359.

69. *New York Times*, 7 June 1971; and *Economic and Political Weekly*, May 8, 1971.

70. R.K. Hazari, "The Implications of the Managing Agency System in Indian Development," in Ashok V. Bhuleshkar, ed., *Indian Economic Thought and Development* (London: Hurst Co., 1969), p. 201.

71. Ibid., p. 204.

72. Amar N. Agarwala, "The Government-Business Relationship in India," *MSU Business Topics* XVI (Spring 1968), 20.

73. Krishnamachari, *Fundamentals of Planning*, p. 180.

74. Agarwala, "The Government-Business Relationship," pp. 21-25.

75. Bruce McFarlane, "India: The Political Economy of Crisis," *The Australian Quarterly* XXXVII (March 1965), 19.

76. Agarwala, "The Government-Business Relationship," pp. 25-27; see also *New York Times*, 26 December 1968.

77. Agarwala, "The Government-Business Relationship," p. 17.

78. Quoted in Government of India, Administrative Reforms Commission, *Report on Public Sector Undertakings* (New Delhi: Manager of Publications, October 1967), p. 8.

79. McFarlane, "India: The Political Economy of Crisis," p. 21; Government of India, Planning Commission, Perspective Planning Division, *Notes on Perspective of Development, India: 1960-61 to 1975-76* (New Delhi: Manager of Publications, April 1964), p. 29.

80. India, Administrative Reforms Commission, *Report on Public Sector Undertakings*, p. 52.

81. Ibid., pp. 14-19, 120-122.

82. Ibid., p. 15.

83. Ibid., pp. 17, 23.

84. Ibid., p. 58.

85. Hanson, *The Process of Planning*, p. 477.

86. Venkatasubbiah, *Indian Economy Since Independence*, p. 180.

87. Spencer, *India, Mixed Enterprise and Western Business*, p. 120.

88. Gupta, "The Changing Structure of Industrial Finance," pp. 14-15.

89. "Survey of Ownership of Shares in Joint-Stock Companies as at the End of December 1965," *Reserve Bank of India Bulletin* (February 1968), p. 146.

90. Government of India, Deputy Prime Minister and Finance Minister, "Memorandum on Public Undertakings," *Lok Udyog (Public Enterprise)* II (March 1969), 1287-1295.

91. M.G. Shah, "Management of Public Undertakings in India," *Indian Journal of Public Administration* XIV (April-June 1968), 321.

92. B.L. Maheswari, "Management of Public Undertakings in India," *Indian Journal of Public Administration* XIV (October-December 1968), pp. 1003-1004.

93. Nural Islam, "Private and Public Enterprises in the Economic Development of Pakistan," Asian Survey III (July 1963), 338.

94. Quoted in J. Russell Andrus, *The Economy of Pakistan* (Stanford: Stanford University Press, 1958), p. 159.

95. Ibid., p. 160.

96. See, e.g., Ignacy Sachs, *Patterns of Public Sector in Underdeveloped Economies* (Bombay: Asia Publishing House, 1964), p. 95.

97. Gustav F. Papanek, *Pakistan's Development: Social Goals and Private Incentives* (Cambridge, Mass.: Harvard University Press, 1967), pp. 81-82.

98. Stephen R. Lewis, Jr., *Pakistan: Industrialization and Trade Policies* (New York: Oxford University Press, 1970), pp. 53-54.

99. Papanek, *Pakistan's Development*, p. 95.

100. Government of Pakistan, Department of Advertising, Films, and Publications, *Pakistan Industrial Development Corporation* (place and date unknown), p. 4.

101. Government of Pakistan, Department of Advertising, Films, and Publications, *Industries in Pakistan* (place and date unknown), p. 5.

102. Andrus, *The Economy of Pakistan*, p. 160.

103. See ibid., pp. 160-161.

104. Papanek, *Pakistan's Development*, p. 94.

105. See ibid., pp. 96-101.

106. Ibid., pp. 103-104.

107. A brochure published by the West Pakistan Industrial Development Corporation is the source for this information and that in the remainder of this paragraph.

108. Government of Pakistan, Ministry of Finance, Economic Adviser's Wing, *Pakistan Economic Survey 1969-70* (Islamabad: Manager of Publications, 1970), p. 38.

109. Ibid., p. 39.

110. Ibid., pp. 35-37.

111. Ibid., p. 37.

112. Richard R. Nyrop et al., *Area Handbook for Pakistan* (Washington, D.C.: U.S. Government Printing Office, 1971), p. 383.

113. A.M.K. Mazar, "Observations on Public Enterprises in Relation to Government In Pakistan," in M.A.K. Beg, Robert Abramson, and Iftihar Ahmud, eds., *Problems of Public Enterprises*, Proceedings of a National Institute of Public Administration Seminar (Lahore: National Institute of Public Administration, March 1967), p. 96.

114. Aminul Haq, "Observations on Financial Resources of Public Enterprises," in ibid., p. 231; and A. Rashid Ibrahim, ibid., p. 234.

115. Haq, in ibid., p. 231.

116. Ibid.

117. Ibrahim, in ibid., p. 235.

118. Letter from Mr. S.M. Nasim to Mr. M.A.K. Beg, vice-chairman, West Pakistan Enemy Property Management Board, dated December 23, 1969, in response to the circulation by Mr. Beg of a draft of this chapter.

119. A.T. Chaudhry, "Observations on Public Enterprises As Seen Through the Eyes of the Citizen and the Private Sector," in Beg, Abramson, and Ahmud, eds., *Problems of Public Enterprises*, p. 116.

120. Andrus, *The Economy of Pakistan*, p. 161.

121. See Government of Pakistan, Department of Investment Promotion and Supplies, *Guide to Investment in Pakistan*, 2nd ed. (Karachi, n.d.), p. 39; and Government of Pakistan, Planning Commission, *The Fourth Five-Year Plan, 1970-75* (Karachi: Manager of Publications, July 1970), pp. 90, 543.

122. Tajammal Hussain, "Financial Resources of Public Enterprises," in Beg, Abramson, and Ahmud, eds., *Problems of Public Enterprises*, p. 225.

123. Beg, Abramson, and Ahmud, ibid., p. 19.

124. Ibid., p. 16.

125. Government of Pakistan, Ministry of Finance, Economic Adviser, *Government Sponsored Corporations and Other Institutions, 1968-69* (Islamabad: Manager of Publications, 1969), p. 33. The information on PICIC is from Hussain in Beg, Abramson, and Ahmud (eds.), *Problems of Public Enterprises*, p. 226.

126. Papanek, *Pakistan's Development*, p. 88.

127. S.A. Abbas, "Observations on Financial Resources of Public Enterprises," in Beg, Abramson, and Ahmud, eds., *Problems of Public Enterprises*, p. 240.

128. Papanek, *Pakistan's Development*, p. 91.

129. Government of Pakistan, Ministry of Finance, Economic Adviser, *Central Government Corporations* (Rawalpindi: Manager of Publications, 1969), p. 91.

130. Pakistan, *Government Sponsored Corporations*, p. 43.

131. Ibrahim, in Beg, Abramson, and Ahmud, eds., *Problems of Public Enterprises*, p. 237.

132. Pakistan, *Government Sponsored Corporations*, p. 87.

133. Ibid., p. 89.

134. Beg, Abramson, and Ahmud, eds., *Problems of Public Enterprises*, pp. 16, 19. In 1970, this was still a recommendation for the East Pakistan Road Transport Corporation—Pakistan, *The Fourth Five-Year Plan, 1970-75*, p. 458.

135. J. Russell Andrus and Azizali F. Mahammed, *Trade, Finance and Development in Pakistan* (Stanford: Stanford University Press, 1966), p. 173.

136. Pakistan, *Central Government Corporations*, p. 125.

137. Guthrie S. Birkhead, "Government by Corporations: The Case of West Pakistan WAPDA," in Guthrie S. Birkhead, ed., *Administrative Problems in Pakistan* (Syracuse, N.Y.: Syracuse University Press, 1966), p. 125.

138. Pakistan, *Government Sponsored Corporations*, p. 128.

139. Ibid., p. 101.

140. Ibid., p. 169.

141. Ibid., pp. 154-155.

142. Pakistan, *Central Government Corporations*, p. 32.

143. Ibid., p. 92.

144. See Lewis, *Pakistan*, pp. 23-24.

145. Ibid., pp. 33-34.

146. Government of Pakistan, Planning Commission, *The Second Five-Year Plan, 1960-65* (place unknown, 1960), p. 222.

147. Ibid., pp. 222-223.

148. Ibid., p. 227.

149. Government of Pakistan, Planning Commission, *The Second Five-Year Plan (Revised Estimates)* (place unknown: Manager of Publications, March 1961), p. 9.

150. Government of Pakistan, Planning Commission, *The Third Five-Year Plan, 1965-70* (Karachi: Manager of Publications, 1967), p. 74.

151. Papanek, *Pakistan's Development* pp. 85-86.

152. Lewis, *Pakistan*, p. 35.

153. See Swadesh R. Bose, "Pakistan's Development—The Role of Government and Private Enterprise," *Pakistan Development Review* VIII (Summer 1968), pp. 264-280.

154. Mahbub ul Haq, *The Strategy of Economic Planning* (Karachi: Pakistan Branch, Oxford University Press, 1963), p. 195.

155. Keith B. Griffin and Bruce Glassburner, "An Evaluation of Pakistan's Third Five Year Plan," *Journal of Development Studies* II (July 1966), 457.

156. Pakistan, *Fourth Five-Year Plan*, pp. 10-12, 18, 25-27.

157. Pakistan, *Second Five-Year Plan*, p. 226.

158. Ibid.

159. Ibid., p. 38.

160. Pakistan, *Third Five-Year Plan*, p. 32.

161. Ibid., pp. 32-33.

162. Ibid., p. 33.
163. Ibid., p. 117.
164. Ibid.; Nyrop et al., *Area Handbook*, p. 379. The quotation in the text is from Pakistan, *Third Five-Year Plan*, p. 117.
165. Pakistan, *Third Five-Year Plan*, p. 120.
166. Ibid., p. 124.
167. Ibid., p. 450.
168. Ibid., p. 125.
169. Ibid., p. 450.
170. Pakistan, *Fourth Five-Year Plan*, p. 363.
171. Ibid., p. 120.
172. Ibid., pp. 120-121.
173. Ibid., p. 445.
174. Ibid., p. 543.
175. Ibid., p. 541.

Chapter 6
Diverse Experimentation: Israel, Mexico, and Taiwan

1. Howard Pack, *Structural Change and Economic Policy in Israel* (New Haven: Yale University Press, 1971), p. 2.
2. Nadav Halevi and Ruth Klinov-Malul, *The Economic Development of Israel* (New York: Frederick A. Praeger, 1968), pp. 4, 11-12.
3. Abraham Cohen, "The Emergence of the Public Sector of the Israeli Economy," *The Jewish Journal of Sociology* X (December 1968), p. 251.
4. Halevi and Klinov-Malul, pp. 43-44.
5. Cohen, "Emergence of the Public Sector," pp. 262, 264.
6. Falk Project for Economic Research in Israel, *Sixth Report, 1961-1963* (Jerusalem, 1964), p. 16, n. 3.
7. Ibid., p. 18.
8. Benjamin Ahzin and Yehezkel Dror, *Israel: High-Pressure Planning* (Syracuse: Syracuse University Press, 1966), pp. 22-23.
9. Ibid., p. 23.
10. Government of Israel, Prime Minister's Office, Economic Planning Authority, *Israel Economic Development: Past Progress and Plan for the Future*, final draft (Jerusalem: S. Monson, 1968), pp. 411-412.
11. Ibid., p. 412.
12. Cohen, "Emergence of the Public Sector," p. 264.
13. Halevi and Klinov-Malul, *Economic Development*, p. 42.
14. Ibid.
15. The term was used by the deputy director, Government Companies Authority, Ministry of Finance of Israel. Shimon Shapiro, *A Review of Public*

Enterprise in Israel, prepared for United Nations Seminar on Organization and Administration of Public Enterprises, English translation, mimeo (Jerusalem, 1966), p. 24.

16. Israel Association of Political Science, research committee (hereafter cited as the Moses Committee), *The Management of State Enterprises*, English translation (Jerusalem: Israel Association of Political Science, 1965), p. 12.

17. Shapiro, *Public Enterprise*, p. 28.

18. Mordechai Bentov, in Moses Committee, *Management*, p. 83. The quotation in the text is from ibid., pp. 18-19.

19. Quoted in Shapiro, *Public Enterprise*, p. 26.

20. Moses Committee, *Management*, p. 11.

21. Ibid.

22. Government of Israel, Ministry of Finance, Government Corporations Authority, *Supplement to the Report on Government Investment in Corporations Up to March 31st 1966*, English translation (Jerusalem, 1967), p. 5.

23. Moses Committee, *Management*, p. 38.

24. See Government of Israel, Ministry of Finance, Government Corporations Authority, *Supplement to the Report on Government Investments in Stock Up to March 31st 1964*, English translation (Jerusalem, 1965); *Supplement 1966*; and *Report and Account on Government Corporations and Government Investments in Them*, Hebrew original (Jerusalem: Medenot, 1970).

25. Israel, *Supplement 1966*, p. 12.

26. Moses Committee, *Management*, p. 17.

27. Ibid., For details, see Bank of Israel, *Annual Report 1969* (Jerusalem: The Jerusalem Post Press, 1970), pp. 320-335.

28. Shapiro, *Public Enterprise*, p. 22

29. "Changes at Zim," *Israel Economists* XXIII (February 1966), 43-44; and "The Story of El Al," ibid. XXIV (January 1968), pp. 12-17.

30. Shapiro, *Public Enterprise*, p. 46.

31. Ibid., p. 27.

32. *Time*, March 1, 1963, p. 77.

33. Shapiro, *Public Enterprise*, p. 25.

34. Ibid., p. 27.

35. Halevi and Klinov-Malul, *Economic Development*, p. 43.

36. Meir Heth, *The Legal Framework and Economic Activity in Israel*, (New York: Frederick A. Praeger, Inc., 1967), p. 21.

37. Ahzin and Dror, *High-Pressure Planning*, p. 24.

38. Ibid.

39. Halevi and Klinov-Malul, *Economic Development*, p. 43.

40. Ibid., pp. 201-202.

41. Ahzin and Dror, *High-Pressure Planning*, p. 68.

42. Ibid., p. 70.

43. Ibid., pp. 71-72.

44. Ibid., pp. 73-74.

45. Israel, *Israel Economic Development*, pp. 423-424.

46. Michael Tzur, "The Public Corporation and the Private Sector," in Graeme C. Moodie, ed., *Government Organisation and Economic Development* (Paris: Organization for Economic Cooperation and Development, 1964), pp. 47-48.

47. Ibid., p. 48.

48. Pack, *Structural Change*, pp. 141-142.

49. Ibid., p. 168.

50. Moses Committee, *Management*, p. 26.

51. Ibid., p. 74.

52. Tzur, in Moodie, ed., *Government Organisation*, p. 55.

53. Ibid.

54. Ibid., p. 56.

55. Ibid.

56. Michael Tzur, "Industrial Development in Israel," in Albert Winsemius and John A. Pincus, eds., *Methods of Industrial Development* (Paris: Organization for Economic Cooperation and Development, 1962), p. 142.

57. Shapiro, *Public Enterprise*, p. 56.

58. Israel, *Supplement 1966*, p. 15.

59. "The Financial Structure of Public Sector Companies," *Bank of Israel Bulletin* 23 (March 1965), p. 43.

60. Shapiro, *Public Enterprise*, p. 56.

61. Ibid., p. 57.

62. Ibid.

63. Leopold Laufer, *Israel and the Developing Countries: New Approaches to Cooperation* (New York: Twentieth Century Fund, 1967), pp. 140-141; Mordechai E. Kreinin, *Israel and Africa: A Study in Technical Cooperation* (New York: Frederick A. Praeger, Inc., 1964), pp. 133-146.

64. Raymond Vernon, *The Dilemma of Mexico's Development* (Cambridge: Mass.: Harvard University Press, 1963), p. 11.

65. Charles W. Anderson, "Bankers as Revolutionaries: Politics and Development Banking in Mexico," in William P. Glade, Jr. and Charles W. Anderson, *The Political Economy of Mexico* (Madison, Wisc.: University of Wisconsin Press, 1963), p. 118.

66. Frank Brandenburg, "The Relevance of Mexican Experience to Latin American Development," *Orbis* 9 (September 1965), 191-193.

67. William P. Glade, Jr., "Revolution and Economic Development: A Mexican Reprise," in Glade and Anderson, *The Political Economy of Mexico*, pp. 16-17.

68. Roger D. Hansen, *The Politics of Mexican Development* (Baltimore: Johns Hopkins Press, 1971), p. 95.

69. Leopoldo Solís, "Mexican Economic Policy in the Post-War Period: The

Views of Mexican Economists," *The American Economic Review* LXI (June 1971), Part 2, Supplement, p. 25; Hansen, *Politics*, p. 50.

70. For a summary of various writers' views, see Wilfried Gruber, "Career Patterns of Mexico's Political Elite," *Western Political Quarterly* XXIV (September 1971), 467-482; and Hansen, *Politics*, pp. 102-109, 217-221.

71. Hansen, *Politics*, pp. 221-222.

72. See, e.g., ibid., pp. 43-45, 55-56, 221; Solís, "Mexican Economic Policy," pp. 17, 54; and Timothy King, *Mexico: Industrialization and Trade Policies since 1940* (London: Oxford University Press, 1970), p. 46.

73. William O. Freithaler, *Mexico's Foreign Trade and Economic Development* (New York: Frederick A. Praeger, Inc., 1968), p. 10.

74. Vernon, *Dilemma*, pp. 6-7; Robert Jones Shafer, *Mexico: Mutual Adjustment Planning* (Syracuse: Syracuse University Press, 1966), p. 27.

75. Frank Brandenburg, *The Development of Latin American Private Enterprise*, National Planning Association Planning Pamphlet 121 (Washington, D.C.: National Planning Association, 1964), p. 62.

76. Frank Brandenburg, "A Contribution to the Theory of Entrepreneurship and Economic Development: The Case of Mexico," *Inter-American Economic Affairs* 16 (Winter 1962), 9-10.

77. Brandenburg, "Relevance of Mexican Experience," p. 195.

78. Vernon, *Dilemma*, p. 26.

79. Brandenburg, "Relevance of Mexican Experience," p. 195.

80. Shafer, *Mutual Adjustment*, p. 25.

81. Raymond Vernon, "Introduction," in Raymond Vernon, ed., *Public Policy and Private Enterprise in Mexico* (Cambridge, Mass.: Harvard University Press, 1964), p. 4.

82. David H. Shelton, "The Banking System: Money and the Goal of Growth," in Vernon, ed., *Public Policy*, p. 114; Vernon, *Dilemma*, p. 149.

83. Vernon, *Public Policy*, pp. 4, 5.

84. See, e.g., James W. Wilkie, *The Mexican Revolution: Federal Expenditure and Social Change Since 1910*, 2nd ed., rev. (Berkeley: University of California Press, 1970), pp. 82-96.

85. See, e.g., John J. Womack, "The Spoils of the Mexican Revolution," *Foreign Affairs* 48 (July 1970) 677-687.

86. King, *Industrialization and Trade*, p. 46.

87. Vernon, *Dilemma*, p. 3.

88. Shelton, "The Banking System," in Vernon, ed., *Public Policy*, p. 114.

89. Joseph S. La Cascia, *Capital Formation and Economic Development in Mexico* (New York: Frederick A. Praeger, Inc., 1969), p. 27.

90. Glade, "Revolution and Economic Development," in Glade and Anderson, *Political Economy*, p. 92.

91. Anderson, "Bankers as Revolutionaries," in ibid., pp. 134-135.

92. Government of Mexico, Secretaria de la Presidencia, Direccion de

Inversiones Publicas, *México, Inversion Publica Federal 1925-1963* (México, D.F.: Tallares Graficos, de la Nacion, 1964), pp. 115-127.

93. Calvin P. Blair, "Nacional Financiera: Entrepreneurship in a Mixed Economy," in Vernon, ed., *Public Policy*, p. 194.

94. Nacional Financiera, S.A., *Informe Anual* 1968 (México, D.F.: Banco de México S.A., 1970), pp. 16-17.

95. Sanford A. Mosk, *Industrial Revolution in Mexico* (Berkeley: University of California Press, 1950), pp. 94-97.

96. Glade, "Revolution and Economic Development," in Glade and Anderson, *Political Economy*, p. 73.

97. Blair, "Nacional Financiera," in Vernon, ed., *Public Policy*, p. 194.

98. Glade, "Revolution and Economic Development," in Glade and Anderson, *Political Economy*, p. 89.

99. Ibid.

100. Anderson, "Bankers as Revolutionaries," in ibid., p. 137.

101. Ibid., p. 138.

102. Ibid.; see also La Cascia, *Capital Formation*, p. 33.

103. Anderson, "Bankers and Revolutionaries," in Glade and Anderson, *Political Economy*, p. 139.

104. King, *Industrialization and Trade*, p. 54.

105. Bertram M. Gross, "The Dynamics of Competitive Planning," Preface in Shafer, *Mutual Adjustment*, ix-xiii; Anderson, "Bankers as Revolutionaries," in Glade and Anderson, *Political Economy*, p. 182.

106. Gross, "Competitive Planning," in Shafer, *Mutual Adjustment*, pp. ix-xviii.

107. Shafer, ibid., p. 127.

108. Ibid., p. 120.

109. Womack, "Spoils," p. 680.

110. Shafer, *Mutual Adjustment*, p. 39.

111. Vernon, *Dilemma*, pp. 8-9.

112. King, *Industrialization and Trade*, p. 57.

113. Shafer, *Mutual Adjustment*, p. 84.

114. Ibid., pp. 84, 36.

115. Ibid., p. 38.

116. King, *Industrialization and Trade*, pp. 47-48.

117. See Raymond W. Goldsmith, *The Financial Development of Mexico* (Paris: Organization for Economic Cooperation and Development, 1966), p. 23.

118. Blair, "Nacional Financiera," in Vernon, ed., *Public Policy*, p. 193.

119. Ibid., p. 212.

120. Ibid., p. 213.

121. *Industrial Revolution*, p. 138.

122. Blair, "Nacional Financiera," in Vernon, ed., *Public Policy*, p. 221.

123. Ibid., pp. 225-226.

124. Ibid., p. 197.

125. Nacional Financiera, S.A., *Informe Anual Correspondiente a 1964* (México, D.F.: Tallares Graficos de la Nacion, 1965), pp. 89-93.

126. Blair, "Nacional Financiera," in Vernon, ed., *Public Policy*, p. 197.

127. Ibid., p. 201.

128. William E. Cole, *Steel and Economic Growth in Mexico* (Austin, Texas: University of Texas Press, 1967), p. 25.

129. King, *Industrialization and Trade*, p. 73: Blair, "Nacional Financiera," in Vernon, ed., *Public Policy*, p. 236.

130. Blair, ibid., p. 237.

131. King, *Industrialization and Trade*, p. 71.

132. Blair, "Nacional Financiera," in Vernon, ed., *Public Policy*, p. 202.

133. King, *Industrialization and Trade*, p. 71.

134. Blair, "Nacional Financiera," in Vernon, ed., *Public Policy*, p. 203.

135. Anderson, "Bankers as Revolutionaries," in Glade and Anderson, *Political Economy*, pp. 160-161.

136. Ibid., p. 161.

137. Ibid.

138. Blair, "Nacional Financiera," in Vernon, ed., *Public Policy*, pp. 227-228.

139. Ibid., p. 228.

140. Cole, *Steel*, pp. 37-40.

141. Norman Schneider, *Government Competition in the Mexican Steel Industry* (Davis: University of California, Institute of Governmental Affairs, 1967), p. 40.

142. Blair, "Nacional Financiera," in Vernon, ed., *Public Policy*, p. 235.

143. Quoted in Anderson, "Bankers as Revolutionaries," in Glade and Anderson, *Political Economy*, p. 164.

144. Ibid., p. 165.

145. Shafer, *Mutual Adjustment*, p. 27.

146. Blair, "Nacional Financiera," in Vernon, ed., *Public Policy*, p. 233: see also La Cascia, *Capital Formation*, p. 41.

147. King, *Industrialization and Trade*, p. 74.

148. Samuel P.S. Ho, "The Development Policy of the Japanese Colonial government in Taiwan, 1895-1945," in Gustav Ranis, ed., *Government and Economic Development* (New Haven: Yale University Press, 1971), p. 320.

149. Ibid., p. 325.

150. J.C. Huang, "Transfer of Public Enterprise to Private Ownership: An Experience in the Republic of China," United Nations Seminar on Organization and Administration of Public Enterprises, mimeo (New York, 1966), p. 3.

151. Tchin-Chung Liu, "The Process of Industrialization in Taiwan," *The Developing Economies* VII (March 1969), 64.

152. Neil H. Jacoby, *U.S. Aid to Taiwan: A Study of Foreign Aid, Self-Help and Development* (New York: Frederick A. Praeger, Inc., 1966), p. 38.

153. K.T. Li, "The Growth of Private Industry in Free China," Part 2, *Industry of Free China* 16 (August 1961), 17.

154. See Jacoby, *U.S. Aid to Taiwan*, pp. 53, 138-139.

155. Ibid., p. 49.

156. Ibid., p. 51.

157. K.T. Li, "The Growth of Private Industry in Free China," Part 1, *Industry of Free China* 16 (July 1961), p. 8.

158. Jacoby, *U.S. Aid to Taiwan*, pp. 146-147.

159. S.Y. Dao, "Fostering New Attitude Toward Private Enterprise," *Industry of Free China* 23 (June 1965), 30.

160. Li, "Growth of Private Industry," 2, p. 15.

161. Ibid., pp. 12-13.

162. Ibid., pp. 13-14.

163. Huang, "Transfer of Public Enterprise," appendix.

164. Hui-Sun Tang, *Land Reform in Free China* (Taipei, 1954), p. 164.

165. Wolf Ladejinsky, "Agrarian Reform in Asia," *Foreign Affairs* 48 (April 1964), pp. 451-452; see also Hui-Sun Tang and Jen-Lung Chen, "Land-to-the-Tiller Policy and Its Implementation in Formosa," *Land Economics* 31 (August 1955), p. 201.

166. Sino-American Joint Commission on Rural Reconstruction, *Annual Report on Land Reform in the Republic of China* (October 1965), pp. 73-74.

167. Tang, *Land Reform*, p. 167.

168. Anthony Y.C. Koo, *The Role of Land Reform in Economic Development* (New York: Frederick A. Praeger, Inc., 1968), p. 45.

169. Tang, *Land Reform*, p. 169.

170. Kao-Tang Chen, "Free Enterprise for Prosperity," *Free China Review* 14 (June 1964), 13-17; Koo, *Role of Land Reform*, p. 61.

171. Ibid., p. 48.

172. *New York Times*, 26 December 1968.

173. Chen-fu Koo, "Fostering New Attitudes Toward Private Enterprises," *General Report*, Far East Regional Private Enterprise Workshop (Taipei, April 26 - May 3, 1965), p. 179.

174. For details, see Lloyd D. Musolf, "Public Enterprise and Developmental Perspectives in South Vietnam," *Asian Survey* III (August 1963), 362, 369.

175. Shigeto Kawano, "A Remarkably High Economic Growth Rate," in *Economic Development Issues: Greece, Israel, Taiwan, Thailand*, Committee for Economic Development Supplementary Paper No. 25 (New York: Committee for Economic Development, 1968), p. 147.

176. K.T. Li, "Economic Development Strategy," *Industry of Free China* 23 (May 1965), 16.

177. *China Yearbook*, 1969-70 (Taipei: China Publishing Co., n.d.), p. 203.

178. Quoted in John D. Montgomery, *The Politics of Foreign Aid: American Experience in Southeast Asia* (New York: Frederick A. Praeger, Inc., 1962), p. 49.

179. See ibid., pp. 97-98.

180. See ibid., pp. 98-99; and Li, "Growth of Private Industry," 2, p. 18.

181. Li, ibid.

182. S.Y. Dao, "Investment Incentive and Promotion Measures," *Industry of Free China* 23 (May 1965), 46.

183. H.H. Ling, *Industrial Development of Taiwan* (Taipei: China Culture Publishing Foundation, 1953), p. 6.

184. C.K. Yen, "The Trend of Our Economic Development," in *General Report*, Far East Regional Private Enterprise Workshop (Taipei, April 26 - May 3, 1965), p. 261.

185. Allan B. Cole, "Political Roles of Taiwanese Enterprises," *Asian Survey* VII (September 1967), 653-654.

186. Jacoby, *U.S. Aid to Taiwan*, p. 141.

187. United Nations, Economic Commission for Asia and the Far East, Asian Industrial Development Council, *Asian Industrial Development News* 3 (New York: United Nations, 1968), p. 26.

188. United Nations, *Economic Survey of Asia and the Far East 1969* (Bangkok: Economic Bulletin for Asia and the Far East, United Nations, 1970), p. 135.

189. Jacoby, *U.S. Aid to Taiwan*, p. 142.

190. United Nations, *Economic Bulletin for Asia and the Far East* XVII (December 1966), p. 55.

191. United Nations, *Economic Survey 1969*, p. 135.

192. Kawano, "High Economic Growth Rate," pp. 155 and 139-140.

193. Cole, "Political Roles," p. 653.

194. Ibid., p. 654.

195. Statute for the Transfer of Government-owned Enterprises to Private Ownership, Promulgated on January 26, 1953, Article 8.

196. Huang, "Transfer of Public Enterprise," p. 9.

197. Jacoby, *U.S. Aid to Taiwan*, p. 148.

198. Yen, "Trend," p. 260.

199. *Time*, February 23, 1968.

200. Dao, "Investment Incentive," p. 45.

201. *New York Times*, 18 January 1971.

Chapter 7
Perspectives on Mixed Enterprise and Development

1. Marshall E. Dimock, "Les Entreprises Mixtes," *National Municipal Review* 20 (November 1931), 638-641.

2. John Thurston, *Government Proprietary Corporations* (Cambridge, Mass., 1937), p. 273.

3. Sir William Hart, "Mixed Undertakings," *Public Administration* 10 (April 1932), 151-152.

4. Daniel L. Spencer, *India, Mixed Enterprise and Western Business* (The Hague: M. Nijhoff, 1959), pp. 210-211.

5. David E. Apter, "Nationalism, Government and Economic Growth," *Economic Development and Cultural Change* 7 (January 1959), 126.

6. Jan Tinbergen, *The Design of Development* (Baltimore: Johns Hopkins Press, 1958), p. 67.

7. S.K. Allen, "Development of Private Industry through Public Aid," prepared for the International Cooperation Administration, mimeo (Washington, D.C.: International Cooperation Administration, 1958), pp. VII 13-14.

8. A.H. Hanson, "Report of Preliminary Study," *Organization and Administration of Public Enterprises*, Selected papers submitted for discussion at United Nations Interregional Seminar, Geneva, 1966 (New York: United Nations, 1968), p. 5.

9. A.H. Hanson, *Public Enterprise and Economic Development* (London, 1959), p. 192.

10. Yaacov Arnon, "Role of Government in a Mixed Economy," in David Krivine, ed., *Fiscal and Monetary Problems in Development States*, Proceedings of the Third Rehovoth Conference (New York: Frederick A. Praeger, 1967), pp. 86-93.

11. See ibid., pp. 90-91, 93.

12. Ibid., p. 93.

13. Jack Wiseman, "Nationalism," in David L. Sills, ed., *International Encyclopedia of the Social Sciences* 11 (New York: Macmillan Co., 1968), p. 74.

14. Ignacy Sachs, *Patterns of Public Sector in Underdeveloped Economies* (Bombay: Asia Publishing House, 1964), p. 103. All other questions in this paragraph are from the same page.

15. See, e.g., Spencer, *India, Mixed Enterprise*, p. 191.

16. See A.H. Hanson, *Managerial Problems in Public Enterprise* (Bombay: Asia Publishing House, 1962), p. 133; Pasquale Saraceno, "Public Enterprise in the Market Economy," in Albert Winsemius and John A. Pincus, eds., *Methods of Industrial Management* (Paris: Organization for Economic Cooperation and Development, 1962), p. 241; Spencer, *India, Mixed Enterprise*, p. 191.

17. Hanson, *Managerial Problems*, p. 133.

18. Spencer, *India, Mixed Enterprise*, pp. 191-193.

19. Saraceno, "Market Economy," pp. 243, 246-247.

20. Ibid., p. 243.

21. Ibid., p. 244.

22. Ibid., p. 247.

23. Andrew Shonfield, *Modern Capitalism, The Changing Balance of Public and Private Power* (New York: Oxford University Press, 1965), p. 190.

24. Spencer, *India, Mixed Enterprise*, p. 93.

25. Ibid., p. 97.

26. Ibid., p. 102.

27. Fred W. Riggs, *Administration in Developing Countries, The Theory of Prismatic Society* (Boston: Houghton Mifflin Co., 1964), p. 296.

28. Ibid., pp. 105-116.

29. Ibid., p. 296.

30. Ibid., p. 295.

31. Fred W. Riggs, *Thailand: The Modernization of a Bureaucratic Policy* (Honolulu, 1966), p. 251; see also Riggs, *Administration*, pp. 189-193.

32. Riggs, *Administration*, p. 309.

33. Frank P. Sherwood, *The Problem of the Public Enterprise*, Comparative Administration Group Occasional Paper, mimeo (Bloomington, Ind.: Indiana University, International Development Research Center, 1966), p. 6.

34. Ibid., pp. 16-17.

35. Spencer, *India, Mixed Enterprise*, p. 94.

Index

169

About the Author

Lloyd D. Musolf has been director of the Institute of Governmental Affairs and professor of political science at the University of California, Davis, since 1963. Earlier he served as chief of party of the Michigan State University technical assistance group in South Vietnam and taught at Michigan State and Vassar College. His other international experience includes a year of research leave in Ottawa, Canada, and three years in the Pacific as a naval officer during World War II. A Johns Hopkins Ph.D., he is the author or editor of seven other books, including *Legislatures in Developmental Perspective* and *Public Ownership and Accountability: the Canadian Experience*. His current research is on the interrelationships among economic regulation, notions of development, and the roles of legislatures in several developing countries.